Old Cane Springs

A *Story of the War between the States
in Madison County, Kentucky*

OLD CANE SPRING CHURCH, BUILT 1812-1813.

OLD CANE SPRINGS

A Story of the War between the States
in Madison County, Kentucky

Revised and Supplemented By

JONATHAN TRUMAN DORRIS, PH. D.

Professor of History and Government
Eastern Kentucky State Teachers College

From the Original By

JOHN CABELL CHENAULT, Attorney

City Judge of Richmond, 1881-1884
County Judge of Madison, 1884-1894

Introduction By

IVAN E. McDOUGLE, PH. D.

Professor of Sociology, Goucher College
Author "Slavery in Kentucky"

Published in Recognition of the
Sesquicentennial of the Organization
of Madison County, Kentucky,
in 1786

THE STANDARD PRINTING CO.
Incorporated
LOUISVILLE, KENTUCKY

COMMONWEALTH BOOK COMPANY
St. Martin, Ohio
2023

Copyright © 1936 by Jonathan Truman Dorris.
Originally published by The Standard Printing Company in 1936.
This edition copyright © 2023 by Commonwealth Book Company, Inc.

All rights reserved. No part of this book may be reproduced in any form or by any means without the prior written consent of the publisher, excepting brief quotes used in reviews. Printed in the United States of America.

ISBN: 978-1-948986-54-0

FRONT COVER IMAGE: CIRCA 1930S POSTCARD VIEW FROM BIG HILL LOOKING TOWARD RICHMOND (SEE PAGE 129).

Dedicated

to the

Sacred Memory

of

the Boys in Blue and the Boys in Gray

of

Madison County, Kentucky

*whose descendants are living
happily together under the
Stars and Stripes*

FOREWORD

IN JANUARY, 1927, the eminent Southern historian, Dr. E. Merton Coulter, in a letter requesting John Wilson Townsend, an author of Lexington, to review his *Civil War and Readjustment in Kentucky,* said, "You are quite right about money-making in literary writing. I have had no illusions about the matter for some time—I would be greatly surprised if I could come out even. But Kentucky has such interesting history that I think a person can afford to indulge in it now and then as a luxury. . . ."

It was with something of the spirit that animated Dr. Coulter that I determined to publish *Old Cane Springs.* The original manuscript came into my possession a few years ago. I appreciated its worth and resolved to secure its publication, if ever occasion warranted it. On being unable to prepare a history of Madison County in time to publish it in recognition of the sesquicentennial of the county's organization, I resolved about a year ago to produce this volume instead.

Judge John Cabell Chenault, who died in 1924, lived as a boy in Old Cane Springs during the War between the States. His experiences then and associations later with older persons who participated in one way or another in that lamentable conflict inspired him to tell late in life its influence on the community of his boyhood. Evidently his thesis was to reveal the very favorable condition of slavery in a prosperous part of Madison County, Kentucky, and to indicate what he regarded as the economic and social misfortunes attending the disturbance of that condition by the war and its consequences. Augustine Hart, for whom he speaks in the story, was his first cousin, who died in young manhood.

My task has been to improve the author's composition and correct his inconsistencies and factual errors; to divide the story properly and determine its chapter headings; to incorporate a few other facts to give the narrative a stronger appeal; and to supplement the whole with notes, excerpts and other material to show the actual historical basis of the story. The notes, illustrations, maps, and addenda, therefore, are my contribution.

In publishing *Old Cane Springs* I do not express my own opinion concerning the desirability of slavery in any form or at any time or place. I might state, however, that the setting of the story is in a county adjoining the one (Garrard) in which Harriet Beecher Stowe is believed to have found much of her material for *Uncle Tom's Cabin*.

Many persons have aided me in this work. Trying not to omit anyone to whom credit is due, I venture to acknowledge my appreciation of such assistance by personal references. Mr. J. P. Chenault allowed me to use his father's original manuscript of *Old Cane Springs*. From Mrs. James W. Caperton and Mr. J. W. Deatherage I also obtained valuable material. Mr. W. C. Griggs and Mr. Eugene Berryman permitted me to use the minutes of Old Cane Spring Church. Certain other material came from Mrs. J. P. Chenault, Miss Nettie Oldham, Mr. Eugene Barnes, Mrs. Laura Clay Garland, Mrs. Nanny May (N. B.) Deatherage, Mrs. Lyman Parrish, Miss Lucia Burnam, Mr. Milton Elliott, Mrs. A. W. Williams, Rev. W. E. Arnold, Mr. Jesse Bogie, Mr. Burton Roberts, Dr. William Goodell Frost, and Mr. Long Tom Chenault. I used copies of Beers' valuable 1876 historic map of Madison County belonging to Messrs. Chowning Todd and Tevis Huguely. Others whose reminiscences and information of equal import have materially contributed to the content of the book are: Mrs. Margaret Jane (R. C.) Boggs, Mrs. Margaret Adams, Mr. and Mrs. Green Noland, Mr. and Mrs. J. B. Noland, Mrs. T. M. Oldham, Mr. C. W. Tribble, Mrs. J. W. Martin, Mrs. John Chambers, Mrs. Robert Dunn, Mrs. Alene Jackson Boggs, Mrs. A. R. Gibbs, Mr. Robert Turpin, Mrs. E. H. Bybee, Mrs. Charles L. Searcy, Mr. T. E. Baldwin, Mr. John Noland, Mr. Douglas Chenault, Mr. S. D. Parrish, Mr. H. H. Brock, Mrs. Geo. W. Mason, Mrs. Joe Gilbert, Mrs. Shelby Jett, Miss Mary Q. Covington, Mr. W. C. Brandenburg, Mr. J. R. McKinney, Mr. D. B. McKinney, Mrs. Waller Bennett, Mrs. Bland Ballard, Mr. G. M. Brock, Mrs. Stanton G. Hume, Miss Bessie Miller, Mr. J. L. Kanatzar, Miss Ann DeJarnett, Mr. C. C. Wallace, Uncle Mose Chambers (colored), and Aunt Ann Bradley (colored).

Professor R. A. Edwards, Mrs. Mary Barnhill, and Rev. Clyde L. Breland read almost the entire manuscript and, with Dr. Noel B. Cuff, made suggestions. I am especially appreciative of Dr. Ivan E. McDougle's encouragement. My wife and daughter, Dorothy Helen, have helped in putting the work in final form for the publisher, the latter as typist. Russell McKee Childs, my student secretary, did all the preliminary typing. Finally, I appreciate the courtesies of the Ogg and McGauhey Studios, the services of H. deB. Forbes and E. Bennett Rose in preparing the maps, and the loan of cuts by the Richmond Daily Register Company and the Berea College Press.

JONATHAN TRUMAN DORRIS.

Richmond, Kentucky,
September 15, 1936.

PREFATORY NOTE TO THE SECOND EDITION

THE FAVORABLE reception of *Old Cane Springs* at home and at large has encouraged the printing of another edition. Some improvements have been made in the book, and it appears now as an actual Madison County sesquicentennial publication, since the county's organization in 1786 is to be appropriately commemorated on October 13-17, 1937. The celebration, which was authorized early in 1936, by the county's fiscal court, is being sponsored by the Madison County Historical Society. The Boonesborough Chapter of the Daughters of the American Revolution and various other organizations in the county are also supporting the enterprise. This edition of *Old Cane Springs,* therefore, is in keeping with the spirit of the celebration, which will include recognition of the sesquicentennial of the making of the Constitution of the United States. A statement concerning the celebration may be found on the last two pages.

J. T. D.

September 30, 1937.

TABLE OF CONTENTS

		Page
	Foreword	v
	Introduction	xv
I	The Garden of Eden	3
II	Aunt Millie	6
III	Negro Servitude	10
IV	More About Negro Servitude	17
V	Mary Ann Oldham	20
VI	The Honest Miller and Green Noland	23
VII	Aunt Creech Sally	28
VIII	Nathan Bird Deatherage and the Fox Hunters	33
IX	Excursions, School Days, and Kentucky Hospitality	36
X	Negro Melodies and the Corn Shucking	42
XI	Old Cane Spring Church	50
XII	A Merry Christmas	56
XIII	War on the Horizon: Will the Negro Revolt?	59
XIV	Dissension and Division	62
XV	The Home Guards	66
XVI	The Rock House	68
XVII	Mary Ann as Confederate Postmistress	73
XVIII	Salt for Cattle, but Food for Men	76
XIX	Mary Ann and Nath at the Rock House	79
XX	Preparations to Move Union Troops Through Madison County	84

		Page
XXI	MARY ANN'S SPEECH SAVES THE DAY	87
XXII	A NEGRO SAINT PASSES	93
XXIII	A FAITHFUL NEGRO OVERSEER	98
XXIV	THE BATTLE OF RICHMOND	106
XXV	TWO OLDHAMS CONDEMNED AS SPIES	110
XXVI	PRESIDENT LINCOLN'S CLEMENCY	115
XXVII	THE DRAFT	121
XXVIII	THE LOST CAUSE AND ANTICIPATIONS OF THE FUTURE	123
	NOTES (See index of important notes, page xi)	131

ADDENDA

- A. Colonel James B. McCreary's Integrity 217
- B. Letters Written by Prisoners in Camp Douglas to Relatives in Madison County 225
- C. The Eleventh Kentucky Cavalry, C. S. A. 231
- D. Deaths in the Eleventh Kentucky Cavalry at Camp Douglas 241

BIBLIOGRAPHY 243

INDEX 249

THE MADISON COUNTY SESQUICENTENNIAL ANNIVERSARY 258

IMPORTANT NOTES

	Page
Madison County and Richmond	131
Silver Creek, The Madison County Rhine	135
The Ethnological Justification of Slavery	138
The Scriptural Argument for Slavery	140
John G. Fee Mobbed Near Old Cane Springs	141
Berea College and Central University	147
Cassius M. Clay	149
The Expulsion of the Bereans	150
Cassius M. Clay vs. John G. Fee	155
The Economic Evils of Slavery	156
Boonesborough	159
The African Background of American Negro Superstitions	163
Nathan B. Deatherage	165
Robert Turpin's Reminiscences	170
Aunt Ann Bradley's Reminiscences	171
Old Cane Spring Church	173
Elbridge J. Broaddus	178
Basket Dinners at the Church and the Norris-Hisle Family Reunion	179
The Clay Battalion	180
Home Guards and State Guards	182
Military Roads in Kentucky	185
Slavery in the Church	186
The Battle of Richmond	190
Reminiscences of the Battle of Richmond	191

Important Notes

	Page
Ante-Bellum Homes Remaining on the Battlefield of Richmond	193
An Ante-Bellum Autograph Album Returns to Richmond	195
General John Miller	196
The Eleventh Kentucky Cavalry, C. S. A.	198
Othniel Rice Oldham	200
Major James B. McCreary and Miss Juan Phillips	202
Curtis Field Burnam	204
James W. Caperton	205
General Burbridge	207
A Madisonian's Response to the Draft	208
Securing the Release of Confederate Prisoners	210
The Deatherage-Oldham Wedding	213

ILLUSTRATIONS

Old Cane Spring Church	*frontispiece*
	Facing page
Panorama of Kentucky River	4
Colonel John Noland's Home	5
Spring near Cecil Willoughby's Home	5
The Jack Martin House	12
Spring in the rear of the Jack Martin House	12
The Rock House	13
Baking Pottery at Waco and Bybeetown	13
Joel T. Hart's Bust of Cassius M. Clay	36
Thomas M. Hart	36
Nathan B. Deatherage	36
Mary Ann Oldham	36
Mrs. John Cabell Chenault	37
John Cabell Chenault	37
Colonel David Waller Chenault	37
Mrs. David Waller Chenault (nee Tabitha Phelps)	37
Beach at Boonesborough	44
June Meeting, 1936, at Old Cane Spring Church	44
Weddle's Mill	45
Cannon used to Defend the *True American*	45
Rev. William Rupard	56
Captain Nathan Noland	56
Othniel Rice Oldham	56
Dr. Jeremiah Ayres	56
William Q. Covington	57
Coleman Covington	57
Cabell Chenault	57
David and Anderson Chenault	57
The Thomas Palmer House	108
Mount Zion Church	108
Madison County Courthouse	109
Madison Female Institute	109

Illustrations

Facing page

Abraham Lincoln	112
The Clay Battalion	113
Major Curtis F. Burnam	120
Colonel James W. Caperton	120
General John Miller	120
Captain P. P. Ballard	120
Merritt Jones's Tavern	121
White Hall	121
Mr. and Mrs. Nathan Bird Deatherage	128
Big Hill View, looking toward Richmond	129
Bogie's Mill	136
Cascades near Silver Creek	136
The Andrew Bogie House	137
The Gen. Samuel Estill House	137
Rev. John A. R. Rogers	144
Rev. John G. Fee	144
Rev. Lindsay Hughes Blanton	144
Rev. Robert L. Breck	144
Main Building of Central University	145
John G. Fee Memorial Union Church	145
"Castlewood"	196
"Cumberland View"	196
"Woodlawn"	197
The Solomon Smith House	197
Colonel James B. McCreary	204
Mrs. Milton Elliott (nee Juan Phillips)	204
Mrs. Margaret Jane Boggs and Mrs. Margaret Adams	204
The Fort at Boonesborough	205

MAPS

Madison County	*cover pages*
Old Cane Springs and Vicinity	*page 2*

INTRODUCTION

MANY BOOKS have been published in which the authors have considered the peculiar position of Kentucky in the Civil War period. Some of them have been pure political treatises; others have been confined to accounts of military exploits; while some of our best writers have chosen the field of historical fiction. In spite of all this material there is still much to be learned. When something comes along to fill a gap left by others we should be more than glad to receive it.

The manuscript left by the late Judge John Cabell Chenault is a rare discovery at this late date. It differs from nearly all other works covering this epoch in Kentucky by being confined to the life of a small rural community. The author deals only with what he saw and personally knew. The human aspect of conditions predominates. The presentation of slavery as it existed in Madison County is not so much an argument for an institution as it is a picture of its everyday life. To the older persons who read this book, especially if they are Kentuckians, the various chapters will stand out as very accurate accounts of central Kentucky three-quarters of a century ago. To younger persons the story will no doubt appear as a description of another world, or, as Professor Dorris calls it, another "Garden of Eden."

Judge Chenault's manuscript, which is valuable in itself beyond all our powers to reconstruct, becomes vastly more intelligible today by the numerous notes and illustrations which have been gathered together by Professor Dorris. This additional material will enable those who live in Madison County to see the background of their own citizenry. To others it will portray a connecting link with many other records of Kentucky which have been published. Furthermore, for the student of this period in American history these notes and illustrations will serve to round out the picture painted by Judge Chenault and to act as a check on his statements. The book as a whole also presents as complete a picture of the life of a small country community in the Civil War period as we can ever hope to have today.

It is eminently fitting that this work should be published in connection with the celebration of the sesquicentennial of the establishment of Madison County in 1786. While it does not go back to the very beginning, it does consider a type of rural economic independence which had changed very little in the 1860's from that which was enjoyed when Kentucky first became a state. In these days of rapid social and economic change it is well that students of history read such an account as this to realize what tremendous transformations have occurred in the social order in the past century. Moreover, the book merits reading by students of the social sciences as well as by those who are primarily interested in antiquities.

IVAN E. MCDOUGLE.

Baltimore, Maryland,
September 8, 1936.

Old CANE SPRINGS

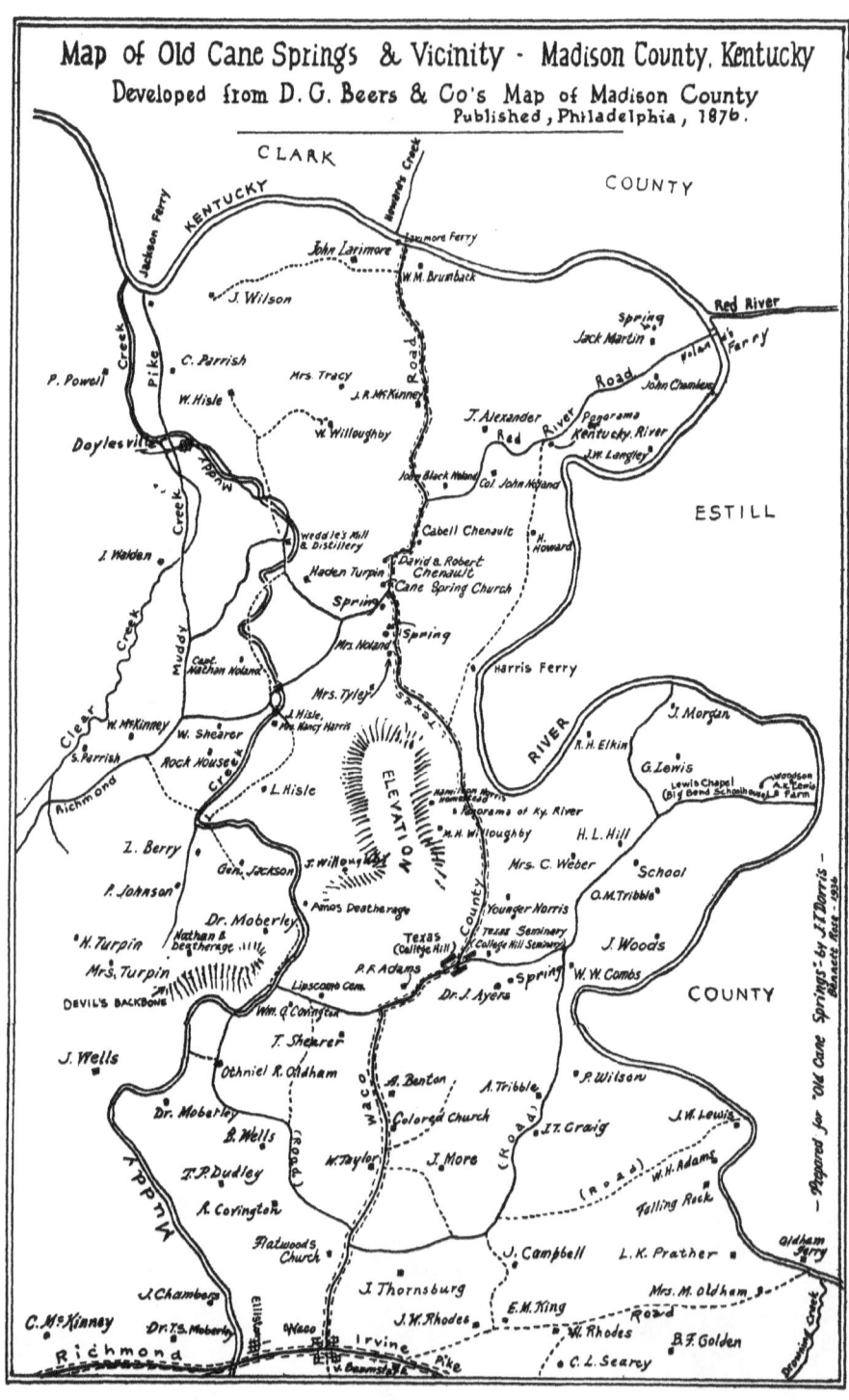

CHAPTER I

THE GARDEN OF EDEN

BEFORE the War between the States, Madison County,[1] Kentucky, was divided into communities, well known by their local names. For example, when Poosey was mentioned everyone understood that reference was made to the extreme western part of the county. The mention of Foxtown directed attention to the region near the home of Cassius M. Clay. When Old Cane Springs was mentioned it was well understood the reference was made to the fertile region in the northeastern part of the county, the prosperity and wealth of whose inhabitants were known not only in Madison, but also in the adjoining and many remoter counties of the State.

I had been promised from early childhood that some day I might visit Old Cane Springs, and many fanciful pictures had I drawn of the wonderful spot from descriptions given by those who had seen its splendor and wealth. Now the day of my dreams had come and I was on the way to the home of my Aunt Josephine Chenault, who, I had been told, lived almost under the eaves of the old church which stood in the midst of this land that flowed with milk and honey; and I was going with the promise that I might remain for four or five years.

It was in the autumn of 1860 and I had left my home on Silver Creek to meet my Uncle Robert Chenault[2] at Waco. I found him waiting with two saddle horses and we soon arrived on an elevation of the Waco-Red River road about a mile north of the village of Texas and were viewing the magnificent scene beyond. On our right we beheld the Kentucky River flowing toward us in a westerly course until it disappeared from sight. On looking a little to the north I saw that the water, on meeting the impassable barrier on which we stood, had turned abruptly to continue on its way in a northern direction. From this vantage point I could also discern the stream's course mile upon mile until it reached the mouth of Red River. Thence it took a generally western direction, passing the mouth of Howard's Creek and soon receiving the waters of Muddy Creek. The distance from the point on the Kentucky River where the stream appeared to pass under us and the mouth of Muddy Creek, as the water flowed, was and still is about fifteen miles.[3]

On looking westward, I saw Muddy Creek flowing toward us until it also touched the eminence on which we stood. Thence it turned and ran for a distance in a northwestern direction, pursuing finally a generally northern course to the Kentucky River about five miles away. From our position I could see the threads of these two streams by reason of the tall white sycamores[4] lining their banks and making the land between them look like an island.

The region through which I had just passed from the Richmond and Irvine turnpike at Waco[5] to this point has never been very fertile, and at that time it was covered mostly with blackjack and sourwood. Around Texas[6] the soil was sandy and appeared to have little fertility, and I felt that I had just passed through a rather barren country; but as I looked northward from my elevation, I saw that I was entering a beautiful and fertile land. I could see broad fields of ripened corn, and the straw stacks in the distance indicated that there had been a bountiful wheat harvest. There were giant trees everywhere, and places that had the appearance of small villages were scattered throughout the country. Cattle, horses, mules, and sheep by the thousands were feeding on the luxuriant pastures beyond, and as I gazed in rapture at the magnificent scene before me, I almost involuntarily exclaimed: "The Garden of Eden!"

Near the center of this garden spot I saw a large clump of towering elm,[7] beech, hickory, and oak trees, and just discernible through their glorious autumnal foliage I could see a rather large brick building. I exclaimed: "Old Cane Spring Church!"

I inquired of my uncle the name of the village just before us, the one about a mile farther on, and another possibly three miles away to our right. He informed me that none of the places I believed to be a village was such, as generally understood.

"The first group of buildings there," he explained, "belongs to my father. The cluster of houses you see to the right and left

Panorama of the Kentucky River, seen from the "Elevation." See map of Old Cane Springs. The foothills of the mountains are dimly shown in the distance.

Col. John Noland's Home. Built more than a century ago. (See Map of Old Cane Springs.) The Chambers-Noland cemetery is in the clump of trees in the rear, overlooking the Kentucky River.

Spring on the road near the home of Mrs. Noland, as shown on the map of Old Cane Springs. Cecil Willoughby now occupies this ante-bellum residence.

of the large brick house are Negro quarters. My father owns about fifty Negroes and it takes quite a lot of buildings for them. The next place beyond is the home of Colonel John Noland.[8] He has hardly as many Negroes as my father, for he has given many away to his children. The other group of houses that you inquired about belongs to Captain John Chambers.[9] His place really looks like a town, for he owns nearly a hundred Negroes. Looking farther on you will see the home of Jack Martin,[10] and the houses around are quarters for his Negroes. Near the center yonder, on the river near the mouth of Howard's Creek, is the home of John Lariemore; and a little farther to your left is the home of Captain Nathan Noland.[11] Under the hill there, hardly in view, is where Haden Turpin lives, and to the left yonder is the home of Amos Deatherage, and a little farther up the creek—that large white house—is the home of Othniel Oldham.

"On that high point yonder, just a little to our left, is where Colby McKinney lives. Just before us is the home of John Black Noland,[12] and a little beyond is that of Walter Norris. Just back of the church you see a few houses; that is where you have come to live. Nearly every home in Old Cane Springs can be seen from this point, and all the houses you see around them were built for the Negroes. There is really no village or post office closer to Old Cane Springs than Texas, through which we have just passed. No one around Texas or on the road back to Waco over which we have just come owns Negroes, but everyone down here does. Taking them all together, at the places I have pointed out to you, I would guess there are nearly a thousand Negroes."

We then rode on to my new home. Aunt Josephine greeted me affectionately and, after much talking, gave me a very good supper. She and Uncle Robert made many glowing promises of what I might do to make my stay with them pleasant; and with bright visions for the morrow I was at last tucked away in a warm bed, where I dreamed of learning more of the Negro quarters which I had seen in the distance that afternoon.

CHAPTER II

AUNT MILLIE

ON THE MORROW, I was up bright and early and was informed by my uncle that he had secured from his father a spotted mule named Whizaker, that I was to ride about the country at my pleasure.

My first great desire was to visit the Negro quarters. In our part of the county there were very few Negroes, and only now and then had I seen them. Bogie's mill on Silver Creek was near our home,[13] and occasionally they came there with wheat or corn. Most of them were happy, bright-faced boys. When their grain was ground they left immediately for their homes, leaving me to wonder how they actually lived and behaved. My father was an emancipationist. Mr. Lincoln had just been elected President, and during the campaign I had heard repeatedly of the cruel treatment of the slaves; and now that I was among them, I was anxious to see and know for myself whether they were humanely or inhumanely treated.

My Aunt Josephine made me feel as welcome in her home as I had been in my own before the death of my mother. She realized I would be with her for years and at once made me feel that I was one of the family. Before the day was far spent, I was in the cabin talking to Aunt Millie, an old darky that my Grandfather Cavins had given my aunt. She hugged and caressed me with the same apparent pleasure that my aunt had the night before. She would hug me, push me off and look at me, call the name of my dear mother, and then pull me back to her and cry. She said she saw in me her old master and mistress and all of her young misses and especially "yo' deah ma," she said, referring, of course, to my mother. Then she would grab me and hug me again. Soon her two sons, Harvey and Martin, came in. They had known me as a baby many years before in the Cavins home, and they also appeared very glad to see me. They, too, had been allotted my aunt after the death of my grandparents in Fayette County. My father, being an emancipationist, would not take any of the slaves when my Grandfather Cavins' estate was wound up. I was very small when this was done, and, having spent my earlier years in the hills of Silver Creek[14] and knowing nothing whatever about Negroes and their attitude toward those with whom they lived, Aunt Millie's talk and conduct were a surprise to me.[15]

I had believed that Negroes, to a large extent, were held almost as criminals, that they were writhing under a heavy yoke and constantly planning some means of escape. To meet this old Negress and have my features revive in her memory visions of her old and young masters and my mother and aunts, none of whom she had seen for many years and most all of whom had gone to the Great Beyond, and then to see her rejoice at the pleasant memories aroused by my presence, were certainly a revelation.

She spoke of all those who had been near and dear to me, as if they were her own. She recalled and told something extremely interesting about every one of them. "You'll nevah know, chile, how purty yo' ma, Miss Car'lin', wuz de night yo' pa come an' tuck 'er 'way," she said. Then she related some kindness my mother had shown her and told of presents she had given her, and said, "Po' chile, dead, but I'll see 'er yit in heben."

I was about fifteen years old then and able to see that her emotions were genuine and that she really loved those with whom she had grown up, even though she was a slave. I said, "Aunt Millie, since you thought so much of them all, how did you decide which one to go with when they broke up the old home?"

"Dat wuz hard, chile, to decide," she replied. "I did love 'em all, but yo' Aunt Jose wuz de baby gal, de last un I'd nussed, an' I loved 'er jis like she wuz my own chile, an' I wanted to be close to 'er an' see 'er evah day, an' she knowed it an' wouldn't heah to nothin' 'cept I wuz to come wid 'er. I wanted to bring both of dese black niggers wid me, so w'en I lets yo' Aunt Jose know w'at I wanted, she up an' tole Marse Robert, an' so heah we all is. Heah is our home, an' we's all happy. Cou'se, it ain't de ole home in Fayette, whar all de darkies am a singin' in de fields an' 'round de quarters an' whar ole Marse an' Missus an' all de white chillun wuz 'roun'."

"Dat sho wuz a home, honey," Aunt Millie continued. "Time an' nothin' else could change it. I hate to t'ink back on it. Ole

Marse an' Missus, you know, died an' am burr'ed dar close to de road in de old burren groun'. Marse Robert an' William had bin burr'ed dar befo' 'em, an' since den yo' ma an' some of yo' aunts hab bin laid dar by 'em. My ole man an' some ov my chillun am burr'ed neah. The burren groun's am close—not furder 'part den de big house an' de qua'ters. I wish I could be burr'ed dar too, so dat w'en dat great resurrectin' day comes, ez soon ez I've hugged an' kissed my ole man, Mose, an' our chillun, I can run right down an' hug Ole Marse an' Missus an' de chillun. But dat is too fur off to hope fur, an' if me an' Miss Jose is burr'ed out heah, we kin jis fly over togedder w'en dat great day comes."

"Aunt Millie," I said, "you look like you are happy and would rather be here than any other place. You know Mr. Lincoln has been elected President, and the talk is that he is going to free all the Negroes. Don't you want to be free?"

"Shut yo' mouf, chile," she commanded. "I's already de frees' pusson on dis place. I's ole an' nobody 'spects me to work, 'cept w'en I wants to. I sho am de boss heah now, ez I's de oldes'. Miss Jose an' Marse Robert ain't nothin' but chilluns. Dey ax me 'bout ebert'ing dey do. Dis heah talk 'bout free niggers is all fur nothin'. Dem white folks whar dey ain't no niggers keeps talkin' 'bout freein' de niggers, but ef dey would come 'round heah an' see de diffur'nce 'tween us niggers dat has homes an' de free niggers, dey would shut up. W'y, heah is Hen, Jim, an' Noa Brock, free! W'en der ole marster died, he had no chillun to gib 'em to, so he sets 'em free an' gib 'em each a home. Dey is great big, stout lookin' men an' dey cain't make a livin' an' nobody wants 'em 'round. None ov de young nigger gals wid a home will hab 'em for a beau, an' won't t'ink ov marryin' 'em. Dey comes to see my gal Lucy, an' ez dey is sech good lookin' niggers, Marse Robert, he 'courages der comin'; but my gal she tole 'em she wouldn' marry no free nigger. Marse David Chenault set ole Harry free w'en he died, an' gib 'im thirty acres a lan' down by de riber, an' he cain't make 'nough to feed an' clothe hisse'f. Marse Cabell has to feed 'im all de time. Sally, 'is old woman, she won't stay down dar wid 'im. She say she cain't raise her chillun right ef dey ain't 'round white folks."

"But, Aunt Millie," I interrupted, "don't you think the Negroes would soon learn to do their work well, if they were freed?"

"I tells you, honey-chile, a free nigger ain't no good, an' dem white folks dat am cuttin' up 'bout it 'll find it out w'en dey come down heah. A free nigger gits so he don't love nobody an' nobody loves a free nigger. De good Lawd nevah 'tended it dat way. A nigger can't t'ink 'bout layin' up. He can work good, but de t'inkin' an' de plannin' an' de layin' up fur winter an' a rainy day must be done by old marse. Ef all de niggers wuz set free—you's young an' you'll see dat it's wuss fur de nigger."

"Well," I said, "that may be true; but I have never lived where there were many Negroes and I have always been taught that they should be set free. I believe they would be better off."

"Honey, you say you ain't eber seen many niggers?" Aunt Millie questioned. "Well, you'll l'arn all 'bout 'em. I 'member w'en de ole home ovah in Fayette wuz broke up. Yo' pa, Marse Hart, he wouldn' 'low Miss Car'lin', yo' ma, to buy eny ov us folks, though yo' ma wanted some ov 'em an' dey wanted to go wid 'er. You'll see some day dat yo' pa done wrong to rob yo' ma ov de folks she loved an' dat loved her an' would a worked fur 'er an' nussed 'er to de day ov 'er death. I tells youse, honey, a free nigger don't know nothin' 'bout makin' a livin' an' bein' a good man. You kin go to eny ov de homes 'roun' heah whar a nigger has a home with a marster an' you'll see fat, sleek, happy singin' niggers; but you go to de home ov dem free niggers, an' dey is a heap ov dem 'roun' heah, an' you'll see a rusty, shabby nigger. If dey has chillun, dey looks sceered like a varmint. A nigger 'way frum a white pusson can't raise der chillun right. Sally, ovah heah at Marse Cabell's, knows dat, an' she made 'im build 'er a house in de qua'ters an' she keep 'er chillun dar so dey will grow up some 'count."

At this point Aunt Jose came into the cabin and remarked that my mule had been hitched to the fence all morning and that at least a dozen young Negro boys from my grandfather's had been waiting out at the road to meet me. She said that it was now too late for me to go riding until after dinner, so, after telling

Aunt Millie I would come to see her again, I walked to the big house with my aunt.

I told Aunt Jose and Uncle Robert at dinner about the pleasant morning I had passed with Aunt Millie, about her hugging and kissing me and that I did not push her away. I said that I came to feel that she had been one of the old home which I had so often heard my mother speak of when I was a child, and which I had hardly ever heard mentioned since her death and father's second marriage. I also admitted that, big boy though I was, I had cried with her.

Chapter III

NEGRO SERVITUDE

After dinner I mounted Whizaker, my spotted mule, and rode first to the home of Cabell Chenault. A group of little Negroes, with shining eyes and open mouths grinning a welcome, were on the road to meet me. They had heard that a new boy—a nephew of Missus Jose, as they all called my aunt—had come to the neighborhood. They indicated that they thought I was one of their kinsfolk and that it was their special duty to try to entertain me and make me feel welcome. Without any formal introduction, they gathered around my spotted mule and escorted me to the big house. Mr. Cabell Chenault greeted me pleasantly and invited me to alight, hitch my mule, and come in. There was, however, no hitching for me. As soon as I alighted, more than half of the little Negroes had hold of my bridle, each wishing to do me the honor of hitching, and a general row for the privilege at once ensued. About half of them held the bridle on one side and half on the other, so the mule could not move, until Mr. Chenault ordered them all to let loose and permit me to hitch.

I found Mr. Chenault to be one of the most kindly disposed men I had ever met. When I expressed surprise at his being so gentle with the little Negroes, he said it was the only way to get on with them.

"I always try to show no favoritism with my people, large and small, men, women, and children. I own forty-nine," he went on to say, "and while I am positive with them, I dare not have favorites among them. If I had designated any one of those boys to hitch your mule, you would have seen a frown of disapproval come over the faces of all the others. As I treated them all alike, you could see that no one of them was offended. I have to be just as careful with the grown-up ones."

"On my plantation here," he continued, "various kinds of work have to be done. I study the inclination of each and assign him the work he appears to like best. My man, Amos, is the oldest of my people. He has been a faithful servant and now he acts as my general overseer, and by reason of his age, all the others appear to approve the responsibility assigned to him and none envies him the position. Jerry is gentle and kind with my stock, and for that reason he is head wagoner. I learned early that Alfred was inclined to be a carpenter and shoemaker, so I encouraged him along that line. He makes all the chairs you see here in the house and all in the quarters. He made all the beds on which the Negroes sleep and he built most of the houses in which they live. As winter is approaching he is now working hard to get a pair of shoes for each of them as well as for each of my own sons."

"My sons work in the field with my servants and no discord or dispute ever occurs. David, Cabell, and Anderson are now with them shucking corn, and if you should be here when they come in at night you will know from the merry and jolly mood in which they go to their quarters that they are as happy as my own children."

I asked him if he locked them in their quarters at night and if he was not afraid they would run off. He answered that he had never thought of such a thing; that he had owned and had worked Negroes for forty years; that he did not have many at first; that most of those he now owned had grown up to be his; and that they considered his place as much their home as he and his children did.

"I never speak of them as my slaves,"[16] he explained; "I always call them 'my people'. I believe they think I am simply the head of a big family, and I doubt if any one of them thinks any more of running away from home or being dissatisfied with his lot than do my own children. Every one of them has a desire to beat all of our neighbors in getting out our crops in the spring. They all want to keep my corn clearer of weeds than that of my neighbors. They want to lay it by first and they want to be first in harvesting and cribbing. They are shucking corn now, and I can gather from their talk that they expect to have our corn shucked before Colonel Noland or Captain Chambers has finished. So you can see that everything runs smoothly and all work is done cheerfully. The same spirit appears to prevail among all the Negroes in Old Cane Springs."

"Our Negroes marry whom they choose in this community,"[17] he continued. "Several of my men have wives in other quarters and men from other quarters have married my women, and if they do not live too far away, they are here every night and my men are at the homes of their wives. If they live too far away, they generally come or go every Saturday night and spend Sunday with their families."

I told Mr. Chenault that I knew nothing about Negroes, since there were scarcely any in that part of the county where I lived. I also told him that my father thought they should be free, and now that Mr. Lincoln was to be President, he thought they would be freed. I observed further that if there was any danger of the Negroes' being freed it might be well to sell them so as not to lose so much.

"Yes, my son," he explained, "you will find that those who know least of the Negro and the nature of his bondage are far more interested in his freedom than those who know him well. I know that your father[18] was reared in the North and that he is opposed to slavery. As an abstract proposition, it is wrong for any one man to own another, but the system was here when I was born. I had nothing to do with its establishment. I have become greatly attached to those I own and who depend on me for their well-being. I believe they are all attached to me and my wife and children. We are really one big family. As to selling

The Jack Martin House. Built about 1861. The third porch built to the front is shown.

Spring in the rear of the Jack Martin House. The water flowed continually, as shown in the cut, throughout the dry seasons of 1930 and 1936.

Hide-out of Confederates near Muddy Creek, called the Rock House—as it looks today. (See map of Old Cane Springs.)

BAKING POTTERY AT WACO AND BYBEETOWN

A superior and varied quality of ware is still turned out at Waco and Bybeetown, and is shipped to all parts of the United States. It is interesting to note that some of Morgan's raiders visited Waco during the Civil War and on learning that the operator of the plant, Valentine Baumstark, was a Union sympathizer, broke up the ware ready for the market and in other ways damaged the establishment.

them, I cannot. I have never sold a Negro except at his request, so that he might live in a home with his wife and children. I have bought them under the same conditions. I have given some to my married children, fixing on them a price simply that I might equalize my children's inheritance.[19] Beyond circumstances of that kind, no one can buy one of my Negroes, not even if I knew every one of them would be set free. My son, should they ever be set free I will be as solicitous of their welfare as for my own children. Were they liberated in a land where nature supplied most of their wants, they might get on fairly well, but here I fear they will never succeed."

"Do you think that differences between the white and black races justify slavery?" I asked.

"Yes, I do," Mr. Chenault answered. "The all-wise Creator has made a great difference between the white and black man. Slavery is right, for the Creator made the two races different.[20] Furthermore, the Negroes are happier in service than any other people. They sing when at work as no other folk sing. They appreciate a kindness as much as anyone. Their domestic ties are strong and in everything they are a good and faithful people. The Negro is not a thinker and planner, but he is a fair executor, when he understands a plan. I fear that if it happens that the Negro will have to plan and execute for himself, he will be unable to do so, and degeneracy of the race will be the ultimate end. I conclude this from what I see of the free Negroes around me. If a Negro is freed after he has passed middle life, he appears to do fairly well, but if he is freed before he has been taught lessons in economy and accumulation, he never appears to catch on. None of those I know raise and lay by in summer enough to carry them through the winter. Their stock starve and they themselves almost freeze. They appear to have no knowledge or thought of making arrangements for the future."

"Do you really believe, Mr. Chenault, that slavery is necessary for the Negroes' moral and religious welfare?" I questioned.

"It seems to me that it is," he replied. "I notice further that those who are born free and who grow up with free parents have neither the moral nor religious sentiment of those raised in the quarters around homes of white persons.[21] I fear, therefore, that should they all be set free, as soon as the older ones, who have been trained in economy and the necessity of providing and laying up for the future, pass away, the entire race will begin to degenerate. A great portion of those coming on after the old ones have died will naturally drift into petty thieving, and thereby be a great annoyance to the community in which they live. With these impressions, my son, I fear those who are now clamoring for the freedom of the Negroes, if they finally succeed, will bring to them a far greater calamity than they now endure. I know that those who are working for their freedom believe they are directed by Divinity, and, therefore, I hold no animosity towards them."

I said that I had heard Uncle Robert tell about some men mobbing John G. Fee over in the big bend of the Kentucky River east of Texas for preaching abolition doctrines. "What do you think of that?" I asked.

"That was all wrong, my son," he replied. "Mr. Fee wanted a whipping and so he provoked and encouraged certain men of the community to give it to him.[22] He has his admirers and abettors in the North. A few years ago he opened a church and a school for Negroes and whites at a place he has named Berea in the extreme southern part of the county.[23] There are several families of free Negroes near there. Cassius M. Clay,[24] an emancipationist of this county, gave him land and money for his work in the beginning and his northern admirers also sent him money to carry on his efforts to abolish slavery. Clay is not as radical as Fee, but both are playing with fire. I have no sympathy whatever with their views and I heartily approved the expulsion of Fee, Rogers, and others last winter from the county.[25] I hope their school and church never open again. Even Clay doesn't approve of Fee's radical teachings."[26]

"But what effect has Mr. Fee's efforts had upon the Negroes?"

"None. If our people had only left Fee alone he never could have accomplished anything. Neither my Negroes nor Colonel Noland's nor Captain Chambers' pay any attention to him. I have heard some of them talk about him and they all referred to him as some 'po' white trash tryin' to kick up trouble.' They actually regarded him with contempt, and if the people around had not mobbed him, it would not have been known outside of Old Cane Springs that he had been here. Now this community is spoken of in the North as being owned by people who cruelly drive their slaves to their daily tasks and beat and threaten to hang any good, God-fearing Christian who may dare speak a kind word for the poor Negro."

"The Negro is satisfied with his condition," Mr. Chenault concluded, "and no man or set of men can make him dissatisfied. If freedom ever comes to him, it will not come as a request of the Negro but it will be forced upon him by the fanatics of the North, who know absolutely nothing of the conditions and desires of his race."

While Mr. Chenault was making this last statement, he saw that I heard the sound of many voices in song. Seeing that my attention was diverted, he arose and said: "We will walk to the door and see my people and hear them sing as they come in from work."

I had never seen more than five or six men working together before, and until I beheld a much larger number coming from the fields I could hardly believe anyone could work so many on a farm. The older ones were walking with Mr. Chenault's sons in the rear. The youngest ones were apparently playing tag as we children did at school. The middle-aged were in the midst of the procession and were singing in perfect accord all the parts of a song I had never heard before. It was melodious, however, and I stood charmed by the great wave of sound rolling from those fifteen or twenty voices. We moved out to the county road which was in front of the big house. The entire procession had to pass us to reach the gate that led to the quarters. We had hardly reached the stiles leading from the road over the fence into the yard, when the young Negroes in front began in one accord: "Yon's Ole Marse! Yon's Ole Marse!" They kept up the exclamation as they ran until they were near us.

Mr. Chenault spoke to each of them as kindly as a father would to his sons. "Andy, how are you getting on shucking corn?" he asked.

I noticed two rows of white teeth showing from a tall, good looking brown-faced boy and I knew by his becoming smile which one was Andy.

"Fine, Ole Marse, fine. Me an' Pete shucked ten shocks since dinnah,". was the reply.

Mr. Chenault then pleasantly addressed something to every one—Pete, Frank, Letch, and Bob—and each cheerfully rendered an account of himself.

Next came the singing crowd. They ceased to sing when about fifty yards away. Everyone bowed as he passed and, with a look and smile which almost spoke adoration, said: "Evenin', Ole Marse." Then came Amos, Bill, and Jeff with Mr. Chenault's sons, David, Cabell, and Anderson. He bowed a welcome return to them, and they greeted him respectfully.

Sounds back toward the quarters caused me to look that way. The little Negroes, who had escorted me that afternoon to the big house, were scampering like so many lambs to meet their fathers and larger brothers, and with them came their little sisters and brothers. The children ran to their elders, and every worker held in his arms one or two of the little affectionate Negroes as he walked on towards the quarters. At the quarters, the married men were met by their wives, who greeted them pleasantly. A look of happy contentment appeared on the face of everyone.

I marveled at such happiness and asked Mr. Chenault whether his people were often as happy as they appeared that evening.

"Always," he answered, "except when someone on the plantation dies. A death in my home or the quarters causes a sadness that will not wear off for two or three weeks, but after that they are as merry as ever."

Presently I bade Mr. Chenault and his sons, "Good evening," mounted Whizaker, and rode back to my aunt's, musing along the way over the "oppressed Negro" that my father had caused me to believe should be freed. I told Aunt Jose what I had seen and on retiring dreamed of the poor slave, but I did not see him as a man dissatisfied with his lot in my dreams that night.

CHAPTER IV

MORE ABOUT NEGRO SERVITUDE

EARLY the next morning I called for Whizaker and set out to see more of the life of the Negroes. I rode at once to Mr. Cabell Chenault's to continue my interview of the previous day. I learned from him that on the day before his force had finished shucking corn, and that now they were preparing to cut and bring in the winter wood. Nearly every able-bodied man had an axe. Two grindstones were running, putting the axes in shape for use. He said that Bill, Jerry, and Jeff were his wagoners, and that the three would possibly haul wood in and stack it in the yard as fast as the other ten or twelve would cut it. He stated, further, that if the weather remained favorable during the next two weeks, they would likely get in a hundred cords, which would probably last through the winter. Amos and his sons, he said, would not assist in gathering the wood; they would have to see to getting in enough corn for the hogs, which must be well fed until the latter part of November or the first part of December, so as to be ready for killing as soon as the weather was favorable.

I had just noticed the great number of hogs he had and said: "I suppose you will send most of them to the Cincinnati market?"

"No, my son," he replied, "I will not send any of them to market. It will require all of them for my family. During the summer we kill six or eight beeves, fifteen or twenty sheep, and with our hams and bacon and our turkeys and chickens we manage to have enough meat to last until time to kill hogs again."

"Who-ee!" I exclaimed, "a hundred cords of wood to keep your family warm and nearly a hundred hogs to feed them! It must take nearly all the corn you raise to feed the hogs and bread your family. Where do you get any money from all your labor?"

"Your astonishment looks reasonable, my son," he answered. "I have to watch close to see that I do not come out behind.[27] All of my people have to be clothed as well as fed. They must all have plenty of good bed-clothing. But nearly everything they need is made here on the farm. Your grandmother has always looked after making the cloth and then the garments. My women hardly ever work in the field. Some of the girls assist in pulling flax, and they weave the cloth. Nell and Minerva are the regular spinners. Most all the women join in making the garments. Jennie and Judy are the principal weavers. My wife assigns each her work and she goes to it as cheerfully as my men. That old woman you see yonder does nothing but cook. Dishes are washed by young girls."

I told him I wanted to go that day to Colonel John Noland's and Captain John Chambers'. "I understand," I said, "that the Captain has a few more Negroes than you have."

"Yes," he stated, "Captain Chambers has a few more than I have, and we both have more than we need. But he, like myself, has no money value on his people. I conclude, therefore, that he will never have fewer than he has now, unless Lincoln frees them, as they say he will."

Then he turned to a lean-looking, long-legged Negro boy, almost as black as the ace of spades, and said, "Letcher, you have nothing to do; catch one of the mules and ride with Gustin here to Colonel Noland's and Captain Chambers' or anywhere else he may wish to go. Be sure to come home before dark."

Letcher sprang about three feet in the air and lit running toward the barn, and in a short time returned leading a mule. The bridle was of homemade rope, except the bit, and there was no saddle. We both mounted and went on our way to Colonel Noland's.

To give Letcher a start at talking, I said: "Letch, does Mr. Chenault treat you darkies well?"

His eyes brightened, and he showed two beautiful rows of teeth. "Yes, suh, he's good to us all, an' we all loves 'im. All de grown up ones say Ole Marse is de bes' man in Ole Cane Springs. Marse John Nolan's niggers say dey hab de bestes' marster, an' Marse John Chambers' niggers say dey hab de bestes'; but Uncle Amos say he knows Marse Cabell is de bestes' man, an' he knows. Marse John Nolan', he works his niggers jis' like Marse Cabell, but Marse John Chambers b'lieve his niggers too good to work. His niggers run 'roun' heap more than any niggers in Old Cane Springs. He done use up all de wood on his place."

"You know Marse John Chambers' house is down yonder close by de riber," Letch continued. "Dey git der wood frum de drif; dey cain't git in big stack ov wood like we-uns an' Marse John Nolan' git. W'en Chambers' Mart wuz up to our house de udder night, Aunt Judy, she say to 'im: 'Mart, w'y you allus beggin' me fur sumpin' to eat? You is jis like some free nigger, allus askin' fur sumpin' to eat.' "

Letch gave his mule a kick in the side to urge the animal along and then continued: "Marse Chambers' niggers mighty proud dough. Dey t'ink dey am de bestes' niggers in Ole Cane Springs. Uncle Amos, he say Marse Chambers make 'em b'lieve so. Marse John Nolan', he ain't got but one big feelin' nigger; dat's ole Harrison. He's his ovahseah. Dey say he wuz named fur a pres'dent. Dat's w'at dey say makes 'im so stuck-up-like. He won't walk out wid de han's like Uncle Amos do wid our folks. W'en he go whar dey work, he rides one ov Marse John Nolan's big bay mares."

I noticed Letcher's eyes flash to one side. He said: "You can see ole Harrison now. Look how big he rides dat ole mare."

Harrison was the most portly looking Negro I had ever seen. He appeared to be at least seventy years of age. Though he was very dark, every feature about his face was pleasant. He rode up to us, bowed politely to me, and then spoke to Letcher: "Who am dat you ridin' wid?"

"Marse Cabell calls 'im Marse Hart. He kin to Miss Jose ovah at Marse Robert's. He'll tell you who he am; you ax 'im."

Harrison laughed heartily at Letcher's introduction, and simply said, "I'll find out"; and we three rode on to the Noland home together.

Colonel Noland came out to meet us as we rode up through the yard. I saw at a glance that he was a very old man, possibly eighty; but he walked as straight and erect as if he were not more than half that age. He spoke to me first:

"You are some of my neighbor Chenault's kin or guest, for I know your mule. You must alight and take dinner with us."

"Boy," he said, addressing Letcher, "you take the mules to the barn. Jerry is there and he will feed them."

Then Colonel Noland turned to Harrison and asked whether he was through shucking corn and whether arrangements had been made for getting wood.

After Harrison had explained satisfactorily, his master said: "You see that the boy who was with this young man gets something to eat. Take him with you to the quarters." Then turning to me, he said: "We'll go to the house now."

CHAPTER V

MARY ANN OLDHAM

WE HAD hardly been seated on the porch before a young lady came out. Our eyes met, but I looked at her only a second, for my eyes dropped with boyish bashfulness, and I thought in that one short glance I had beheld the prettiest face I had ever seen. I saw that she was two or three years my senior, but I could not look up until she spoke.

"Grandpa," she said, "you seem to have company whom you want to enjoy all to yourself. Why don't you introduce him to me?"

"Bless you, honey," he replied, "you walk so lightly that I did not know you were here, and now that I do know I am unable to tell you who he is. He rode into the yard just a few minutes since with Harrison and a boy who I think belongs to Mr. Cabell Chenault. I know the spotted mule he is riding. There is not another in Old Cane Springs like it, and I doubt if there is another in the county, and I know by the mule he is either Cabell Chenault's relative or a visitor of the owner of the mule. In either event, he is welcome to my home, but he will have to introduce himself to both of us."

I told them that my name was Hart—" 'Augustine Hart,' is the way my mother wrote it in the Bible," I explained, "but they just call me 'Gustin.' I am not stopping with Mr. Cabell Chenault, as the mule makes you think. I am staying with my Uncle Robert Chenault. He married my Aunt Josephine Cavins. My mother is dead, and my father, Thomas Hart, has married the widow Bogie[28] over on Silver Creek. They all consented for me to come and stay a while with my aunt, possibly four or five years. Uncle Robert borrowed the mule for me."

"Well, Master Hart," said the Colonel, "you have given a splendid introduction to yourself. I will now introduce you to my granddaughter, Miss Mary Ann Oldham. She is a little too old for you to expect anything more than an introduction, but she has three little sisters that will be up about the time you may begin to sigh after the girls, and it may be well that you know the older sister."

Miss Oldham ran up, grabbed me as if I had been a small child, and kissed me in spite of my bashful dodging. She said my Aunt Jose was the dearest, sweetest woman she knew, and that we were to be the best of friends. I was glad to hear her say that, for I felt sure I loved her then, and that I would grow fast and catch up with her and then we would be more than friends. I did not know then that she was at an age when she would grow faster than I.

In a little while we had a very good dinner. In the meantime, I had explained why I had started on my itinerary among the homes of the community. It appeared strange to them that I had never seen Negro quarters and knew so little of them. Miss Oldham, whom I soon came to call Mary Ann, let me know she would be my escort that afternoon and show me the Kentucky River as well as the quarters. Shortly after dinner, Jerry, a handsome black boy, brought my mule and Mary Ann's pony. He assisted her to mount as though she were some ethereal being and appeared as though he was as delighted in his work and service as if waiting on a goddess.

Letcher appeared to realize that his time to entertain me had ceased, so Mary Ann and I rode first past the Noland quarters. At that hour only old women and the children who were too small to labor occupied them, but they all knew Mary Ann. Old heads were thrust out of the cabin doors and the little children came running to us, and all shouted: "Howdy, Miss Mary," and every now and then some of the old women would say, "Bless yo' heart, honey, you is de purt'es' t'ing in de worl'." Others would say as we passed, "Don't she ride like a lady," and "De boy's some of Marse Cabell's kin; I knows dat mule."

Presently we were on the Red River road. Mary Ann said that we would go to the mouth of Red River first and that she would show me the Negro quarters and all the Negroes I wanted to see when we returned. As we rode along, she interested me by pointing out homes in Estill and Clark counties across the river, and by telling me the neighborhood's history. She also explained how the community came to be called Old Cane Springs, by stating that there was never any other spot on earth better watered than the land between the Kentucky River and Muddy Creek; that there were about ten thousand acres of land between the river and the creek below the narrow place up the road towards Texas; that there was a spring for nearly every one of those acres; and that the largest of cane grew around these springs before the county was settled. Furthermore, she was of the opinion that this community was the earliest part of Madison County to be settled except Boonesborough,[29] which was a few miles down the river.

We found the river very low. After we had allowed Mary Ann's horse and my mule to drink, we started for the Martin home. The Negroes there knew my companion and greeted her with "Howdy, Miss Mary." Everyone looked as happy as if it were a holiday and no one appeared as I had pictured slaves to be.

After a short delay at the Martin place we went on to Captain John Chambers', who was Mary Ann's uncle. All the Negroes there knew my companion, and when they saw she was coming to the quarters instead of the big house, they rejoiced. It was "Howdy, Miss Mary. God Bless yo' purty soul! How she looks like 'er deah ma, befo' Marse Oldham tuck 'er away."

Mary Ann knew all the Negroes and called each one by name. I watched and listened with amazement and I said to myself, "Are these the unhappy homes my father wishes to break up? Is this the bondage he has taught me to abhor?"

We rode up to the big house, where I was introduced to Captain Chambers as a lad who had never seen many Negroes and wanted to see them in their quarters.

A very handsome man greeted me pleasantly and said he knew by my mule that I had come from one of the Chenaults. He insisted on our staying for supper, but on remembering Mr. Chenault's charge to Letch, we had to decline, and were soon on our road home. I was grieved when Mary Ann bade us good-afternoon and turned in at the Noland gate, after she had promised to see that I had a good time and that she would come to visit my aunt the next Sunday.

On arriving home, I tried to tell Aunt Josephine where I had been and what I had seen, but I soon became too sleepy to talk and, with the promise that I would find something else interesting on the morrow, I was sent to bed.

Chapter VI

THE HONEST MILLER AND GREEN NOLAND

THE FOLLOWING morning Uncle Robert suggested that, since I had already been to the mouth of Red River and from points on the road had seen much of Old Cane Springs, if I would go down to Weddle's Mill and follow the Muddy Creek road to the Othniel Oldham plantation and return home, I would then have a pretty good idea of the neighborhood in which I had come to live. He assured me that I would meet some very interesting and pleasant people if I took that route.

In a short time Whizaker and I were on the road to the mill. I learned on arriving that there was a distillery operated at the same place. The mill and its arrangements were just as interesting as the one near where I had lived on Silver Creek, but the still was a feature which Bogie's Mill did not have, and consequently I had never seen one.

"Young man, what Chenault are you?" the miller asked.

When I explained that I was not a Chenault, but only a visitor who expected to be in the neighborhood for a few years, he became very accommodating and kindly offered to show me around the place. I told him of my familiarity with a mill, but that I had no idea how a still was operated.

He explained that his mill ground corn and wheat for everybody in Old Cane Springs and that out of the toll he made whiskey, which he sold. That was about the only way he had to make money, since there was no sale for meal and everybody raised his own corn. Very few people, he said, made whiskey, so he virtually supplied the whole community.

"Does your whiskey make people drunk like that we sometimes have on Silver Creek?" I asked.

"Yes, my son, I suppose it will make people drunk just like any other whiskey, but it's very seldom that anyone in Old Cane Springs gets drunk. There is not a man in the community who would not feel that he was eternally disgraced if he should drink to drunkenness. He would have no more standing in this community than a glutton. We believe here in a man's being a man, temperate in all things and an extremist in nothing."

Our conversation was interrupted by the sudden appearance in the mill of a very stout, matronly looking woman. The miller said, "My wife, young man"; and I bowed and said, "Mrs. Weddle, I'm happy to know you."

She gave a peculiar look at the miller. I had not told him who I was nor had I asked him his name. Thereupon the miller explained: "My name is not Weddle, young man; my name is Walden, but you are not to blame for calling my wife Mrs. Weddle, from the fact that this mill is known by that name near and far.[30] However, its builder was a good, honest miller, and when people say nice things about him, nobody objects or says it is untrue."

"My son," Mr. Walden continued, "when people speak kind words about a miller and say he is honest, never doubt them. Very, very few are so spoken of. No one is tempted as often as a miller. I often grind for many different people in a day and I take my toll out of every sack that comes. I generally do it when no one interested but myself is around. The temptation to toll deep strikes you every time you put the piggin in the bag. A man to be a miller should be not only honest but also God-fearing. He should feel that there is an all-seeing eye that is watching him for the absent one. If he is that kind of man, temptation is soon gone, and with pleasure he deals honestly. George Weddle, the man who built this mill, must have been just that kind of person, and for that reason I do not object, even though I am now its owner, for it to keep the name of its builder."

"Oh, Mr. Walden, you'd talk all day about an honest miller," said Mrs. Walden. "Everybody knows you are as straight in your dealings as Mr. Weddle. I want to know who the young man is."

I told her my name and where I was stopping and explained further that I would be going to school to a Mr. Harris, who was to begin teaching the next week.

"I'm glad to know you," she said; "my boys, General and Elijah, will be in school with you."

Mrs. Walden and her husband invited me to dine with them, but I explained that Uncle Robert had mapped out a long ride for me, and, with many thanks, I started up the creek by the deep, blue mill pond, and as I rode along I wondered if I would find everyone in Old Cane Springs as good and kind as those I had already met.

Presently, as I was passing a modest little farm house near the creek, a very handsome man of about forty appeared and said, "Hey, there, Whizaker, where are you taking that boy? He wants to stop here. Do you think you'll get to grass quicker by going on? Young man, hold him up and turn in or he'll carry you by."

His suggestion was equivalent to a command, so into the yard I turned and dismounted. Whizaker at once went to eating grass with as much relish as if he had been invited for that purpose. I had never before been in the presence of a stranger at whose home I felt so welcome even before I knew who the gentleman was. I saw that he was a good, kind man, who knew my mule and intended to know me, so I concluded there was no use to demur, but let the acquaintance begin. I learned that he was Captain Nathan Noland. He asked me many questions about myself. He pointed up the creek only a few hundred yards distant to a house where my aunt first lived and said that my uncle had been living by the church only a short time.

When Mrs. Noland came out he told her who I was, and when he explained that I was Mrs. Josephine Chenault's nephew, she grabbed and hugged me as if I had been her nephew, saying she felt as if she almost knew my mother, since she had heard my aunt speak of her so often. She told me how she and Aunt Jose, when they lived so close together as young housekeepers, had spliced their tableware together on various occasions, so as to make a creditable showing when one or the other had company. She also related many other interesting things in their young married lives.

Mr. and Mrs. Noland insisted on my remaining for dinner. "The boys will soon be in from work," they said, "and one of them can ride with you this afternoon." I felt so welcome that I accepted their invitation. Presently the boys and one Negro came in, and I was introduced to Elbridge, John, James, and Green.[31] After enjoying Captain Noland's hospitality to the fullest and after Green had been chosen as my companion, we started up Muddy Creek.

Green, a handsome brown-eyed boy with curling locks, genial and agreeable from the start, appeared to believe it his special duty to point out and tell about everything he thought would interest me. When we had passed the creek ford, he pointed over to the left and said: "That's Lion Run branch, and all that land way over there, as far as you can see way up the creek, belongs to Mr. Cabell Chenault. He's got more land than anybody else in Old Cane Springs, and more niggers too, except Uncle John Chambers, who has more big, fat, lazy niggers than anybody else, and he hardly makes them work enough to feed themselves. I don't know why they call that branch Lion Run. I never heard of a lion being on it, but Uncle Caesar, one of Grandpa Noland's old niggers, saw a bear on it not long ago. That nigger shouted so loud when he saw that bear that he waked folks up clear down to our house. Pa heard him shouting and ran up the creek nearly to the ford, when suddenly Old Caesar passed him going down to the house. Pa tried to stop him, to learn what he was yelling about, but he couldn't do it. He said that nigger certainly flew by him like the wind. When Pa got to the house it was nearly an hour before Old Caesar quit blowing long enough to tell him that he had seen a bear up the branch."

"Do you suppose Old Caesar ever did see a bear?" I questioned.

"Yes Sir - - ee! Uncle Caesar had seen bears long ago," Green answered. "He says there were plenty of them in the canebrakes when he was a boy, and that he used to keep a lookout for them; but he was not expecting to see any bears now since the country had been settled. Uncle Caesar said that he had his umbrella to fight him with, and that he gave him some good punches with it until he got a chance to run."

I laughed and said, "Some bear story!"[32]

"See that little mouse-colored mule over there?" Green asked, letting go his bear story. "That's the mule your Uncle Robert let Dick Ward ride to see Hawkins hanged. Your uncle told my Pa that he wanted Dick to see Hawkins hanged, because he was inclined to be a bad boy, and he thought it might scare some of the meanness out of him. But when Dick returned he said he'd rather die like Hawkins than any other way, for women gave him flowers, and he made a big speech at the scaffold and was the best looking man there.[33] Mr. Chenault was mighty sorry he had let him ride old Mouse after he talked that way."

"That house up there is where your Uncle Robert lived until last year," Green continued. "He was our closest neighbor before he moved away. Your Aunt Jose and my Ma used to be together all the time—seemed to love each other like they were related. We must go by and see Aunt Creech Sally. She's always called that. Mr. Cabell Chenault has got another Sally—old man Harry's wife. Mr. David Chenault set old Harry free, but didn't set his wife free. She had twenty-two children. She had lots of them after Uncle Harry was freed. You see, if his Sally had been free, there would have been a lot of those niggers born free, just like the Brock niggers. I suppose Mr. Chenault knew that and for that reason he didn't set her free. She is a great big, fat, yellow nigger."

"What about Aunt Creech Sally?" I asked.

"Oh, Aunt Creech Sally is a good nigger and the best cook you ever saw. I wish we could have gotten started before dinner.

I just love to eat up there. She makes gravy out of butter, and she cooks everything well. There isn't any plate of butter on her table. It is in a great big bowl. She carries the keys to the smoke-house, just like Ma."

Chapter VII

AUNT CREECH SALLY

BY THIS TIME we were at the stiles. Aunt Creech Sally had seen us coming and had started out to welcome us.

"Git down, honeys; I's so glad to see you all," was her greeting. "Who's dis young stranger? Must be some ov Marse Cabell's folks. I see he's on Whizaker."

We alighted and Green told her who I was. She grabbed me in her arms and hugged me and said, "You looks jis like yo' aunt, Miss Jose. I oughtah knowed you by dat, but I warn't thinkin'. Yo' aunt is de deahes', bes' chile in de world. You know Marse Robert brung 'er heah w'en dey furst marri'd, an' dey lived heah wid me fur five yare. Lawdy, honey, how I did hate to see 'er move 'way; but she's close 'nough fur me to see 'er eber now an' den. A heap a de life ov dis place went w'en she moved 'way."

"Aunt Sally, why don't you move up to the home with the rest of the folks?" I asked.

"Lan's sake, chile! Marse Cabell, he allus atter me to do dat, says ez I be gittin' ole, he wants me to come up close to de big house, whar he kin see atter me an' hab someone wait on me ef I git sick. Dat's mighty good ov 'im, but I jis cain't make up my mind to leabe heah. I's bin heah fur nigh on to forty yare, an' I wants to die right heah an' be burr'ed out heah in de orchard by my Sam."

"Where did you live, Aunt Sally, before you came here?"

"I lived in ole Virginny, dat's whar I lived. I had a good marster out dar. He had lots ov niggers an' he wuz de kindes', bes' man—Marse Jonathan Abney, he wuz. He thought all ov 'is niggers wuz too good to be worked hard. He sp'iled all ov us. He wouldn't have no ovahseah, an' his farm got po' raisin' t'ings to feed so many niggers, so he gits in debt. I wuz marri'd den an' had three chilluns. My man, Sam, wuz a mighty likely man. I know'd times wuz hard an' dat my marster wuz gittin' in debt an' we all used to say, 'Marster, you orter let some ov us go'; but he'd say he'd jis ez soon sell some ov his own chillun ez eny ov 'is people. At last somebody sued 'im, an' den de sheruff, he comes an' levies on all de niggers fur de debt. Honey, you don't know w'at a time it wuz dat day, way back in our ole Virginny home. Ole Marse an' Missus an' all de white chillun an' all de niggers wuz a cryin'. Marse John, he comes out to de qua'ters cryin' like 'is heart would break, an' all de niggers stood 'roun' lookin' scared-like, fur dey all knowed some ov 'em had to be sole an' leabe de old home furevah."[34]

Then Aunt Creech Sally went on to relate how her "Marse John" had assembled his Negroes and had told them of his financial difficulty and had explained that the sheriff was there to sell one or enough of them to satisfy the debt. He reminded them that he had never bought any of them, but that he had inherited them or they had been born to those whom he had inherited; nor had he ever sold one of his "people," as he kindly referred to his slaves. He explained that he had borrowed money to feed and clothe them, hoping that conditions would change and that he would finally make enough off of his plantation to pay his debts. He stated further that he had a number of young men, any one of whom without his family would sell for enough to pay the debt then due, but he wanted a man and his family sold together. Mr. Abney closed his remarks by promising to try to get a kindly disposed person to purchase them, and then he asked for someone to offer himself for sale, since he did not want to choose the family to be sold.

"W'en Marse John stop talkin'," Aunt Sally continued, "we alls wuz quiet fur de longes' time. It wuz not 'cause we alls wuz 'fraid to be sole down Souf, like dey do now.[35] Dar wuz no sellin' niggers down Souf den, but dey wuz 'fraid dey would hurt Ole Marse' feelin's if dey 'peared willin' to go. When Ole Marse had waited a long time an' de sheruff stan'in' right dar by 'im, he said someone must speak up or he'd haf to let de sheruff say who'd go."

"I felt like cryin' w'en my Sam, he steps out an' say: 'Ole Marse, I knows nothin' 'bout eny place 'cept dis ole farm an' de neighbors 'roun' heah. I's neber bin enywhar but heah an' de neighbors' qua'ters, an' I don't b'lieve eny ov de neighbors'll want my Sally an' our chillun, but I b'lieve dat somebody'll pay 'nough fur us to pay dat debt. I knows dey will ef you'll 'low dat little boy Jake to go wid us. You know my wife, Sally, tuck 'im w'en 'is muvver died, an' we've kept 'im eber since. He feels like one ov us, he do, an' he'd hab nobody to look atter 'im ef we all lef'. He won't be worf much fo' a long time nohow, an' he's half white an' looks like he might be del'cate. 'Low me dis an' I knows Sally'll make de sac'fice wid me an' gib up de bes' marster an' missus an' de bes' home in ole Virginny. Fur de good ov de res', I b'lieve de Lawd'll bless us fur dis sac'fice.'"

"When Sam wuz talkin' he suttinly look gran' to me. I wuz rebellin' all de time 'till he mentions li'l' Jake. Soon's he mentions li'l' Jake, I gives up, I do, feeling like it wuz all right. Ole Marse promised to bring us all in to de county seat on de day ov de sale, an' de sheruff lef'. How it did hurt to leabe dem all, but Sam wuz brave an' say he'd please whoevah bought us."

Aunt Sally stated that the day of the sale was just like a funeral at the plantation. When she and her family arrived in town they were all put on a platform, after which the sheriff read a paper, and they were sold at the first bid, the offer being enough to pay the debt and costs, and Mr. Abney having declared he would not accept any money from the sale. He was disappointed, however, when he learned that a Mr. Mullins, from Winchester, Kentucky, had bought his people. He told the purchaser that he had expected someone near his plantation to buy them and that he had hoped the family would not be separated.

Mr. Mullins explained that he was buying Negroes for speculation in Kentucky, where the soil was rich and the forests and cane were heavy and where strong men like Sam and his wife were needed. He said further that the children would be an expense for years and could not be sold for much. In all probability he would have to separate the family.

This statement caused Mr. Abney much anxiety and he said, according to Aunt Sally, that he had hoped Mr. Mullins wanted the Negroes for himself, and that he was not a "regular nigger trader." He reminded him that he had bought the family cheap and expressed the desire that he would be satisfied with a fair profit when he returned to Kentucky and would allow Sam and his wife and children to be bought by some kind, considerate person who would keep them all together.

Thereupon Mr. Mullins assured Mr. Abney that he was not a "regular nigger trader" and that he wanted only a few of the people he had purchased. The others he would dispose of to farmers near Winchester. Especially did he promise to find someone who wanted just such a family as Sam and Aunt Sally's.

"Den Marse John grab 'is han' an' shake hit hard," Aunt Sally related. "He tole 'im w'at a good man he wuz, an' den he tuck me an' Sam by de han' an' say he hate to part wid us, an' he hope we all'd meet again, ef not heah, den in heben. Atter dat he went away, an' we all ain't nevah see 'im no mo'."

Aunt Sally's voice trembled as she uttered these words. She stopped talking long enough to wipe her eyes with her apron, and then continued.

"Our new marster said now he had all de niggers he wanted an' wuz ready to start home. He tuck us to a place whar we could git sumpin' to eat an' whar we could sleep dat night. W'en he call fur us next mornin', we all went out on de street, an' dar wuz a great big drove ov niggers. Some wuz tied tugedder, an' dar wuz some mo' women an' chillun. He had one wagon an' said de women an' chillun could ride in dat w'en dey got tired, but de men 'ud haf to walk, 'cept de driver. It tuck us near two weeks to git to Winchester. Sam drove mos' ov de way, an' me an' de chillun rode. Marse Mullins, he wuz good to us all de way, an' we alls liked 'im an' wanted 'im to keep us, but he said he couldn't—it 'ud break 'im.

"Well, de day atter we gits to Winchester, Marse Cabell comes 'roun' an' looks at us, an' he an' Marse Mullins takes a long time a talkin' an' at las' he come back an' say to us, 'You all b'long to me. Git all yo' t'ings tugedder so we all kin go home.' So we come heah wid 'im an' heah I haf bin eber since."

By this time Green began to get restless and indicated a desire to go, but I encouraged Aunt Sally to continue.

"Well," she said, "Sam sho' wuz a big he'p to Marse Cabell. He tole 'im many times how he happen' to be sole, an' he listen to 'im, an' it looks like Marse Cabell not a-goin' to make no mistake like Marse John did. He's careful an' he make money ebery yare, an' he keeps on buyin' lan' 'til he now own mo' lan' den eny man in Ole Cane Springs. He bought Marse David's farm an' moved up to de big brick house beyon' de chu'ch an' lef' me an' Sam heah on de creek to run dis fa'm. W'en Marse Robert come he run it. Den my deah, po' Sam, he dies. An' w'en Marse Robert buys 'is farm up at de chu'ch, Marse Cabell want me to come an' lib wid 'im, but lan' sakes, honey, I couldn't leabe Sam. I tole Marse Cabell I couldn't; dat while he wuz burr'ed up heah in de orchard I seen 'im ebery day, or at leas' I thought I did. I could heah 'im singin' jis like he sung in ole Virginny befo' we come heah, an' I wuz 'fraid ef I got too fur 'way I couldn't heah 'im no more, an' I told Marse Cabell it wouldn't be long befo' I would lay up dar in de o'cha'd by 'im, an' ez we had allus bin neah each udder, I couldn't leabe 'im, so dey jis let me stay heah."

At this point Green exclaimed impatiently, "Look here, Gustin, Aunt Sally will keep us here all evening! We must go."

So Aunt Sally said, "Good-by, honeys; you all mus' come back to see me"; and we rode away.

I could not help meditating deeply over Aunt Creech Sally's life story, and I thought possibly Green was also touched, as he was silent for the first time since we had left his home, except when Aunt Sally was talking. Presently he looked back toward the house and indicated that he wanted to see if he was out of hearing of the old woman. He must have judged that he was, for he said: "That old nigger certainly believes in ghosts. I kinder got scared when she began to talk about hearing old Sam sing. I know old Sam is dead. I was at the burying, and when she began to talk about his singing, I tell you, boy, I wanted to get away from there. I don't want to hear anybody I have seen buried singing around. I expect old Sally just imagines she hears him. Don't you think so?"

"I have been taught that there are no such things as ghosts," I replied, "and, of course, I don't believe in them."

"Well, if you stay around niggers, you'll change your mind about ghosts," Green explained. "Nearly any nigger you talk to can tell you of lots of ghosts he has seen, but we'll talk about ghosts some other time when you have been here longer."[86]

CHAPTER VIII

NATHAN BIRD DEATHERAGE AND THE FOX HUNTERS

As MY COMPANION ceased speaking of ghosts, we approached an attractive residence on the west side of the creek.

"There is an interesting place," I observed. "Who lives there?"

"General Israel Jackson lives up there,"[87] Green replied. "He is the fattest man you ever saw. He is low and fat. You just ought to see him on a horse. His legs stick out straight from the horse. You see that fat old nigger woman way up there? She is the wife of old John, the same boy you heard Aunt Sally talking about. Of course he is a man now. The woman's name is Violet. I expect she looks like a violet to Mrs. Jackson. The Jacksons haven't many niggers and I suppose they all look good to them. I wish Mrs. Jackson was out where you could see her. She is fat just like Mr. Jackson. They are all the fattest people I ever saw."

Green in no wise shirked what he apparently regarded as his commission to entertain me, so he kept on rapidly and loudly talking about every object he thought of interest.

"There on the hill lives Mr. Amos Deatherage,"[88] he explained. He has lots of niggers and owns a thousand acres or more of these rich hills and bottoms. They are all fine folks. I tell you, Gustin, his boys are all gentlemen and they have three of the best looking little sisters you ever saw. That other big white house you see farther up the creek is where my Uncle Othniel Oldham lives. Yonder come Killis Deatherage and Kie Oldham now. They are going fox hunting."

I looked and saw two young men on horses coming up the creek road, and at least twenty hound dogs following them. When we met, one of the two said, "Green, I thought Harvey or Jephtha had come home, but I see you have captured a stranger."

I waited, thinking Green would tell them who I was, but instead of an introduction he began telling them about Aunt Creech Sally's account of seeing old Sam's ghost. One of the boys interrupted him by saying, "I am not interested in old Sam's ghost"; and, looking at me, said, "My name is Killis Deatherage, and this is my neighbor, Kie Oldham. We want to know who you are."

I told him who I was and explained why I was in the neighborhood, and we soon drifted into friendly conversation. The boys insisted on my going to the hunt with them. I declined, explaining that my aunt might not excuse me and that I had better go on. At their earnest invitation I promised to visit them, and being favorably impressed I begged that they first call on me, which they promised to do; and we parted, they going on towards the cedars for a chase and Green and I riding on towards the ridge road.

Green continued to point out places and things he thought might interest me. "That place over there is the devil's backbone," he went on to say. "I don't know how it got its name, but it looks just like the backbone of a hog, only you see it's a heap bigger than a whole drove of hogs. That backbone turns the creek and runs it over yonder like it was going into the river way up here, but that hill yonder is too much for it and it turns back the way we came.[39] Yonder comes Nath Deatherage.[40] I expect he has been up to Uncle Oth's. He and my cousin, Mary Ann, are mighty thick."

By this time we were near the rider, who said, with a broad smile, "Hello, Whizaker, where are you taking that young man? Green, haven't you lost your way up here?"

"No, Pa got me to ride around with this boy," Green replied. "His name is Hart—Gustin Hart. He has come to live with Mr. Bob Chenault. We are going to school together next week." As my companion continued to rattle on, Nath listened to him with an expression of amusement on his countenance.

I had never seen a young man that I was better pleased with than I was with Nathan Deatherage. He was riding a high-headed bay horse, fat and sleek, with a new saddle and bridle. He was dressed in a light cashmere suit, and wore a becoming hat. I thought he was the handsomest man I had ever seen. Presently he said, "If you are going home by the church, you had better hurry along, for it's getting late." Then he passed on towards his home.

Green kept me well entertained until we got to the old church, where we parted, he turning to the left down the road that went to the creek and I going on by the church to my uncle's.

That evening I related to my aunt the trip I had taken and told her of the acquaintances I had made and how charmed I was with the appearance of Nath Deatherage. She said that all the people I had met were fine folks and that I should cultivate their acquaintance. She was glad, however, that I had declined to take in the fox chase, saying that, while there was no special harm in the sport, there was certainly no profit in it.

"Fox hunters never want to catch the fox," she explained, "and if they do, it is not fit to eat; and, besides, its pelt would not bring enough to pay one to take it to market. It is not often a chase is had in the daytime; such sport is most always at night, so you will understand that about all anyone gets out of it is the sound of barking dogs. Killis Deatherage says he enjoys beating the other fellow's dogs. I am unable to see any good in it, and I will be pleased if you continue to decline such sport."

"Oh, Aunt Jose," I said, "you are too hard on fox hunters; I'm sure I'll like the sport."[41]

"Well, I hope not; but I am glad you are so well pleased with the appearance of Nath Deatherage," she continued. "I know him well—have known him since he was younger than you are now. His mother is one of my dearest friends. I am often in their home and I have seen a great deal of Nath. Should circumstances lead you to know him better, you will find him one of the most manly young men you have ever met. It is generally believed that he and Mary Ann Oldham, the pretty young lady you met at Colonel Noland's, will marry, and if they do it will certainly be a happy union; and I shall expect their home to surpass, if possible, any other home in Old Cane Springs for genuine Kentucky hospitality."

She then told me that I had taken in generally the community in which I had come to live and that I would have to be in school the following Monday, so we did some planning for school before retiring.

Chapter IX

EXCURSIONS, SCHOOLDAYS, AND KENTUCKY HOSPITALITY

I SPENT the rest of the week in going from one plantation to another and in watching the Negroes at work. It mattered not whose plantation I visited, the happiest people I saw were the Negroes. Whether I was at Jack Martin's, near the mouth of Red River; or at John Lariemore's, near the mouth of Howard's Creek; or at Othniel Oldham's, four or five miles away on Muddy Creek, every Negro I met addressed me pleasantly, saying, "Howdy, Marse Chenault." They thought, because of Whizaker, that I was a Chenault. I afterward learned that Harvey Chenault, the youngest son of Mr. Cabell Chenault, who was then away at school, always rode Whizaker when at home, and that his squirrel hunting and fishing carried him to all the neighboring farms and to many places on the creek and river; and that explained why I was always addressed as "Marse Chenault."

CASSIUS M. CLAY

Joel T. Hart's bust of Cassius M. Clay, now in the possession of Mrs. Brutus J. Clay, Richmond.

THOMAS M. HART

(From a portrait now in the possession of his grandson, Eugene Barnes, Madison County.)

NATHAN B. DEATHERAGE

Confederate Soldier, September, 1862, to April, 1865. The photograph was taken in 1928 when he was 84 years old.

MARY ANN OLDHAM

This cut was developed from a picture said to have been taken for Nathan B. Deatherage while he was a prisoner of war in Camp Douglas, Chicago.

MRS. JOHN CABELL CHENAULT
(nee Nettie Oldham)

JOHN CABELL CHENAULT
See title page and Foreword

COL. DAVID WALLER CHENAULT
Eleventh Kentucky Cavalry, C. S. A.

MRS. DAVID WALLER CHENAULT
(nee Tabitha Phelps)

The fertility of the soil in Old Cane Springs was not surpassed in any other part of the county. Walnut, wild cherry, and bur oak grew taller and larger than any other I had ever seen. There were many miles of crooked stake-and-rider rail fences with every rail from top to bottom either cedar,[42] walnut, or wild cherry. The fields were thick with the largest shocks of corn I had ever seen. Abundance appeared everywhere. There were large orchards and vegetable gardens on every farm, and ice and milk houses were at every home. Happy Negroes were singing at their work. Those too small to work, both boys and girls, were playing around the quarters like young lambs in grassy pastures. Melodious feminine voices could be heard everywhere.

In my excursions the enchanting springs especially attracted my attention. There were several near my uncle's home. One bubbled from beneath an overhanging ledge of rock about fifty yards from the house. The great elm and other trees shading this spring contributed to the enchantment of the spot. Another such interesting watering place was located about two hundred feet in the rear of Jack Martin's home. This spring had a continuous hourly flow of three or four hundred gallons of wholesome water for both man and beast.[43]

The rank growth of cane, which in earlier days grew about these springs, of course, had long since been cut away; but even then a small growth here and there still justified the name Old Cane Springs, by which the community is known even to this day. Mary Ann was surely correct when she said that there was never any other spot on earth better watered than this land between the Kentucky River and Muddy Creek.

As everyone knows who has ever seen a Kentucky autumn, the trees and shrubs were most beautiful. The season was late and the foliage still retained its magnificent autumnal colors. Wherever I went the gorgeous hues of sumac, dogwood, maple, oak, beech, and ash, intermingled with the emerald green of the cedars, the ghostlike whiteness of the sycamores, and the brown tints of hickory, elm, and cherry—not to mention the equally glorious colors of numerous other shrubs and trees—caused me to feel that I was in a veritable fairyland. And as I followed the meandering courses of Muddy Creek (whose water was really as clear as crystal) and the Kentucky River and passed over the rolling productive hills and crossed the fertile intervening valleys between these streams, I was keenly impressed with the wonderful environment that an ingenious and benevolent Providence had provided for the inhabitants of Old Cane Springs. Truly I might have paraphrased and exclaimed with the Psalmist, "The heavens declare the glory of God and the *Earth* showeth his handiwork."

When the week ended I told my aunt that I had never before enjoyed such an experience. She said that such cheerful environment naturally made one agreeable and that it was apparent from my conduct every evening that I was taking on the happy disposition and good humor of the people of the community.

School had not always been pleasant to me, and I told my aunt that I disliked to give up my new pleasures for study. She stated that a new teacher had been employed and that he came well recommended. She also assured me that new acquaintances at school would make the coming week as pleasant as the one just ended.

Monday morning Uncle Robert went to the old church with me. The country school building had been allowed to become dilapidated, and besides it was too small to accommodate the children, so consent had been given to teach in the church.[44]

My uncle presented me to the teacher, Mr. John Harris, who was rather short and slender and had a well shaped head covered with reddish-brown hair. His eyes were dark blue and he had a pleasant manner. I felt from the start that I would like him. My young friend, Green Noland, was on hand to welcome me, and I felt that the number of my acquaintances in the community was going to be greatly enlarged. While my uncle and the teacher were chatting I spent the time taking a minute survey of the pupils. Every one was neatly dressed and I thought they all looked well. There was not a mean or vicious looking boy to be seen, and I felt that I would like them all. In a short time Uncle Robert left and I was shown a seat. During the day I was assigned to various classes in which I was to recite.

I returned home in the afternoon perfectly delighted with my new school. My friend Green appeared to have learned a lesson when he failed to introduce me on our ride up the creek, and made amends by giving me a rather formal introduction to all the boys and girls during the long recess. I was not deceived in my first impression of the pupils, for I found them to be what I first thought, little ladies and gentlemen.

The school days were from Monday to Friday, inclusive, and I expected Saturday to be a holiday. I was informed by my uncle on Friday, however, that he had a big day's ride for me on the morrow. It would be necessary, he said, for me to ride all over the neighborhood to let it be known that there would be a corn shucking at Walter Norris' on Wednesday night next. He stated that I would have to see only some of the white people at each place and let them know that the neighbors expected to shuck out Mr. Norris' corn on that night, and invite them to be on hand with as many of their colored men as would volunteer to come. If anyone invited could not come, he was expected to send as many men as he could, for the crop was to be shucked in one night.

I was up early the next morning and off to carry out orders. Uncle Robert said I need not stop at his father's, for he would tell him. I was instructed to take the Red River road first, and then go down the Kentucky River to John Lariemore's and from there to the mouth of Muddy Creek. Then I was to pass up the creek as far as Othniel Oldham's, from which place I would return home. I was cautioned to make Whizaker jog along at a good gait, if I made the entire trip by nightfall.

I found the mission most agreeable. Everyone received me pleasantly and assured me in every instance that either all or a liberal number of his men would be on hand at the appointed hour of the day designated. By noon Saturday I rode up to the home of Othniel Oldham. At my hollo, Mary Ann came to the door. She recognized me at once and invited me to alight and come in. I explained the object of my call and stated that I did not have time to visit.

"Oh, yes, you have," she persisted. "There are only a few other places for you to visit. You must take dinner with us, and I will ride with you this afternoon and see that all who are to be notified get your message."

A grinning, good-natured Negro boy was already near me and in a moment had my mule by the bridle rein and my saddle gripped so as to steady me in alighting. I saw that it was useless for me to resist further, so I alighted. A spirit of bashfulness crept over me as I prepared to enter the house. I recalled how charmed I had been with Mary Ann when I first met her, and how my spirits had drooped when my aunt had said she was too old for me, but that she had three pretty younger sisters. I dreaded to meet others of the family and, if I could have done so, I think I would have run away, for sheer fright. But Mary Ann had already walked out to the place where I alighted and had taken hold of my arm, and we were on the way to the house. She continued to talk, so there was nothing I could do but go along with her.

Mr. and Mrs. Oldham met us in the large hall. After the greeting Mary Ann explained the object of my visit and said, "He wanted to run off after he delivered the message, but I captured him and will hold him prisoner until after dinner."

Presently a girl apparently two years younger than Mary Ann came into the hall. "This is my daughter, Susan,[45] Mr. Hart," Mrs. Oldham said; and before she had scarcely finished the introduction two little tots came running in and she said, "These are my two baby girls, Tempie and Nettie."

I had hardly uttered a word since alighting, but now I was beginning to feel that they would conclude I was dumb if I did not say something, so I blurted out, "Mrs. Oldham, you certainly have four pretty daughters." Then, thinking I had said the wrong thing, I almost pushed the bottom out of my chair; but she thanked me kindly for the compliment, and I concluded that I had probably said the right thing.

I had spoken the truth; the girls were all pretty, but I was literally charmed with the youngest, Nettie. When she looked up at me, I knew I looked down into the most beautiful pair of soft black eyes I had ever seen. "You little darling," I said, as I tried to take her up; but she was out of reach as quick as a fawn. Since she was the pet and adored one of the family, no one appeared surprised that I appreciated her as they did, and they all appeared to like me more, when they saw that I had fallen in love with the baby, who was then only a little more than three years old.

Soon Kie, the boy I had met with the dogs on the creek, came in, and then James, Charles, and Thomas Moberly appeared, and I was told that I then knew the entire family. The noonday meal was announced and we all filed into the dining room. The food indicated abundant crops. Nothing that grew on a Kentucky farm could be missed on that table. Father at one end and mother at the other appeared to look with delight at four daughters on one side of the table and four sons on the other. No meal was ever more agreeably eaten. Business, pleasure, and the neighborhood news were discussed and even state and national happenings were mentioned. I had been permitted to sit next to little Nettie and that pleased me very much. I was sorry to see the dessert come, for I knew with the eating of it my visit would soon end. I had never felt so much at home with strangers before and I was in no hurry for the time to come when I could not look into the beautiful eyes of little Nettie.

But all such delightful times must cease. Dinner was over and Mary Ann soon announced: "Our horses are ready, Gustin—or rather my horse and your mule—and we had better be off."

With a keen feeling of reluctance I bade the Oldhams good-by. Especially did I dislike to leave little Nettie, who by this time had lost her shyness and told me, on her mother's prompting, that I must come again. She permitted me this time, however, to take her up in my arms, and I kissed her and said, "You can bet your life, honey, I will come back to see you more than once."

Mary Ann and I rode down the creek road. We first told Mr. William Q. Covinton[46] of the shucking on Wednesday night, and then after him everyone else in that vicinity. When we were near the old church, Mary Ann reined her horse ready to return home. I offered to accompany her saying, "You will be lonesome riding by yourself."

"Then I would have to come back with you to keep you from being afraid," she said, "for it would be dark before you could return and from what the Negroes say, no one wants to pass that church burying-ground after dark."

While my companion was talking, I looked up the road towards the old church and saw a man approaching. I thought I recognized Nathan Deatherage on the high-headed bay that I had seen him riding the day I went up the creek. As the rider approached I saw that I was not mistaken and I felt a keen desire to see him and Mary Ann meet, so I allowed her to talk on without saying a word about his approach. When Nath got in reasonable hailing distance, he said, "Hello, Hart, have you captured my girl already?"

Mary Ann was not expecting Nath's voice. I was observing her closely when he spoke, and I saw from her looks that no other man could hold her a prisoner if he was near. One blush assured me that what Green and Aunt Jose had said was true. I answered that I had not captured her, but that I had simply been the recipient of genuine Kentucky hospitality in her home and that she had been my pilot, since she feared I could not find my way home. I also told him that I had just offered to repay her by escorting her home but that fortune had brought a better protector and I would allow him the pleasure. Presently they rode off together looking supremely happy.

Chapter X

NEGRO MELODIES AND THE CORN SHUCKING

THE SECOND WEEK of school began, but my thoughts were wound up in the anticipation of the corn shucking. It was a new thing to me. I had never heard of one's neighbors coming and doing his work on such a scale. I told my teacher that I could not keep my mind off the shucking and that I was puzzled to know how they expected to shuck at night. He referred me to Uncle Robert for information, saying that there were very few Negroes in Harrison County where he was born and reared and especially in that part of the county where he had lived. He stated further that he had heard of corn shuckings around Cynthiana and on up towards Paris, but he had never been to one.

That evening I asked Uncle Robert to explain the nature of the corn shucking that was to come off the next night at Mr. Norris'. He said there were a number of persons in the neighborhood who had but few hands. They generally raised large crops of corn and could with their limited force do all their work in due season, except the shucking.

"Unless corn is gathered promptly after it is dry enough to crib," he explained, "there is likely to be considerable loss—in fact, the longer the corn remains in the shock the greater the loss. Our Negroes are fond of going to corn shuckings. I understand that tomorrow night they will set a night to shuck out Colby McKinney's crop, and on that night they will arrange for some other crop, and so on until every man who is short of hands will have his corn shucked. It is some expense, but that is trivial. Mr. Norris will get several gallons of whiskey, which will cost him fifty cents per gallon. He will prepare a good supper for the shuckers and the neighbors who may come. I shall not try to explain to you the pleasure the Negroes will get out of these shuckings. You will simply have to go over tomorrow night and see for yourself."

I awaited with great impatience the coming of the following evening. We were the nearest neighbors to the Norris home and the first to arrive. Uncle Robert said he would go over and talk politics with Walter. Aunt Jose went to help Mrs. Norris. The great quantities of turkey, chicken, shoat, cake, and custard I saw on my arrival made me think of some weddings I had attended on Silver Creek.

I listened to Uncle Robert and Mr. Norris discuss the recent election. Presently Mr. A. K. Lewis came, then Colby McKinney, Captain Nathan Noland, and other neighbors, and finally my teacher arrived. After speaking to the other guests and the host, he came over to me and said, "Gustin, I am glad to see you here. I hope to hear you do some reciting after tonight."

I admitted that thoughts of the novelty of this night's performance had disturbed me so that I could not study, but after it was over I believed I could get down to work again.

Uncle Robert and Mr. Norris continued to discuss politics, and the other callers joined in by way of assent. I soon discovered that they were not pleased with the election of Mr. Lincoln. They generally spoke of him as "Old Abe," and I could not help disliking their reference to my father's choice for president in that way.

Presently a great volume of song a few hundred yards away caught our attention. Some one spoke: "They are beginning to come."

I ran out into the yard and was soon joined by Mr. Norris, who said, "Those singers are my very welcome guests to-night and I must be out to greet them."

Nearer and nearer the singers approached. I had never heard the song before and I could not distinguish the words very well, but the harmony was beautiful. At first I believed that all the Negroes in the community had gotten together, for it seemed to me that there were a hundred voices or more; but on the arrival of the singers, I learned that they were only the men from the Cabell Chenault plantation. Mr. Norris met them in his front yard and greeted them with "Howdy, Amos; howdy, William; howdy, Jeff," until Shed, Jerry, Jim, Horace, Scott, Big Joe, George, Cuff, Little Joe, Andy, and all the others had passed on towards the residence.

The night was pleasant and the moon by this time was shining brightly. The Negroes began to drop around on the grass and joke one another about first one thing and then another, but all in the best of humor.

Presently I caught the sound of voices that appeared to be a mile or more away to the north. The Negroes sprang to their feet as if by order of a commander. There was speculation as to who the singers were. Presently Scott said, "I catch de voice ov one ov 'em. It's Lariemore's Pleas."

The voices were so far away that I thought it impossible to distinguish any particular voice, but they all agreed that Scott was right. At this moment off to the northeast, but much closer, other voices were heard. Nearly every one present recognized the voice of Noland's Allen. Still farther to the northeast singers were heard, and someone said, "That bunch must be Marse Jack Martin's niggers."

Boonesborough Beach today. Scene of stirring events in 1775-1783. The Daniel Boone Bicentennial Commission (created by the State Legislature, January 30, 1934), with proceeds from the sale of commemorative Boone coins, plans to buy Boonesborough and give it to the Government to develop into a Pioneer National Monument, as provided by Congress in laws, approved May 26, and June 18, 1934.

June meeting, 1936, at Old Cane Spring Church. Only about a third of those in attendance are shown in the picture.

Weddle's Mill, built about 1830, as it looks today.
See Map of Old Cane Springs.

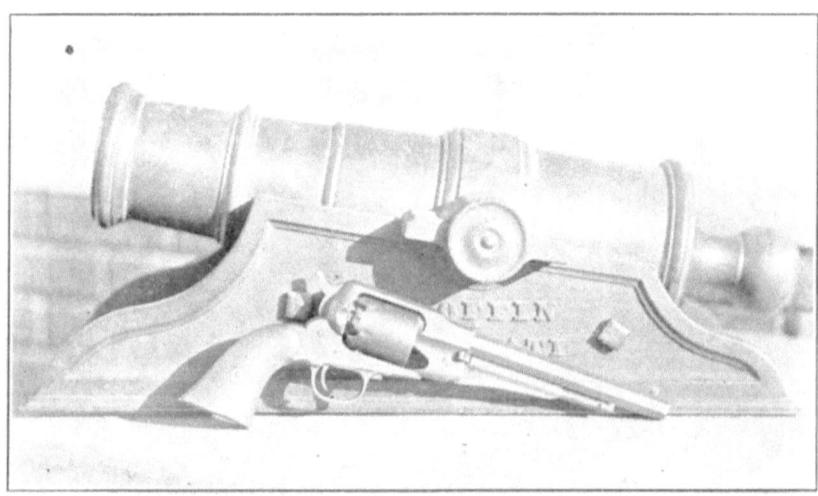

Cannon used in 1845 by Cassius M. Clay to defend The *True American*. Colt Revolver presented to Mr. Clay by President Lincoln, in 1861, in appreciation of his defense of the White House and Navy Yard in Washington during the excitement occasioned by the siege and surrender of Fort Sumter. The cannon is in the possession of Mrs. Brutus J. Clay, and the revolver, Rollins Burnam, Richmond.

Then from farther up the river the sound of other voices came. Pete, a little black Negro said, "I knows dat crowd; I heahs Chambers' Pud."

The voices came nearer and nearer until less prominent singers were recognized. Presently someone said, "All ov them niggers 'll git togedder out yonder at de forks ov de road; den you'll heah some singin' sho' 'nough."

Just at this time voices to the south of us caused all to turn and listen in that direction. Someone in the crowd said, "That's Deatherage's Henry." Then another exclaimed, "Yeah, there's Giles, and now they're jis toppin' de Muddy Creek hill."

Finally off to the southeast came another volume of song and we all turned in that direction, with hands, palms forward, placed behind our ears. I could plainly hear a voice very different from any other I had heard that night. It sounded in the distance like the clarion notes of wild geese in their migratory flights. All were quiet and listening, but no one named the leading singer, whose voice was a clear, distinct tenor, that leaped and bounded far above any of the other singers. It was simply charming, entrancing. White and black, men and women, stood in silence looking up the Texas road as if bound by some spell in that direction. The silence was broken by Cuff's saying, "I heah Moberly's Otaway in dat crowd, too."

No one answered and as I could not restrain my anxiety to know the tenor singer, I said to Uncle Amos, who was standing near, "How is it that none of you recognize that tenor voice?"

"Oh, we all knows dat voice. Dat's Oldham's Pike. He's sech a good singer, dat we all jis stand an' listen w'en we fust heah 'im. Ef anyone had said dat wuz Oldham's Pike, all de res' would ov laughed at 'im. His voice can be recognized jis ez fur ez you kin heah hit."

By this time voices in song were heard coming from every direction. The sound was simply fascinating. Melodies echoing and re-echoing from the hills beyond the river and from the hills across Muddy Creek sounded like the intermingling of voices singing in unison near and far away.

As the Negroes drew nearer they all ceased singing except the Oldham crowd. When they came within a hundred yards of the Norris home, Pike could be plainly heard lining the song; then those already in the yard and others coming along the road took up the melody. No camp meeting I had ever attended had in any way equaled that singing. When the approaching singers heard those in the yard, it seemed to be a signal for all to stop singing. Mr. Norris greeted every one with a familiar "howdy," which made the Negroes feel welcome and then returned to the front portico, rapped for silence, and said:

"Men, you have done me the kindness to come here tonight to shuck my corn. I have only three hundred shocks. I am unable to tell how many there are of you, but I imagine you will not have to shuck over three shocks each if you finish my crop. There is to be no boss or overseer. You can arrange the manner of your work, or if you prefer, you can select a leader and let him arrange the way you are to work. I know you will be careful and shuck the corn clean. I want to give each one of you a dram before you begin. I imagine you would all like to have a little something to drink first."

"Yes, suh; yes, suh; we all's mighty thusty," came from all over the yard.

"After you have finished shucking you can have another drink and your supper. And for fear I may not be able to thank you when you quit work, I thank each one of you now for his volunteer service tonight, for I know that you are not here by order of your masters."

"No, suh; no, suh. We come 'cause we wanted to he'p you all," came from many voices.

"Now, here are four jugs of whiskey, as good as Walden can make, and here are plenty of glasses. I will ask you, Amos, to take this jug, and you, Harrison, this one, and you, Henry, this one, and you, Pleas, this one.[47] Each of you pour for the boys. Now come on, fellows, and when you have drunk, go over there to the cornfield and arrange the manner of shucking to suit yourselves. I will now go in and spend the remainder of the evening with my neighbors."

The Negroes were eager to get a drink, but as soon as served, they filed off to the field. When they were in the field, someone suggested that Colonel Noland's Harrison and Mr. Chenault's Amos be general bosses to see that all the men worked orderly and missed no shocks. This suggestion was promptly agreed to.

It was arranged that the shucking was to be by pairs, or two men to a stack. Harrison and Amos were to pair them off, so as to equalize the pairs. The best two shuckers, according to the decision of Amos and Harrison, were to receive special mention at the supper as the best workers. The pairs were shortly arranged. Generally where two expressed a desire to be together, they were thus assigned. In a very short time the teams were at their shocks. Oldham's Pike was to give the signal to begin by starting a song.

All these arrangements were very interesting to me. I doubted, however, that so many men would ever be kept successfully at work. Pike and his partner were given the first shock in the first row, nearest the county road, and Amos and Harrison went with the other men until all were properly placed, and then returned to Pike at the first row, and said, "Start your song." At the command he began:

"Old Marster shot a wild goose."

A hundred voices answered from all parts of the field, and each man grabbed a stalk for shucking.

"Ju-ran-zie, hio ho."

"It wuz seben years fallin'."

The multitude of voices cried out as at first—

"Ju-ran-zie, hio ho.

"It was seben years cookin'.
Ju-ran-zie, hio ho.

"A knife couldn't cut it.
Ju-ran-zie, hio ho.

"A fork couldn't stick it.
Ju-ran-zie, hio ho."

There was harmony and perfect concord, although the men were scattered. The Norris farm was not far from the Kentucky River but it was higher than the surrounding land. Consequently, the great volume of sound rolled off across the river and echoed and re-echoed in the Estill County hills beyond; and strangely enough these reverberations rolled away across Muddy Creek and echoed and re-echoed in the cedar hills. Such singing this generation will never hear, for I am writing this account many years after it occurred, and only those who have heard something of the kind will believe that echoes from a hundred vigorous voices can cause one to feel that he is listening to thousands of singers scattered over a large area. But it is true, as many yet living will bear me witness—or at least it was true in Old Cane Springs.[48]

I attended many other huskings during the remainder of that season and during my stay at Old Cane Springs, and I was always thrilled while listening to what seemed to be a thousand voices in one melodious symphony. Not only were the common Negro melodies of the ante-bellum period sung, but such Foster songs as *Old Black Joe, Massa's in the Cold, Cold Ground,* and *My Old Kentucky Home* rang out on the cool night air. And when Pike's clarion tenor voice led in these songs, especially in *Swing Low, Sweet Chariot* and *Nellie Was a Lady,* followed by a score of deep bass voices, the melody thrilled one beyond description.

My reverie was finally broken by a call from Uncle Robert to come to supper, and I reluctantly went to the house. A splendid supper had been prepared for the white guests. In my absence, a young man by the name of Willis Hisle had come. I soon discovered that he was the wit of the occasion. He appeared to feel older than he really was. He talked mostly to the older men and pretended to know a joke on every one present.

Hisle spoke to me only once. "Hart, is this your first corn shucking?" he asked.

On my acknowledgment that it was, he replied, "If you stay here long you will get used to them."

Hisle then turned his remarks to the guests generally and said, "Captain Noland has taught me something new in cultivating corn. He told me not long ago that he had discovered that one man at the plow with a fresh, well groomed mule could do more work than two, where the stock was not properly cared for. Well, I passed down the creek by his house during the latter part of May and found the Captain taking a nap under a nice shade tree, and, as I thought, his plow mule was hitched nearby. I wanted to know how he could afford to sleep that way while Wash, his man, was plowing. He said he had discovered that currying and resting a mule for an hour made him very brisk and that he and Wash had talked it over and had finally agreed that Wash would do the plowing and he would do the feeding and currying."

I was not certain that I caught the joke, but the rest of the company laughed heartily. Captain Noland accused Hisle of making up a lie without any foundation whatever, but his denial and defense caused more laughter.

Hisle continued to rap first one and then another until the meal was over. About nine o'clock I heard an unusual noise out in the field and was about to run out to learn the cause of the commotion when someone near me remarked: "The field is finished, and they will be here in a few minutes." Like a great black cloud the men began filing into the yard, merry and cheerful as when they started to work.

Mr. Norris went to the front of his portico and said: "Boys, I must thank you again for helping me out as you have. My wife and her good neighbors have prepared, I think, a good supper for you. I wish I had a table of sufficient length and chairs so that you could each sit and enjoy your supper more, but as that is impossible, you will have to eat as they do at the Baptist Association."

"Good 'nough; good 'nough," was heard from all sides of the yard, which was full of Negroes by this time.

"Would you prefer to have your drink before or after supper?" Mr. Norris asked. "There is enough left for each of you to have another drink, even if Willis Hisle has had hold of my jugs."

Everybody—white and black—laughed, for this was the first joke on Hisle. He denied emphatically that he had had the jugs. After the laughing subsided, the Negroes exclaimed, "Stimulant furst, stimulant furst."

They were all promptly served, and then Mr. Norris announced, "Boys, you will find plenty of chicken, turkey, shoat, and mutton, with other good things for the first course, and a washing tub of custard with enough pound cake for each of you to get a slice to eat with it; so file around to the rear of the house where you can be helped."

It was certainly a sight to see those Negroes eat. Mrs. Norris and three other women stood by a table on which there were large bread trays and pans full of chicken, mutton, turkey, and shoat. Then there was another table with a great quantity of bread, and beyond that were Negro women, who spooned steaming vegetables on the men's bread. There was enough to eat for all, but the food vanished like dew before the sunshine. For dessert everyone was given a cup of custard and a large slice of cake.

While this last course was being served, Uncle Harrison stepped forward and said it was the custom in the midst of an enjoyable meal after a corn shucking to announce who the judges thought had been the best shuckers. He stated that he and Amos had watched closely, and while it had been very hard to decide, they had finally concluded that Cabell Chenault's Scott and Amos Deatherage's Giles had shown the most skill in removing the shucks and shocking the fodder; but all had done well and no complaint was filed against anyone for not doing good work. Three cheers rang out for Scott and Giles.

Soon the Negroes began to say, "good night, Marse Norris," and "Thank you, Miss Norris, fur de good supper. Call on us 'gin w'en yo' all got mo' corn to shuck"; and off they went towards their homes singing as merrily as when they came. Thus ended my first corn shucking.[49]

Chapter XI

OLD CANE SPRING CHURCH

ONE SATURDAY soon after my arrival, I found my aunt and her servants very busy dressing fowls. Uncle Robert and his men had killed and prepared a shoat and a lamb, and I noticed something of this nature going on at other homes I visited during the day. Evidently preparations for a feast were under way. I asked my aunt what it all meant, and she informed me that there would be preaching at the church Sunday. This would be the regular December meeting, and many people were expected to be present from distant parts of the county and from Clark and Estill counties. After the services it would be too far for them to return to their homes before eating, and the preparations I had seen were for the purpose of feeding such of the congregation as came from a distance. The dinner would not be spread at the church, she explained; instead, the people would be invited to the homes nearby, where the horses could also be fed.

The morrow came and I arrived at the church early, since I lived near. The congregation soon began to gather, most of the people coming on horseback. If anyone came in a buggy, I have forgotten it; but there were many carriages drawn by either two sleek mules or well groomed horses. One of the first carriages to arrive was owned by James Noland, of Clark County. Then there came Dr. Thomas S. Moberly from Waco and Henry Dillingham from Speedwell. The carriages of Curtis F. Burnam and David C. Irvine from Richmond also arrived before services began. I came to know the owners and occupants through my uncle. I knew the Oldham and Deatherage carriages and many others by their occupants. Most every vehicle indicated pride and prosperity. A bright-faced Negro driver, who appeared to understand his business and indicated that he was just as proud as any occupant of the carriage, sat high on a front seat especially made for him.

When the Oldhams drove up, a smile from Mary Ann caused me to feel welcome to come to their carriage. Evidently someone else received that welcome smile also, for I had hardly reached the carriage before Nathan Deatherage came up to claim her attention; so I turned to Tempie and Nettie and walked with them to the church door.

As was the custom in those days, men did not sit with the women during the service. Half of the church was for the women and none of them occupied the side assigned to the men until all the seats on that side were filled. When it was necessary, the front seats on the men's side were assigned to the women, the men vacating so that no women were left standing even if the men had to leave the church. The building, while apparently commodious for a country church, was soon filled to its utmost capacity, and the large yard was also well filled with groups of men, discussing all manner of news. Most of them, however, were talking about the late election and its probable consequences.

The preacher, Rev. William Rupard, a young Baptist minister from Clark County, arrived in due time and I noted that he was received as a very important personage. As I felt anxious to hear him, I slipped into the church and secured a seat which I thought would not be needed for the ladies.

The service began with hymns lined by James Noland. Song books were scarce, and reading the lines to be sung was a necessity. The preacher read the scripture lesson and offered a devout prayer. After another song, he went up into the pulpit, which was a boxed-up arrangement in the middle front of the building with a small entrance at one side. The most of his body was hidden from view. The minister opened his Bible and read the entire eighth Psalm, announcing as his text a portion of the fourth verse, namely, "What is man, that thou art mindful of him?" The sermon made such an impression on me that its substance clings to me yet, and I will give it from memory. The preacher paused after reading his text, looked over the audience slowly, and impressively repeated, "What is man, that thou art mindful of him?"

Then deliberately and earnestly he proceeded. "My brethren, no greater question was ever propounded; no greater inquiry can be asked by a man about himself. The man who does not have serious thoughts about himself and his fellow men with whom he comes in contact fails to do justice to himself. He is almost sure to be guilty of conduct that will bring upon him condemnation at the hands of his fellow man. Thus the necessity of jails and penitentiaries. We must ponder the words of our text, 'What is man . . .?' if we would avoid many of the pitfalls along the pathway of life. We have been blessed with a knowledge of the creation from our infancy, but I often wonder what view man has of himself and his fellow man who has not the revelation here opened before us. The wiser he is the greater must be his perplexity and confusion. Darkness—darkness it must all appear to such an one. No light, no life, no immortality.

Can you think of your fellow men being thus conditioned and not be stirred with pity and compassion for them?

"David must have been moved by such feelings when he spoke, as it were, directly to his Creator: 'What is man, that thou art mindful of him?' David was a Jew and he knew that God had been mindful of that people, but in this chapter he caught a broader conception of man. He saw the world with all its resources, with all living things, and knew that it was all for man. Then if all the earth and all the things thereon are for man, man must be something wonderful; and he cries out in the words of the text, 'What is man . . . ?'

"My brethren, man is not a creature that you should kill. Man is not a creature from whom you may steal. Man is not a creature against whom you may bear false witness. You all will agree with me on these three propositions; but man is more than a creature that should not be injured by the commission of any of these wrongs. I thank God that He has not left us in darkness but that it was His good pleasure to reveal to us our true state. All praise to His holy name, for He has revealed to us that in the councils of heaven He determined to create man in His own image, and did create him, 'male and female created He them.'

"I have read books pretending to answer the question concerning the origin of man. I felt it my duty to do so, for if a truth has been discovered I should know it; and if it is a falsehood, I should combat it.[50] I have always noted that those who are worried about man's origin other than as revealed in this blessed book never lay down a code of conduct for him as does this book; nor do they concern themselves about any existence hereafter as revealed in this book. In fact, I find no book that satisfies me as to how man came to exist except this book. I find no book that tells all mankind how to live except this book, and I find no book that tells me truly of man's future existence except this book. If this book is the inspired word of God, if men wrote it as God moved them to write, then all that is in it is true. Since this is true, I must go to this book to find the answer to the question: 'What is man . . . ?' I learn therein, my brethren, that he is something marvelous. When I look at man, I see the greatest creature that inhabits the earth. Instead of seeing a creature that I may defame, rob, malign, and if occasion demand kill, I see something sacred—a creature a little lower than the angels, a creature that the Creator loves and pronounced His work in creating him as good. That is the kind of a creature you are, my brethren."

The minister eloquently reminded his hearers that their lives indicated that they appreciated their exalted position and understood how they should deport themselves. Since they were only a little lower than the angels, who continually do the will of God, they should strive to conform their lives to the will of their Creator, who had revealed himself more clearly to man through his son, Jesus Christ. "Yes," he said, "in fullness of time, 'God did become manifest in the flesh and dwelt on the earth with men.' In His coming we learned all. We not only had confirmed the knowledge of our creation, but we learned our destiny. Instead of feeling that our Creator was an angry God that required of us some great sacrifice to appease His wrath, we were told to call Him Father. We were told that He loves us as does our earthly father love us. We learned that there was no question about His love and care for man. The object of His coming was to have man love Him and do His will on earth as it is done in heaven.

"My brethren, this is my view of man. It is no new thing. It is the old, old story that has been told and retold since man in his ignorance crucified our Lord on Calvary. He died and arose again that we might know Him, and in the knowledge of Him have that peace which passeth all understanding.

"My brethren, I do not wish to flatter you, but I do feel it is my duty to commend you if I think you do those things worthy of commendation. If you were doing wrong it would be my duty to admonish you. I deem it my duty as well to speak of your virtues. You will note in the scriptures that Paul spoke both of the shortcomings and the virtues of the congregations to which he wrote and preached. With this precedent I feel at liberty to say that I believe your faith in our Lord and Savior Jesus Christ is not excelled by any other people. Furthermore, I know your hospitality cannot be excelled, and I know also your obedience to law and the constituted authorities is all that the scriptures say it should be. I have never heard of jealousies, bickerings, and evil-doers among you. Therefore, I feel justified in saying that in Old Cane Springs, man, to my mind, realizes what he is and is showing a due appreciation of his exalted origin and is looking to that eternal destiny promised to all who live and obey Him here.

"Our Father has promised temporal blessings to those who love and obey Him, as well as spiritual. On my way over here, from time to time, I have been impressed with the fact that you are blessed with abundant crops. Your herds and flocks are always well fatted. Your servants have bright faces and are cheerful and contented. Your orchards are fruitful and plenty appears to reign on every hand. You certainly are blessed. Noble men, noblemen you are! Live then that you may be eternally with Him who created you, who loves you, and who has in store for you blessings that will far surpass the blessings with which you are now surrounded as the noonday sun outshines the midnight darkness."

I was electrified with the minister's words and manner of delivery. When he had finished, James Noland announced the hymn and said that possibly there were those who might not be able to shake hands with Brother Rupard after the congregation was dismissed and that it would be in order while the hymn was being sung for anyone or all to come forward and extend to him the hand of Christian greeting.

Amazing Grace was never sung with greater fervor and the audience in one common emotion passed in and out of the seats to shake the preacher's hand. In fact, there was a general handshaking. One corner of the church had been reserved for the Negroes, and master and servants shook hands in Christian fellowship and shed tears of joy together.

After the congregation was dismissed I was especially interested in watching the movements of those who lived close to the church and whom I had noticed the day before making preparations for the Sunday dinner. I could hear, "Yes, thank you, I will go with you"; "No, thanks, I have promised to go with Brother Cabell Chenault." Or it might be Colonel Noland's, or Captain Noland's, or Colonel Chambers', or Walter Norris', or John Black Noland's invitation that was being accepted or declined, as the case might be. Everyone from a distance had several invitations to dinner.

Thus the wholesome Christian influence of Old Cane Spring Church, before the War between the States, permeated and leavened the countryside for miles and miles around.[51]

I learned shortly that the Oldhams were to go home with us and of course their girls would come too. I consoled myself that my little charmer, Nettie, would at least be present to entertain me even if the older boys would prevent me from talking to Mary Ann. Our yard was filled with guests. The prices of cattle, hogs, horses, mules, and all farm products were discussed by the men while waiting for dinner, and everyone appeared to be pleased with the business outlook. Nevertheless, occasionally someone would refer to the mutterings in the North and the fiery demands of the South and then all would become grave. But Willis Hisle was present and would tell some joke, and then all would laugh and declare that the present peace and prosperity could never be disturbed.

And so passed my first church meeting at Old Cane Spring. I attended others with as great evidence of hospitality, until late the following year.

CHAPTER XII

A MERRY CHRISTMAS

THE SCHOOL, which was called a fall or short term, had closed and the Christmas holidays were on. By this time I had come to know well all of the younger men and boys in the neighborhood and had visited most of them in their homes. A round of pleasure was now in store for me, as indicated by plans for parties to be enjoyed at this season of the year. Furthermore, I would witness Christmas in the Negro quarters.

My father had been educated in the East and had come to Kentucky to teach school. My mother, who was his second

DR. JEREMIAH AYRES
The physician of Old Cane Springs.

REV. WILLIAM RUPARD
Pastor of Old Cane Spring Church for more than forty years.

CAPTAIN NATHAN NOLAND
Confederate sympathizer who supported the Union sympathizer, Rev. William Rupard.

OTHNIEL RICE OLDHAM
Sentenced to be shot as a spy but was pardoned.

WILLIAM Q. COVINGTON
A Confederate sympathizer.

COLEMAN COVINGTON
A Confederate sympathizer.

CABELL CHENAULT
He had four sons in the Confederate service.

DAVID AND ANDERSON CHENAULT
Sons of Cabell. Taken while the boys were Confederate prisoners in Camp Douglas.

wife, had died when I was very small, and my father had married a lady on Silver Creek, and there I had grown up under the watchful care of a stepmother, who was exceedingly kind to me, but watched my every step and allowed me none of the freedom and liberty I had enjoyed since my arrival in Old Cane Springs. The prospect for pleasure during the coming Christmas of 1860 was more than I had ever dreamed could be my lot. I was to go to a party on Christmas eve at Captain John Chambers'. On Christmas day my uncle and aunt and their children and I were to dine with Mr. Cabell Chenault and family, and were to remain there until late at night so as to see the merrymaking of the Negroes in the quarters. Later on I was to attend parties at both the Oldham and Deatherage homes. I could not keep from dreaming of the happy things in store for me.

Finally Christmas eve came, and, in company with Aunt Jose, I arrived early at the Captain's grand old home. Only a few of the boys with whom I attended school were present. Green Noland, who was my chum by this time, was there, as he was a cousin; but most of the beaux were an older set whom I hardly knew. I met a very handsome young man by the name of Elbridge Broaddus,[52] who lived near Richmond and was preparing for the law, and I also met David, Anderson, and Cabell Chenault. Nathan Deatherage, Kie and James Oldham, and many other younger men of the neighborhood about my age I had already come to know. Of course, there were many young ladies present. A company of handsomer young men and more beautiful young ladies I had never seen before. In fact, their appearance indicated wealth and culture that could not be excelled anywhere in Kentucky. The men were well dressed in tailored clothes and the ladies wore lovely silk dresses that made them especially charming. Everyone deported himself or herself well, and in due time a very elaborate meal was set before the assembled guests. Bright-faced happy Negroes answered our every beck and call and appeared to enjoy the occasion as much as the host and hostess.

I returned home with my aunt near the early dawn, feeling that a kind providence had placed me in a most fortunate environment.

The next day was as delightful as the evening before. Mr. Cabell Chenault's children and grandchildren were with him for Christmas. John Andrew, Cabell, and Jacob Huguely had come from Danville; Nannie and Ann Shearer, from Kirksville; his sons, Harvey and Jephtha, were home from college; and the older boys were there. Mr. Chenault was happy beyond measure as he looked upon his handsome sons and grandchildren. The richest food that could be produced on a Kentucky farm was well prepared by servants, who took as much delight in its preparation as did the host and his good wife take in seeing their loved ones who ate it.

The main treat to me was yet to come. My father had caused me to believe that slave owners managed their slaves like beasts of burden, and that the Negroes were a restless and unhappy set of human beings, longing for freedom and writhing under their enforced servitude. I might have expected, therefore, to see a dull and dolorous assembling of the family slaves in the quarters that evening; but how different the gathering! The beaux and belles came early from the adjoining plantations. No place in the quarters was large enough to hold all that came. It was thought at first that Aunt Sally's room would do for the dancing, and it had been cleared of furniture for that purpose; but it was soon discovered that the dance must be out in the yard. A great bonfire was prepared and torches and lamps were arranged so as to light the place. Fortunately the night was pleasant, a condition that often happens at Christmas time in Kentucky. The music began and twenty or more couples took their places for a Virginia reel. Such dancing I had never seen before, nor have I ever seen it excelled since. All were equals, there was no cost, and everybody was happy.

The white folks looked on and enjoyed the merry-making. The music for the dancing was produced by Negroes from several plantations. There was no note or sheet music; only familiar tunes were played by ear on violins that were very good instruments.[53]

After an hour or two the dancing ceased for a while and a cry went up for Nannie and Ann Shearer to sing. A little begging brought them out, and, to the great delight and vociferous applause of the darkies, they sang *Nellie Gray, Yellow Rose in Texas,*

Swing Low, Sweet Chariot, Those Golden Slippers, and several other songs. Then the dance was again resumed and continued until refreshments were announced.

Along early in the morning we started for home. As we went away I thought that I had surely seen the happiest folks in the world that night. And I had watched a people that I had been taught to believe oppressed and miserable exhibit such happiness as comes only from those who are contented with their lot in life. If anything occurred during the night to indicate that anyone present was unhappy, discontented, or burdened in any way, it was not noticeable. I felt, therefore, that someone was in error about the oppressed colored race in America. I had been taught that happiness here and hereafter should be the chief aim of man, and I was concluding that if there was anything in appearances, the Negroes around Old Cane Springs had acquired it here, and, as nearly all of them were Christians, they were likely to secure it hereafter.

CHAPTER XIII

WAR ON THE HORIZON: WILL THE NEGRO REVOLT?

WHILE I was enjoying the merriest Christmas I had ever known, my elders often questioned: "Is anything unforeseen likely to disturb the happiness of these good people in Old Cane Springs? Can any calamity arise that would affect these happy homes?" To their minds the answer would invariably come: "Surely no calamity in this good government of ours can change the fortunes of these brave men and these beautiful women. It is their destiny to be happy here; nature has wonderfully blessed them in their location. Furthermore, the law will protect them in their homes and in the possession of their other property, and the community will remain unchanged—one of the brightest and best places on earth."

Winter had passed and the spring of 1861 was advancing. Uncle Robert often talked politics. He took the weekly Cincinnati *Enquirer,* for which I had to ride up to Texas every Saturday. He read it with forebodings, and the neighbors came in to hear him, especially Captain Noland. Many were their surmises in my presence, but I thought they were talking about something away off, something that could never directly affect us. I hardly knew what was meant by the War between the States, which Uncle Robert and Captain Noland seemed to have anticipated during the past few months. My young mind was wrapped up in the pleasant surroundings.

On one Saturday afternoon in April, 1861, I was told to return with the newspaper as soon as I could have it delivered to me by the postmaster. On my return I found Captain Noland and Walter Norris with my uncle anxiously awaiting me. The paper was taken from me before I could alight and I could see that all three were startled at what they read. I caught such remarks as these, which often thereafter as well as at the time deeply impressed me: "The war is certainly on"; "Lincoln says, 'The rebellion must be put down at all hazards'"; "All the States have been called on for volunteer troops to aid in the suppression of the rebellion"; "The fight is on and there is no way to avoid it now."

After everything of interest in the paper had been read aloud I recall that Captain Noland said that he felt sure that Old Cane Springs would know but little about real war. The community was too far away from the main roads north and south to be affected. He hardly believed we would know the war was going on except as we saw reports of it in the *Enquirer.* Uncle Robert, however, took a more serious view. He believed both the North and South would be aided by young men of the community and that their action would bring about a hostile feeling among those who remained at home. He expected persons to come into the community to arouse the Negroes and if possible to array them against their masters; and should they be successful, he believed a desperate state of affairs would exist.

He said with great emphasis: "Captain Noland, has it ever occurred to you that there are not over fifty white men and boys in Old Cane Springs who can fight, and that there are nearly four hundred Negro men and boys here of fighting age? While this community is a small portion of this county, one-sixth of the Negroes of the county are here."[54]

Captain Noland stated that was true, but he knew all the Negroes well and he did not believe it possible for any man or set of men to array them against their masters.

"Take, for instance, your father's Negroes," he said. "There are Amos, Bill, Jeff, and Jerry, among the older ones that are high types of manhood. If you talk with them, you will conclude that they think they share your father's farm in common with him. They speak of 'our farm,' 'our cattle, hogs, horses, and sheep,' and 'our corn and wheat.' They recognize your father as being the owner, but they think he holds everything in common for them all. They are perfectly willing that he should so hold it, and I do not believe anyone can dissatisfy them. The same thing is true about my father's Negroes, Captain Chambers' Negroes, Jack Martin's, John Lariemore's, Amos Deatherage's, and Othniel Oldham's. Now it would be impossible to stir any of them against their masters. These men own more than three-fourths of the Negroes here and those who own the others treat them so kindly that they appear to be as well contented as the members of their masters' families."

"These Negroes are not eye-servants," he continued; "they all appear to regard themselves as a part of the family with whom they reside; and I tell you, come what will out of this war, you will never hear of a Negro in Old Cane Springs being in revolt against the whites here. I admit there are enough of them here to kill every white person in the community in one night, but there will never be enough Yankees south of the Mason and Dixon line to induce them to do it."

Mr. Norris said he agreed with Captain Noland. He feared nothing from the Negro, but his gravest concern was about a class of people who lived in that portion of the county where the land was too poor to support slaves. He believed some of the people in that part of the county had always been envious of the slave-owners. He expected, therefore, to see them take sides with the North, if there was an opportunity, and if they once had the power, he expected to be oppressed by them. Uncle Robert said, as he bade his neighbors good-night on this occasion, that conditions looked gloomy to him from many angles and he only hoped and prayed that things would not be as bad as he feared.

Chapter XIV

DISSENSION AND DIVISION

OLD CANE SPRINGS appeared to be a God-fearing and God-loving community. There was preaching at the Cane Spring Church as usual. Rev. William Rupard was still the minister.[55] The first Sunday in May was expected to be a big day, and the usual preparations were made to entertain those attending who might live at a distance. Lambs, pigs, and chickens had been slaughtered by the dozens, and when the congregation began to assemble, it was evident that no unnecessary preparation had been made.[56]

In a very short time the church was filled with ladies, except the "amen corner" and the extreme rear of the church. The yard was about as full as the church. Men gathered in various parts of the yard, and as one passed among them he heard nothing but war and preparation for war being discussed. One group was vigorously discussing the Clay battalion's recent defense of the White House and the Navy Yard in Washington. Since Cassius M. Clay was a citizen of Madison County, his singular action was especially interesting.[57] The opposing views of the North and South were freely advocated and it was evident that the peace-loving and law-abiding citizens of Old Cane Springs and vicinity were ready to take up arms in defense of one or the other of the sections.

When the services were over, those who had heard the sermon came out either lauding or condemning the preacher, who had spoken of the people of the South as Rebels, bent on dissolving the Union of the States. His utterances on this point were soon known by the crowd on the outside, some of whom received them with condemnation while others approved; and excitement ran high. One man said in a loud voice, "No more of his preaching for me. No true preacher knows anything in his pulpit but Christ and Him crucified."

Most all of the members who owned slaves were grievously offended at the preacher's remarks. Major C. F. Burnam, an attorney from Richmond, who was present, congratulated the preacher on his defense of the Union. His statement, however, was overheard and caused him to be condemned as much as the preacher.

Finally the crowd began to disperse. It was noticed that Rupard and Burnam were still in the yard. When most everyone had left Captain Noland went up to them and remarked: "If you gentlemen do not hurry, I fear you will be late in getting your dinner."

Rupard said, "I have been here at other times when I received many invitations, but I must confess no one has invited me today."

Major Burnam stated that he had been coming to the May meeting at Cane Springs ever since he had united with the church, and that he had eulogized the hospitality of this community above any other of the county; but now he, too, had been overlooked by his brethren.

"Exciting times! Exciting times!" exclaimed the Captain. "I am sure it was unintentional and you must both go home with me."[58]

Captain Noland soon learned that he had incurred the ill will of his neighbors for inviting Major Burnam and the preacher to his home. Men of the community were fast taking sides and excitement ran high. Those with much property and many slaves sympathized with the South, while most of those with small homes and no slaves were for the North. Uncle Robert was very outspoken for the South and boasted that he had seen in the *Enquirer* that General Zollicoffer, of Tennessee, was now in Kentucky with a large Confederate army, and would be in the Blue Grass in another week. Furthermore, he was expected to double his army as soon as he reached the Blue Grass and that no man around there would ever see a Yankee.

In a short time after his boasting speech, word came that the Yankees had met General Zollicoffer at Wild Cat Mountain[59] in Laurel County and had completely routed him. The report also stated that those not killed were being hotly pursued and that the men appeared blood-mad and were killing all citizens who had been boasting about the coming of the Confederates. The news frightened Uncle Robert. He had by no means been guarded in his remarks and prison or death appeared certain if he remained at home. The only alternative was to go South, if possible, and win or die with those whose cause he had espoused.

How miserable we all were when Uncle Robert told my aunt that he felt certain it was not safe for him to remain at home, and that he had determined to go South. No persuasion could change him and with tears and farewells we saw him depart as the first man from Old Cane Springs to aid the Confederacy. When news of Uncle Robert's action became known in the community, many others soon began talking of going.

As usual on Saturdays I rode Whizaker in any direction I fancied, but most often to Muddy Creek, where my friend, Green, would be waiting for me. He and I often fished and hunted, and we generally took dinner with Aunt Creech Sally. We had both learned to love her, and we no longer felt uneasy or so scared when she talked about Sam. In fact, we rather concluded she did hear Sam singing up in the orchard and it was all right for him to be there, but we wondered why we could not hear him just as she did. We told her once that we wanted her to call so that we could hear him.

She replied softly, "Honeys, you all cain't heah 'im. Hit's only 'is spirit dat sings an' hit sings only to me."

Green's eyes always opened wide when Aunt Sally mentioned spirits, and at this remark he looked as if he was truly scared. As we rode away he said, "I can't help feeling queer every time Aunt Sally talks about spirits."

In our hunts we had found a great hole in the side of a hill where a hundred acres or more were covered so thickly with cedars that it was almost impossible to penetrate them. There were young cedars and old ones on this hill. Some of the trees indicated great age. At first we did not examine this opening in the earth, but when I reported our find to Uncle Robert and Captain Noland, they said they had seen it too, but its existence was not generally known. They told us that the place was called the Rock House, and that it could be made a good place to live in if it were more accessible.[60]

Green and I resolved to know more about the Rock House, so one day after being well fed by Aunt Sally, we started for the cedars. After climbing and squeezing through the thick forest, we found ourselves once more at the entrance to this cave. We both felt brave and thought we would go in and see everything. We had not gone many yards until it became so dark we could hardly see each other, and we hastily regained the entrance. We began to wonder what was in there, when it occurred to us that it might be the home of Uncle Caesar's bear. This suggestion frightened us and we returned quickly to the outer edge of the forest where we had hitched our horse and mule. For myself, I was perfectly satisfied with our investigation. Little did I know then that in a short time I would go to that place daily and become familiar with every part of it.

Green wanted to return home by his Uncle Othniel's and I was more than willing. When we rode up to the house we were surprised not to see the children bounding out to greet us as usual. We soon learned that Kie and James had gone the night before to join the Confederate army. They had left with twenty or thirty others to find their way South, if possible. Little Nettie was the only one who did not appear to realize that a happy home had been broken and that the places made vacant by the departure of her brothers might never again be filled. Others, however, could not hide their grief and appeared so unhappy that we soon went away.

Naturally Green and I felt that everyone was joining the Confederates, for we had not learned of anybody's leaving to fight for the North. On this day, however, before we arrived at our place of parting, we learned that Dudley Tiley, a young man we knew well, had gone to join the Yankees. It soon became plain that people in the vicinity of Old Cane Springs were clearly divided and that rancor and discord were being manifested.

CHAPTER XV

THE HOME GUARDS

THE JUNE MEETING at Old Cane Spring Church had come and gone. The congregation was unusually small for June, and now it was the time for the July meeting. Orchards were bowed down with fruit and gardens were full of vegetables. In the pastures were many fat lambs and pigs and the barnyards were well filled with the finest of spring chickens, but the usual preparation for the occasion was lacking.

It was known that up at Texas and Waco a company of Home Guards had begun organizing. The Negroes reported that they had seen them prowling around at night and that the company was composed entirely of "po' white trash," some of whom they named. So as the July meeting day approached no one appeared to realize it and no special preparations were made for it. Only a few persons were present, but from that few all the neighborhood happenings were learned. I was told that Mr. Othniel Oldham had followed his boys down South; that John Lariemore had gone also; that many men from Clark, Bourbon, and Harrison counties were passing through our county every night, trying to make their way into the Confederacy; and that the Home Guards were on the watch and were arresting every man they found going towards the South. Men looked peculiarly at each other and had very little to say. The services appeared not to be enjoyed and the hearty hand-shaking which I first saw was not indulged in at all. The Negroes were the only happy looking people around.

It was said that Mr. Oldham had entrusted his wife and children to his faithful servant, Pike, and that Mr. Lariemore had entrusted his family to his faithful servant, Pleas. (Very seldom in Old Cane Springs did one hear the word slave applied to Negroes.) Uncle Robert had left Aunt Jose and her children in the care of a likely Negro named Harvey. Excepting my aunt, I was the largest white person at our home.

I continued in school, where I learned from day to day that someone else had gone southward from the neighborhood. In almost every instance the person had left through fear of the Home Guards, who were made up of men around Texas and from the sourwood community and the knobs of Estill County. They all appeared to be very patriotic and anxious that the Union be preserved, and it finally became dangerous for anyone to say a word in favor of the Confederacy. A young man by the name of William Reid Wallace happened to be more enthusiastic than discreet in expressing himself about the Confederacy, and at the same time spoke in a derogatory manner about President Lincoln. He was not aware that John Daniel Burgess, a Home Guard, was present. With only the remark that "every d—— Rebel, whether in or out of the army, ought to be dead," Burgess plunged a large butcher knife clear through Wallace. No arrest was made, for not even a warrant was sworn out. From that time on talk for the South could be heard only in whispered conversations when no stranger or Home Guard was near.[61]

Those in sympathy with the South had their secret meetings and kept themselves informed of the activities of the Home Guards. The latter pretended to be organized to protect the homes in the community against both Rebels and Yankees, but it was soon learned that only those who were in sympathy with the North could become members. It was also learned from the Negroes that Home Guards made almost nightly visits to their quarters in the neighborhood and tried to make them dissatisfied with their masters. The Negroes told everything the Guards said, but they would usually wind up with a comment that they were a lot of "po' white trash," going places they would not dare visit in the daytime.

When men from counties north of Madison first began to pass southward through Madison, the hospitality of Old Cane Springs was showered upon them. It was soon observed, however, that it was dangerous hospitality. Richmond had been declared under martial law and Captain P. P. Ballard had been appointed provost judge. Orders had gone forth that no one was to aid or comfort anyone who desired to become connected with the rebellion and that any stranger found in the county traveling towards the South was to be arrested and brought before the provost judge.

Captain Ballard was one of the kindest, best men in the county, and well beloved by most every one in Old Cane Springs; and while many of the citizens were brought before him, he merely admonished and threatened them, and then allowed them to return home. He was a true patriot, anxious that the Union be preserved and ready to send Rebels to prison, but he said the accusers would have to prove more on a man than the fact that he had given some stranger lodging and a meal before he would take him away from his family. Nevertheless, he always ended with the remark: "You must not feed too many strangers, but at the same time you must not forget the Christian injunction to be hospitable to the stranger." Then he would turn to those who had made the arrests and say: "However, you bring in every stranger you see if he is headed South. If he is a trader or on a lawful mission, I will not detain him long, but if it turns out he is aiming to join the rebellion, we will land him in prison, where we hope soon to have all who are now in arms against the Union."[62]

At any rate, the arrests had the desired effect. Those going South appeared to know before they came to the county just where to go, but for fear they might not get off so well on the second arrest, other arrangements had to be made.

CHAPTER XVI

THE ROCK HOUSE

MY FATHER, as I have already said, was an emancipationist, but my short stay at Old Cane Springs had removed the impression he had made on me in that respect. I saw that there was neither misery nor oppression among the Negroes, and I believed the homes to which they were attached were surely the best on earth. Moreover, I had long since concluded that it would be very wrong to change the conditions that existed between masters and servants, and that it was the ideal way of existence for both whites and blacks. But my father had also talked to me about preserving the Union, so I hardly knew where I stood on that question.

One Saturday late in the fall of 1861 I mounted Whizaker and started up the road towards Texas. I overtook Mary Ann, and she and I rode along together, chatting in general about happenings in the neighborhood and all the current war news. I learned from her that Nath Deatherage and several other young men had made an effort to get through the mountains to the Confederacy but they had been cut off and almost captured. Nath was then hiding out and the Home Guards were after him every night.[68] Mary Ann was worried over the situation, but I was so charmed by her and so interested in her talk that I hardly knew I had ridden home with her until we drew reins at the stiles. Of course, I accepted her invitation to alight and visit a while.

I learned that Mr. Oldham and his two sons were with the Confederate army in Tennessee and that the family had already heard from them by the grape-vine route, about which more will be said presently. Tempie and Nettie sang the *Bonnie Blue Flag* and *Dixie,* and matters went delightfully on until I suggested it was time for me to return home. I was preparing to start when I happened to think of the grape-vine route to which reference had just been made, and I asked Mary Ann to tell me about it.

She looked serious for a moment and then took me by the hand and walked with me towards my mule. Finally she said, "Gustin, I have work for you. I have heard you say that you know where the Rock House in the cedars is. I can't tell you now, but if you will meet me next Saturday at ten o'clock at the Rock House, I will tell you all about it and show you how we are evading the Home Guards."

I gladly promised, and on my way home the *Bonnie Blue Flag* and *Dixie* were buzzing in my ears, and I began to think I was certainly a Rebel.

Early the next Saturday I was on Whizaker riding to the Rock House. On my arrival, I found Mary Ann as busy as if she were in her home.

"You see," she said, "here are a number of quilts and comforters. Winter will soon be here and they will be needed."

"By whom?" I asked. "You are not going to come here to live?"

"No," she replied, "but somebody is going to live here."

She lit a candle and asked me to follow her. I found the place to be a rock house indeed. Four large rooms turned off from the main passage and the floor of each was covered a foot in straw.

"How did all this straw get here?" I inquired.

"Oh, it's here, you see, and it does not matter especially how, but it was a task to get it here. The straw had to be brought tied up in sheets and the cedars are so very close together that we could hardly get through; but by flattening and rolling we did finally get here with it. As I came here with one load, I ran right into a squad of Home Guards. I have made it a rule to be on good terms with them. I don't really like a one of them but I would not let them know it for anything. I met them as usual with a smile, and reigned up my horse. I asked if they had recently taken any Rebels before the judge."

"The leader replied, 'I suppose, Miss Oldham, you have made that general inquiry for the purpose of learning whether or not we have been able to catch a certain individual whom you think we are anxious to catch. I must confess, Miss, that Nath has outwitted us. We have not been able to get him before the provost, but we expect soon to march him in.'

"I said, 'Never; he knows the Muddy Creek and river hills as well as any fox that his brother, Killis, chases with his hounds, and you will never catch him.'

" 'If you only wanted to,' continued the spokesman, 'you could tell us just where to find him, and you ought to do it for his good. If we fail to get him he will eventually make his way South and, of course, he will join the Confederates. Consequently, he will either be killed or captured, and, therefore, he is sure to fare worse than if we took him in. Now, be a good girl and let us know where he is. I believe that the tick of straw you have there behind you is for no other purpose than a bed for him while he is lying out watching his chance to get away.'

"He had told the truth, and my, how I did feel for a second or two while my mind was at work trying to throw him off the trail! I spoke up defiantly: 'Captain Adams, how dare you accuse me of acts that would justify you and your men in taking me before the provost? Can't a person carry in open daylight some new straw to a poor old sick Negro woman? Aunt Creech Sally is very sick, and I thought I would take her a new straw bed, and now for doing it you accuse me of aiding and comforting Rebels.'

"The other men broke into a hearty laugh, and one said, 'Captain, she has floored you and you ought to apologize.'

" 'Miss Oldham knows no apology is necessary,' he said. 'She knows I was only aiming to tease and not accuse her.'

"I gave him a smile which lead him to believe I so understood his remarks and we parted as usual, apparently the best of friends. That very night, I expect, Nath slept on some of that straw."

We had, by this time, returned to the entrance of the Rock House and had seated ourselves on a heavy bed of cedar needles.

"You know, I told you last Saturday," Mary Ann began, "that if you met me here today I would explain to you the grape-vine mail route. Well, you are in one of the post offices now. I know I can trust you, or I would never tell you what I am now going to explain, nor would I tell you if I did not need you. I want you to enlist in my service for the Confederacy. You are too young to be a soldier. If you were old enough, I would send you South. Now that you cannot go South, you must serve the Confederacy here. Will you join me?"

"I join you, and I do so with all my heart," I replied quickly.

"I knew it," she said, "or I never would have invited you here. As I said, this is one of the offices on the grape-vine route. I know of only two others, and I must tell you where they are, for you may need to know."

She stepped back into the house and came out with a map, and I soon saw on it every road with which I was familiar.

"That one," she said, "goes to Winchester and this one to Irvine. No one leaving here must go through either town. Those places must be avoided."

She then explained how to go around each place and pointed to certain round spots on the map beyond both Winchester and Irvine where a person remained during the day. All traveling on these routes was done at night.

"In there where I got this map is the post office," she said. "Did you ever get a letter out of the post office at Texas for your aunt from your Uncle Robert?"

I admitted that I had not.

"You knew she has heard from him?"

"Yes," I nodded.

"Was it shortly after I had been there that you learned that she had received a letter from him?"

I looked at her in astonishment. It occurred to me that what she said was true.

"The persons who carry this mail dare not take any risk in asking for food," she continued. "It must be arranged for them. If they want to, they can eat here at any time during the day. If they are going North from here, I show them exactly how to hit that round spot there. That is where John Cunningham lives in Bourbon County; and if they are going South, I show them exactly how to get to that spot. That is where Robert Fluty lives in Estill County."[64]

"What I want you to do is to come here every Saturday. You are always riding that spotted mule and have been for more than a year. You are often down here with a bag of salt, salting Mr. Cabell Chenault's cattle, and everybody knows you eat dinner often on Saturdays with Aunt Creech Sally—oftener, in fact, than you do with your Aunt Jose; so no one will think it strange to see you about here riding on a meal sack. Your aunt will have the sack for you next Saturday and this is where you will put it."

"When you get within a hundred yards of this place," Mary Ann continued, "you must begin to whistle *Yankee Doodle*. We did hate to choose that tune because it had Yankee in it, but we finally concluded that if an enemy heard it, it would attract less attention than any other sign; and now that you are a Confederate you may go home with me and see if the *Bonnie Blue Flag* doesn't sound better than it ever did before to you. My horse is hitched in the upper end of the cedars; I suppose your mule is down there close to Aunt Creech Sally's. I'll wait for you to overtake me at General Jackson's. I want you to speak to me when you come up and pretend it is the first time you have seen me today."

CHAPTER XVII

MARY ANN AS CONFEDERATE POSTMISTRESS

IN A VERY short time I joined Mary Ann at the front yard of General Jackson's residence. She was having a lively chat with Violet, John's wife. I heard her say to Violet as I rode up, that she had heard that Aunt Creech Sally was sick and had started to take her a new straw bed but had learned that some of the men had already furnished her a new bed, so she threw her straw away.

"Oh, Miss Mary, chile," exclaimed Violet, "you is all de time t'inkin' 'bout helpin' dat po' ole woman. She's mighty sick, she is, an' it's purty bad fur 'er to be dar all by herse'f; but Marse Cabell, he allus sends someone to be wid 'er, or he comes hisse'f ebery day to see 'er an' he has my John to look atter 'er all de time. I hea'd Marse Cabell de udder day beggin' 'er to let 'im haul 'er on de ox wagon up to 'is home, but she wouldn' go. She say she didn't 'spect to go enywhar but in de garden to be laid by de side ov Sam. Marse Cabell, he jis tuck on like it wuz 'is own mother talkin', an' he promise' to sen' down 'er gal Minerva to stay wid 'er 'til she gits better, but she's too ole to eber be much better."

Mary Ann was so intent on listening to Violet that she pretended she did not know I had arrived. She spoke to me in such manner that I am certain she made old Violet believe she had not seen me for a fortnight.

As we rode up the creek together towards the Oldham home Mary Ann remarked, "Gustin, I'm afraid you'll conclude I'm a deceitful person; in fact, you'll conclude I'm a regular story-teller. You heard me tell you how I deceived the Home Guards and you heard me fibbing to Violet. I'm not a story-teller and you have no idea how it grieves me to resort to deception; but what are we to do? You know father and my brothers, James and Kie, are with the Confederate army. Your Uncle Robert and many others from around here are down there, too. There are men fighting for the South from every county north of here to the Ohio River. Their people want to hear from them. Nothing can come to them from down there through the United States mail, and some other way had to be worked out; so the grapevine route, as it is called, was established. They could not establish an office without a postmaster. I suppose President Davis appointed me. At any rate I was notified of my appointment and accepted it. There was no red tape to it and no bond required."

"I first kept office at home," she continued, "but since the Home Guards were making so many arrests and were around our house so often, I became afraid they would rob the office, so I moved it to the Rock House, and as I needed an assistant I have selected you. There are two reasons why I selected you. First, you have been riding that spotted mule ever since you came here. At first it attracted attention and everyone learned who you were. Everyone knows at a glance now who you are, and in passing around you attract less comment now than anyone else would. I have been riding up and down this creek and on the roads around here since I was large enough to ride and am known by every white and black person in Old Cane Springs and for many miles farther away. I attract less attention anywhere I go than would any other girl in the neighborhood. Still everyone appears glad to see me, and when I go that is the end of it for that time. I suppose for that reason I was selected as postmistress."

"The second reason for selecting you," she continued, "is that I believe you both brave and true—I mean faithful to any enterprise that you might engage in. Now you have joined me in the business of carrying messages of love to the bereaved ones in the homes of this community. The sight of your spotted mule will make many a heart leap for joy, if we can keep hidden the source of the love messages we carry. Now to keep that secret from being known, don't you think I was justified in deceiving the Home Guards and also deceiving Aunt Violet? She is sure to tell her John, and if any of those Home Guards should ask him about my bringing the straw to Aunt Sally he won't be surprised and say she never brought it. On the other hand he will say that I started here with it, but on learning that Aunt Sally's bed had been filled by someone else I threw my straw away. Now when you look at it as you know I did, do you think there was any wrong in the little stories I told?"

I told her I thought she had done exactly right and that I would deceive in the same way if I could, before I would let anyone know of the grape-vine route. "But," said I, "how do the people way down South know of the Rock House?"

"I named the postoffice," she replied. "By the way, here is a letter for your Aunt Jose."

I examined the address and saw that it read, "Mrs. Robert Chenault, Rock House, Ky."

"You understand now," Mary Ann said; "I do not know whether there is any other Rock House in Kentucky, but I do know there is no other place on this route from Atlanta to Cincinnati. Mail carriers pass each other every night at places half way between here and Cunningham's and between here and Fluty's. So mail is going North and South every night; and every day two of these carriers might be caught, but they live near and no one is likely to connect them with a mail route from Atlanta to Cincinnati."

As the plan of the grape-vine mail system seemed to dawn on me, I exclaimed, "Wonderful! I am glad I am in it, and I will make you the best assistant possible. However, I do not understand all about it yet. If there were only two mail carriers and they were in a room you did not show me, why were you covering those other rooms with straw?"

"You will understand that, too, before you have been assistant very long," she replied. "Only a few suggestions and you can work it out. The Yankees are continually capturing our men. As a rule they are carried north of the Ohio and some of them are constantly escaping from prison.[65] It would be difficult and dangerous for them to try to get back South without a guide, especially since they usually travel by night. Furthermore, there are things going on in the North that the South wants to know. The one who goes for that information is on a dangerous mission. He too must travel by night. From these suggestions you may see how there may be more than the two in the Rock House at the same time. And besides, some of our local boys who are dodging the Home Guards go in there if the weather is bad."

As we rode up to the stiles, I looked at Mary Ann and said inwardly, "You are the prettiest, bravest, best, and smartest girl I have ever known." In fact, I so adored her that right then and there she could have sent me on any kind of mission, however hazardous; and, moreover, I felt sure, in my boyish enthusiasm, that she was competent to direct the affairs of the entire Confederacy.

Nettie and Tempie had spied us as we approached and came bounding out to greet us. After a splendid dinner, followed with songs by the children, I told Mary Ann that I must return home. I knew how anxious my aunt was to see the letter I had. I rode away feeling like a soldier, and, strange to say, for the first time in my life I felt I was a man with a man's work before me to perform.

Chapter XVIII

SALT FOR CATTLE, BUT FOOD FOR MEN

A UNT JOSE did look queer when I handed her the letter, which she knew at a glance was from Uncle Robert, and she continued to look puzzled until I handed her a note from Mary Ann. When she read it, she smiled and handed it to me. It read, "Trust G. He is my assistant. Send him with a good sack of salt Saturday. Mary Ann."

School did pass slowly that week. I was anxious to go to the Rock House with my sack of salt. I understood from that note that the bag I was to carry to the Rock House was to be to outsiders a sack of salt for the cattle on the creek farm.

When Saturday came my sack of salt was filled as usual by one of the Negro men and set on the front porch. In a very short time I was on Whizaker and off for the creek farm. I stopped as usual for a visit with Aunt Creech Sally and learned she had improved some. I congratulated her on being better and told her that I wanted her to be up soon. I reminded her that hog-killing time was drawing near, and told her that Green and I had been saying during the week that we were longing for chitlins and shortening bread and that we both agreed that no one could make them taste like those she prepared. For a few minutes the old woman appeared pleased at my flattery. Then she became serious and said she was too old to do these things again, and while she would like to fix some good things for us and all of Marse Cabell's boys, she feared she would never get up. Besides, she knew Sam was tired of sleeping up there in the garden by himself and she wanted to go to him, since he could not come back to her.

"I sees frum yo' sack out dar on Whizaker dat you is gwine to salt Marse Cabell's cattle," she said slowly. "You've bin a heap ov he'p to 'im since Marse Jephtha an' Harvey went 'way to school."

I told her that I knew she would get better soon, and that Dr. Ayres[66] said she was only bilious and would be up presently. "Ef I does, he'll be 'sponsible fur it," she said. "Some ov dese heah doctors has got so dey can keep a pusson 'live w'en it peers like dey's gwine to die, an' really wants to die."

I bade her good-by, and in a short time I was in the hills, ostensibly to salt Mr. Chenault's cattle. I approached the Rock House whistling *Yankee Doodle* in an unconcerned way. Mary Ann came out to meet me. I had my sack of salt, as I thought, and I wondered why she wanted so much salt. Mary Ann told me to follow her and she would show me where to dispose of the contents of the sack. I followed her to one of the large rooms and through it into a narrow passage along which we went a little way, and then turned to the right into another room. It was not more than one-third the size of the rooms I had seen before, and appeared to have been built for a pantry. Rock shelves about two feet in width ran clear around this room. I could see by the dim candlelight various edibles on these shelves.

"Now we'll see what you have and put it up here," Mary Ann said.

"All I've got is a sack of salt," I explained. "Where shall I put it?"

"Well, we'll see," she replied, as she began to untie the sack.

To my great surprise she first took out two dozen half-moon pies, fried brown and crisp; next she brought forth something wrapped in one sheet of the *Enquirer,* which proved to be at least five pounds of old ham.[67] Then pone bread, light bread, and biscuits were brought out. The last things to be removed were catsup, pickles, rice balls, and an octagon pound cake. I looked on in amazement.

Finally I exclaimed, "Well, I'll be jiggered! I can't see how that occurred. I saw Harve fill that sack with salt and set it on the porch, and when I got ready I picked it up from where he placed it and put it on Whizaker. How in the world did it turn to all this food?"

"You see," Mary Ann replied laughingly, "others are resorting to deception as well as myself. You will be at it too in a little while. Your Aunt Jose could have told you the secret, but I suppose she thought it best for you not to know this time. If Captain Adams and his Home Guards had met you and had looked into the sack, I imagine you would have been as much surprised as was Benjamin and his brothers when the king's cup and money were found in their sacks."

I confessed I certainly would have been, and explained: "By the way, I did meet the captain and his men, but they merely said, 'Hello, Old Spot, how's the cowboy?' and hurried on. I thought when I saw them that if they asked me what I was going to do with that salt, I would invite them to go with me to see me give it to the cattle, and then get Harve to fill me another sack with salt, which I would bring here later this afternoon."

"You see now," she said, "it was best you did not know. Knowledge of the contents of the bag might have made you look guilty or scared. What would you have said if they had examined this sack and found all these things in it?"

I felt puzzled and wondered what I would have done. Finally I replied: "I expect I would have told the captain that it was some delicacies Aunt Jose had got me to take to Aunt Creech Sally."

She tapped me on the head in an affectionate way and said, "I see you are going to learn; but we must not be here too long today. The men in that room yonder will find plenty to eat when they awaken. I know you intend to go home with me, but we must not be seen together today. You can find Green and go hunting, but you must come here every Saturday. Your aunt will always have a sack ready. It may be best for you never to know what is in it until you arrive. I may not meet you here again. I will be at the Rock House every now and then, but I must begin to go in other directions on Saturdays. However, I will see you this week either at your school or at your aunt's. Maybe I shall be down there some afternoon and stay late enough to need you as an escort home. I will explain when I see you."

CHAPTER XIX

MARY ANN AND NATH AT THE ROCK HOUSE

ON THE FOLLOWING Wednesday, I saw Mary Ann pass the schoolhouse riding on towards her grandfather's. Of course, I could not keep from wondering what else she wanted to tell me or wanted me to do. I was already doing enough to be carried before the provost and sent to prison, if it were found out. When I got home from school, to my surprise, there stood her horse, and on entering the house I found her and Aunt Jose deeply engaged in conversation. I could easily see that something had occurred or was about to occur that was of great concern to them. They requested me, much to my disappointment, to stay out awhile, saying they would call me in presently.

But I was not called, though Mary Ann and my aunt talked on and on. It was evident that night was fast approaching, for the Negroes had all come in from the field and were doing their chores. The women were milking when Aunt Jose and Mary Ann came out on the front porch. My aunt began speaking, but in a louder tone than was her habit of talking. "Mary Ann, won't you spend the night with us and let me have your horse cared for?"

"No, thank you; I just can't," she replied. "Susie is away and there is no one at home but mother and the little ones."

"Well, if you must go, Gustin will go with you. Harve, you get my saddle horse for Gustin. It's too late for Miss Oldham to go home alone, and besides he is not afraid to ride late."

In a very short time Harve, a most faithful servant, had the horse for me, and Mary Ann and I started up the Texas road. When we reached the spot where I had first been so entranced at the sight of Old Cane Springs, we could dimly discern the Oldham home a mile or more to our right up Muddy Creek; and almost in the same direction and nearly as far away on the lower west bend of Muddy Creek, we could also dimly see the home of Amos Deatherage. I had often seen these places and was so familiar with them that neither would have especially attracted my attention if it had not been for the songs I heard at both homes.

Mary Ann had hardly spoken to me since we had ridden off together. I tried to get her into conversation one way or another, but, as she did not appear to want to talk, I concluded that I was sent only as a protector and that I would simply act guard and say nothing. We had, therefore, been riding in silence for quite a distance, but when the singing from these two homes broke on my ears, I could not help saying, "Mary Ann, do you hear that?"

She brought her horse to a standstill, as I did mine, and we both listened in silence. There were the old beautiful melodies that I had often heard since coming to Old Cane Springs, but of which I had never become tired.

"Isn't that wonderful!" I exclaimed.

"Yes," she said, "but I have heard it when it was sweeter than that."

"Why, what is lacking?" I inquired.

"There are some voices missing at both places," she explained. "The old men and the women and girls and all the children and boys are singing, but the voices of some of our middle-aged men are missing. Their minds are being disturbed. The Home Guards are in the quarters every night. They are trying in every imaginable way to get them to run off and go to Camp Nelson."

Then after a brief pause, she continued: "I don't see how they can do it. If they only knew how happy the Negroes are they surely would not want to bring the misery on them that is sure to come if they continue to interfere with them. There they are down there supremely happy and contented. They think they own my father's thousand acres just as much as he does or any child of his does. They call it 'our plantation.' They are interested in the various crops and the stock, just as much as any of us whites are."

"As I rode off this morning," Mary Ann went on to say, "Pike said they would finish shucking corn today; and while the quarters of both homes are full of life and song every night, there is always more enthusiasm when some great task like gathering the corn is finished. The Negroes are faithful souls to their masters. They tell us every move of the Home Guards. Pike told me yesterday of a number of persons who are members, who we thought were in sympathy with the South. That is why you are with me tonight. We are not going home as you think; we must go to the Rock House. We must hurry on now and pass through Texas before it is so dark that people there cannot recognize me. Since you are not on Whizaker, they will think I have a new beau. I don't want them to know you tonight."

In a very short time we had passed through Texas and were on the creek road. Many persons said, "You ride late, Miss Oldham," but no one spoke to me. We halted and listened to see if we could hear horsemen coming up or down the creek, but hearing nothing Mary said, "We must go to the Rock House as soon as possible, but we must not ride fast enough to attract attention."

Soon we were at the dense edge of the cedars, and, after securely hitching our horses, we began the ascent to the Rock House. When within about a hundred yards of the place I began to whistle *Yankee Doodle* very softly. In the dim darkness I saw a tall man step out and start towards us. Presently I heard him say: "Derned, if it ain't Hart. I know his little old whistle." He said no more until I was within a few feet of him when he called out, "Who's that with you, Gustin?"

"It's a friend," I answered, "but we had better get inside of the house."

He turned and led the way and we followed. When we had gotten into one of the rear rooms where a candle was lighted, I saw that the man was Nath Deatherage. Almost as soon as I had recognized him, he said, "Dad burn it, Mary Ann, what are you doing here?"

She eyed him with defiance and replied, "Now you quiet down, Nath. Gustin and I are actually in the service. You've not enlisted yet, however anxious you may be to do so. I want you to be able to carry out your desire is the reason I am here. You are so confiding and have so much confidence in the justice of the demands of the South that you think everyone but the 'po white trash,' as the Negroes call them, is on our side; but that is not true. There are men meeting with the Home Guards every night that you think are your friends. You would invite them here if you were let alone, and then when they knew of this place there would be one office on the grape-vine route promptly broken up."

"How do you know all this?" Nath inquired.

"I know it, all right," she persisted. "You know they think father is old and that he will get tired of the army and will return soon, and so they are around our house nearly every night expecting him. Last night two of your friends who live on the road from Union to Big Hill were there, and several of your chums at Waco. You know whom I mean."

"Did you see them?"

"No."

"Then I don't believe it."

"But it is true." Mary Ann declared. "They were there."

"Who told you so?"

"Pike says he saw them and knew them."

"He told you he saw them?"

"You heard me say he did."

"Then it is true; but dad burn it, who would have believed it? You are right, Mary Ann, I would have invited any one of those fellows here and without any hesitancy laid before him our plan to go South."

"Yes, I know you would," Mary Ann said, "and any one of them would have had all the Home Guards in the sourwoods on you before you had gotten as far as Bybeetown."

"Well, you are a trump for coming," Nath said tenderly. "I will not only avoid those you have named, but I will have no more recruits. I know all the fellows stretched out in those other rooms are as anxious to join the Confederates as I am, and we expect to slip out in a few nights. I am certainly glad you came. If you had not, I doubt if any of us would have gotten away, because we expected to try to get one of those Waco fellows to go with us tomorrow."

Mary Ann arose and said, "Well, as my mission is ended; Gustin, we will go."

Nath straightened himself and gazed intently at the fair form before him. I could see in his face that he loved her dearly.

"Mary Ann, must I go?" he asked.

"Yes, Nathan, all true men will go," she replied firmly.

They both appeared to forget I was present.

"Will you hope for my return, Mary Ann?"

"Yes, Nathan, I shall always long for your return, when like a true soldier you can return, a conqueror, a hero; or if vanquished, with no taint of cowardice in the defeat."

"Then good-by, Mary Ann, for I feel almost certain I shall see you no more until this cruel war is over."

"Good-by, Nathan," she said in a trembling voice, which caused me to move away from the Rock House.

Presently Mary Ann joined me and we crept out into the darkness and were soon where we had left our horses. We rode away in silence up the creek road. When we were near her home, she said, "I think it is best for you to go on home, Gustin. Nettie is long since asleep, and besides it would attract attention were you to ride that horse tomorrow. Let me know after you go to the Rock House Saturday what you have seen and heard. I am still afraid to be seen there for awhile."

And then we bade each other good-night.

CHAPTER XX

PREPARATIONS TO MOVE UNION TROOPS THROUGH
MADISON COUNTY

I REPORTED on the following Saturday what I had heard and seen at the Rock House. I carried Mary Ann a letter which she kissed when I handed it to her and cried when she read it. Weeks passed and I continued my weekly visits to the Rock House. War, war, was the subject of conversation everywhere, but it all appeared far away from Old Cane Springs. Soldiers were not uncommon, for they were often passing. We were so far from the scene of conflict that we did not know the real thing. Finally word came that Dudley Tiley had died at Camp Nelson[68] and that his remains would be brought home. He was the only young man in the immediate community who had gone to the Yankee army. Everybody, white and black, went to the burial, and everyone extended the warmest feeling of sympathy to his parents; and it looked as if the old spirit of friendship and love was about to revive.

By the spring of 1862 talk of war was heard everywhere. The winter had been severe and the roads between the North and South were very bad and it was impossible for the two belligerent forces to get at each other, but we often heard through the Home Guards that the Union army would move South as soon as the weather would permit and the roads could be put in condition. Rumor also came over the grape-vine route that the Southern army was preparing to come North. We were, therefore, made to believe that a meeting of Federals and Confederates would occur somewhere in Kentucky, and that we were sure to have some fighting near us and in other parts of the State.

Early in the spring an advertisement was scattered throughout Madison County that it had become necessary for all loyal citizens to aid in suppressing the rebellion. It was also announced that it was imperatively necessary for the proper movement of the army that the public roads be put in good condition, so that the assembled Union troops in Kentucky could be moved South as soon as the weather would permit, to meet and disperse the enemy. Therefore, to accomplish these ends all persons in Madison County owning as many as three or more able-bodied male slaves were instructed to furnish one man out of every three to labor on the public road leading over the Big Hill to the South.[69] The owners of slaves were assured that the men they sent would be well cared for and returned to their various masters as soon as the road was put in good condition. Slaves between the ages of eighteen and forty-five in good health were deemed ablebodied.

The consternation caused by this circular was intense. Many of those who had been inclined towards the Union and had not believed that the North would in any way interfere with slavery now allied themselves with the Confederacy. Young white men from every family began to prepare to go South as soon as an opportunity made it possible. One thing surprised me very much. It was evident that the Negroes were soon aware that the circular in some way directly affected them. I was called on by Negroes on nearly every plantation to tell them what those "bills," as they called them, meant. I explained as best I could, and in several instances I found that they had never heard the word slave. Captain Noland's Allen, his blacksmith, had been taught to read and write, so that he could enter charges against those having work done at the shop. He, Cabell Chenault's Jake, and a few others who could read knew, of course, that they were slaves in the true meaning of the term. Many others, however, appeared indignant when I explained the meaning of the word to them. Often the Negroes seemed to regard themselves as much the owners of the plantations as their old masters.[70]

Such was truly the state of contentment of these happy, lighthearted people in Old Cane Springs. They revolted at the idea of being taken away from home. Not one in the whole community wanted to go and fix roads for the Yankees, and they had no hesitancy in so expressing themselves anywhere and at all times.

While both black and white were at fever heat over this call, another letter came to Aunt Jose from Uncle Robert. To my surprise it came by regular post and was post-marked "Bearwallow, Ky." It had been months since we had heard from him and we had often feared that he had been killed. He told, in brief, that he was in poor health; that on account of his physical condition he had been discharged from the Confederate service; that he had spent a month or more at his Uncle David Chenault's in Gallatin, Tennessee; and that he had finally come to Bearwallow in Barren County, where he had been captured. He stated further that on account of ill health he had been paroled and was then at the home of his brother-in-law, William Hone. He planned to start for Madison County as soon as he was able to ride. The children were awakened and the Negroes called in to hear the news, and there was general rejoicing at our house that night.

The order concerning the improvement of the roads required the masters to report at Richmond with their slaves on the first Monday in April at which time they would get receipts for them and a guarantee for their return. Uncle Robert got home a few days before this order was to be carried out. All the owners of slaves in Old Cane Springs were anxious to see him and to learn whether he would advise them to obey the order. I recall well the arrangement for the meeting at his home. The room in which they were to meet was so arranged that no light could be seen from the outside, and no two were to come together or leave together. I was permitted to be present to report facts that I had gathered at the Rock House.

Finally the men were assembled in an upper room. The general expression at first was to disregard the request and not to send a man. Finally Uncle Robert said he had studied the circular very closely and had come to the conclusion that it was a cunningly devised request, gotten up purposely to get slave owners into trouble.

"I notice," he said, "that the request is only to slave owners who are loyal to the Union. It is to be construed that all who fail to respond with their slaves are disloyal. There is now a general order from the provost that all persons suspected of being disloyal to the Union must be arrested and brought before the provost judge. If they refuse to take the oath of allegiance to the United States they are to be confined in prison until they take the oath, and, furthermore, they may be fined any sum of money at the discretion of the judge. Now, you ought to be able to see the trap set for you. I know every slave owner in Old Cane Springs is generally thought to be disloyal. All the authorities want is some excuse to arrest you, and when arrested, if you fail to take the oath of loyalty, you are certain to be heavily fined and sent to prison."

"Now, I think it best to go with your men," Uncle Robert continued. "I see that the Negroes do not want to go, but if you ask them they will go, and besides the road they are required to work will not be exclusively for the Yankees. I know that Bragg will be in Kentucky as soon as possible—as soon as the roads are dry enough to bring his artillery over them. There is more proof of that fact than my words. What have you to say about that, Gustin?"

I admitted that men at the Rock House had been informed that it was very dangerous to try to go South then, and that they were advised to wait until they would have an opportunity to join the Confederate army in Kentucky. Before the meeting adjourned they all agreed to have on hand their respective quotas of men for road work on the appointed day.

Finally the Negroes returned from the work and the Union army was on the way to the South; and by the grape-vine route we learned that the Southern army was moving northward. News had come that a battle had been fought at Pine Mountain in which the Confederates had been worsted and many killed, wounded, and captured. It was also rumored that Captain Ambrose Dudley and his company were with the Confederate forces. Dudley's company was made up exclusively of Madison County boys and especially those who had gone South from Old Cane Springs. Anxiety and excitement, therefore, were intense, but nothing definite could be learned either by post or by the grape-vine route.

Chapter XXI

MARY ANN'S SPEECH SAVES THE DAY

ONE MORNING I felt I must have some special instruction from Mary Ann and rode up to her home. I had hardly arrived when I saw two persons on one horse coming in our direction along the Waco road. Mrs. Oldham cried, "It is Kie and James."

Although they were nearly a half mile away, a mother's eye had recognized her sons. All of us began to shout for joy, except Mrs. Oldham, who gazed as only a mother can at her children. Presently she said, "Kie is either sick or hurt," and then she fell in a swoon. We revived her and continued to watch the lone horse and two riders. Little, big, young and old, white and black appeared to start at once to meet them.

It was evident that Mrs. Oldham had not been mistaken when she said Kie was either sick or hurt. Both boys looked like mere lads. Kie, the younger, was not yet eighteen and his pale, pinched features showed that he was in distress.[71] James, however, was all smiles and appeared to enjoy the demonstration of joy at his return. When they rode up to the stile, faithful Pike was there to lift Kie down, and no father could have exhibited more tender care than he did in helping the lad into the house. We soon learned that Kie had been shot at the battle of Pine Mountain and that James had been captured and then paroled so that he might bring his wounded brother home. They also told us of the other boys of the community who had been killed, wounded, or captured. They were unable to tell what had become of their father, but believed him to be neither hurt nor captured.

There was no more work on the Oldham plantation that day except cooking. Every Negro on the plantation came in and exhibited as much joy as the mother, sisters, and brothers. The news scattered over the community, and soon the neighbors began to arrive. Mrs. Oldham attended to Kie, but she almost fainted when she saw the ghastly wound where the shot had penetrated the flesh. All were wrapped in smiles except Mrs. Oldham, whose countenance remained very grave after she learned the ball was still in the body of her son.

Dinner had been served before the neighbors began to arrive, but when they did come, they stayed to hear James tell his and Kie's experiences after leaving home to join the Confederate army and especially the battle of Pine Mountain and his effort to get home with Kie. He said that during the battle there was one thing that made them all laugh at a time when men were being shot all around them.

"We were in East Tennessee when we heard that Bragg's army had passed into Kentucky from West Tennessee," James related. "We naturally thought he had driven all the Yankees before him and we decided to cross Pine Mountain and join his army. We were coming down the mountain and not even thinking of seeing a Yankee, when from the upper side of the road the Federals began shooting at us. From the way horses fell it looked as if they were aiming to kill them instead of us. It was evident in a few moments that the Federals were also in front of us. Captain Dudley ordered the men on horses to dismount and run to the ravine on the lower side of the road, which we did. It was soon evident, however, that we were surrounded by a superior force, and that we would all be killed if we did not surrender; so we began to yell at the top of our voices that we wanted to surrender.

"If the Yanks heard us," he continued, "they paid no attention, but kept on firing. Finally some one of us said the way to surrender was to raise a white flag. We began to wave our handkerchiefs, but they were all dirty, and the Yanks kept shooting. At last, Jephtha Cornelison, the oldest man with us, cried out, 'Has anyone here got a white shirt?' Answers came from many voices that their shirts were gray. Charley Breck, however, said his shirt was once white and might look white.

"Cornelison said, 'come out of it quick, and pass it to me, or we'll all be killed.'

"We were all lying as close to the ground as possible. When Breck got his shirt off, he pitched it to Cornelison, who had prepared a temporary pole for the hoisting. He tied the two arms of the shirt around the pole and as he started it up among the underbrush, he shouted, 'Boys, watch me wave her d—— beautifully.' Although we were mighty scared we all laughed at Cornelison's remark. In a short time the firing ceased and as we were marched down the ravine I found Kie wounded."

The neighbors were so intent on listening to Jim, as they called him, and had laughed so heartily at his story about Cornelison, that they failed to notice that quite a company of men had ridden down the creek road and were within a hundred yards of the house. Everyone became as silent as death. The little

Negroes heard someone say "Home Guards," and they scurried away to the quarters like frightened rabbits.

The captain of the squad left his men and walked up to where we were all seated in the yard. "Gentlemen," he said, "I dislike to disturb you but we have been informed that two Rebels came this way this morning and stopped here, and we have come for them."

For a moment no one spoke. James finally said, "I suppose you refer to brother Kie and myself, as there are no Rebels here except him and me."

"I infer," the officer said, "you two are the ones we want in particular and we may want some or all of these gentlemen who are here counseling and advising you."

A look of extreme trouble ran over the countenances of the assembled neighbors.

The captain continued, addressing the crowd in general, "There must have been some concert of action, some plot, or so many would not have been here so soon after the return of these Rebels, and it appears to me that not only the Rebels but their counselors should be carried before the provost judge. Therefore, I declare you all under arrest."[72]

If ever a merry crowd was turned into consternation in a moment it was certainly that assembly of well-meaning neighbors.

"Gentlemen, get your horses," the captain ordered; "we can get to Richmond before night and the provost may possibly be able to hear some of your excuses for being in what appears to be an unlawful assembly. If he is satisfied that no plot against the army or Government was being made, he may allow a part or all of you to return home."

Distress was shown in every face, but no man moved. Defiance was visible in the countenance of James, but as he looked at the crowd of well-armed men only a few yards away he knew that resistance would be useless.

The captain gave the second order for the neighbors to mount their horses, and then turned to James and said, "Where is Kie? Tell him to come out if he is in the house."

Mary Ann had sat by in silence while the captain was giving orders. She appeared to think someone else would surely speak in defense of the presence of her brothers at their home, but the neighbors sat as if none of them had a tongue. I had been watching her ever since the arrival of the Home Guards. At first I saw the spirit of a tigress manifested in her otherwise beautiful and serene countenance, but it was soon followed by the placid smile of the Madonna. I felt sure she would soon say something and I wondered what it would be. Presently she arose from her seat and walked close to the captain and in the most winning way I ever heard a girl speak, said:

"Captain Adams, I have known you since I was large enough to ride, and I believe you are a good man and a gentleman. I know your zeal for the Union is to be admired, but on this occasion you have acted too hastily in arresting your neighbors. My brothers came home this morning. Kie is there in the room with a ghastly wound in his body. I want you to go in the house and see for yourself, if you doubt my word. The news that he came home wounded was scattered over the neighborhood. You know father is away as well as do these good neighbors. You know that one of the characteristics of the people of Old Cane Springs is to visit the sick. You did it before this war began. I believe if you had been at home this morning and had heard that Kie was here wounded you would have come and offered your services.

"I say to you," she continued earnestly, "and I will swear to it, if necessary, that no two of these men came here together. There would have been no harm in it if they had. They came here alone and each one has offered his services to sit up with my sick brother. Now would you dare have your neighbors whose arrest you have ordered make that kind of a defense before the provost judge? I know you would not. You just did not know the circumstances, or you forgot. Now please set aside that order of arrest and let us tell our neighbors that we are happy to have their kind offers, but at present we will have to decline them, for Colonel Wolford has detailed brother James to bring Kie home and nurse him."

As Mary Ann finished she handed the captain a piece of white paper, showing the parole of both Kie and James and their right to remain within the Federal lines until arrangement for exchange could be made.

"Gentlemen," said the captain, "Well may you smile upon this fair young lady. I believed I would have had the whole bunch of you before the provost within an hour, if she had not spoken. Not one of you appeared to know how to explain your presence here. I certainly do not wish to arrest gentlemen out on works of mercy. There are so many of you here, that it never occurred to me that you met without some prearrangement; but it is plain now that you are all visiting the sick and distressed, as is the custom in Old Cane Springs. Therefore, I beg your pardon. My object is to guard the homes in this community and not to disturb them when nothing is being done around them to endanger the Union."

On ending his speech, the captain bowed most profoundly and retired towards his company. Some of his men demanded to know why no arrests were made, but Captain Adams said he would explain to their satisfaction at the proper time and place.

Not one of the men seated in the Oldham yard had spoken a word since the Home Guards came up, but when they were well out of hearing William Covington was the first to speak. "Well, Mary Ann," be began, "I was certain Mrs. Covington would be grieving for me this night. You're certainly a trump and you know just when to play. I believe if any one of us had tried to put up an excuse for our being here, those fellows would have landed every one of us in the Richmond jail."

"By blood, you are right, Covington," exclaimed Captain Noland. "We were all too badly scared to think of a defense; in fact, I never thought of anything but going to town. I was wondering what excuse I would put up to the provost tomorrow. When Mary Ann got through with that speech of hers, I knew we were all cleared. By blood, Mary Ann, how did you think of all that so quickly? You did not have many words but it was the biggest speech I ever heard."

"But, gentlemen," he continued, "we may yet be watched from some of the surrounding hills, and we had better leave as we came. It will not do for us all to go at once. I am satisfied Kie needs no one at this time to sit up with him. If we are needed later, you will be duly informed, and I live about as far away as any one of you, so I will be the first to break the company and bid you good afternoon."

Others began to leave and in half an hour all the neighbors had started for their homes.

CHAPTER XXII

A NEGRO SAINT PASSES

ONE DAY late in the summer of 1862 I informed Mary Ann that I had heard that Aunt Creech Sally was very low and expected to live only a few days. I thought it would be well for her and me to go to see her on the morrow, for sometimes we had been compelled to make it appear that our repeated visits to the cedars were visits to Aunt Sally. I knew Dr. Ayres would be there the next day at 10 A. M., and I wanted Mary Ann to be there with me with some knickknacks for her while the doctor was present. We both knew he was a strong Union man and his seeing us at Aunt Sally's would confirm reports that we frequented the old servant's home. A few minutes past ten o'clock the next day we were both at her home. Mary Ann came down the creek road and I took the main road from the church. We arrived at the same time.

Mr. Chenault had allowed all of Aunt Sally's children and several other Negroes to be present that day. Minerva and Jennie, two of her daughters, and Horace and James, two of her sons, came to the stile to meet us. Mary Ann opened a most tempting basket of food, which she told them she had brought for their mother, and I showed the basket which Aunt Jose had prepared and sent by me.

"God bless you two deah chillun," they all exclaimed.

We had alighted and walked towards the cabin with them just as the doctor was coming out of the sick room. The two daughters, each with a basket, ran to him and said, "See heah, Doctah, w'at goodies dese two bless'd chillun has brung mudder."

Then Dr. Ayres appeared serious as he looked into the two well-filled baskets. Finally he said, speaking to Minerva and Jennie, "God bless these two children for bringing this tempting and delicious food and God bless the homes from whence it came. These acts of kindness show the esteem in which your mother is held. They are from two homes miles apart and are not the acts of these children, but are the deeds of their elders, who know the worth and sterling qualities of a true and faithful servant. I regret to say she will never taste it—no, she will not even see it."

The two daughters did not appear to catch the full purport of the doctor's remarks, but exclaimed, "Bless Miss Jose and Mary Ann's mudder; sech good women neber furgits enybody dat's sick."

Then Dr. Ayres went back to the sick bed, and in a short time he and Jake came out and reported that Aunt Sally had died as peacefully as though she had dropped to sleep. With a smile on her face she exclaimed "Sam!" and breathed no more.

The grief of her sons and daughters was touching indeed. In a short time, Mr. Chenault came and arrangements were made for the funeral and burial on the following Sunday. Mary Ann and I agreed before we parted that we would meet again at the funeral.

As usual, on the Saturday preceding, I carried the customary sack of provisions to the Rock House. On that trip I learned of increasing difficulty one had in getting through to the South. A Mr. Clay and a number of men had been arrested near the foot of Big Hill by Captain Dillon. One or two of the company had gotten away, however, and had been to the Rock House. They had left word for no others to try to go South, but to wait for Bragg's army, which was surely coming that way. I felt that Mary Ann should know this at once and rode by to inform her. I left as soon as my mission was performed. As I went through Texas on my way home, many persons stopped me and blessed Mary Ann and me for trying to comfort a poor old sick Negro. It was evident Dr. Ayres had done the work we hoped he would do. Even Captain Adams patted me on the shoulder and said I would certainly get my just reward for visiting widows in their afflictions.

Information concerning the funeral and burial became known in all Old Cane Springs and for miles farther away. Jake, the clever and intelligent mulatto boy whom Aunt Sally had reared as her own son, had learned to read well and was recognized as a rather learned minister of the Gospel. Consequently, he was engaged to preach the sermon. By two o'clock there were more Negroes assembled than I had ever seen before. All of those in the immediate neighborhood were present and there were also many from Dr. Moberly's[78] and other families near Richmond. There were also more than one hundred white persons present. It was by far the largest assemblage of people I had ever seen at a funeral. The people sat on the grass on the upper part of the yard, the whites on one side and the Negroes on the other side of a table, which had been placed under a large pear tree.

Jake opened his Bible and read from the sixth chapter of Ephesians. He said he would take as the basis of his remarks, in the main, parts of the 5th and 9th verses of the chapter he had just read. He stated, however, before proceeding with his sermon that he would line a song which he wished the congregation would join him in singing. He had chosen an old familiar hymn, which Aunt Creech Sally had often sung softly as she sat in the twilight with her face toward the little cemetery on the hill. Surely the lines,

> "My Father's house is built on high,
> Far, far above the starry sky;
> When from this earthly prison free,
> That heavenly mansion mine shall be,"

with the refrain, "I am going home to die no more," were never sung more tenderly than on that quiet afternoon.

Jake began his remarks by saying: "My good friends, the composer of that song must have had the same experience that Dr. Ayres and I had when we stood by the bedside of dear Mother Sally and witnessed her passing from time to eternity. We both felt that she realized her Savior was present and ready to comfort and cheer her; and not only was her Savior there, but He also brought with Him those she loved in the flesh. They were certainly there, for she spoke to them. She saw her old master and other loved ones she knew back in old Virginia. Finally with arms lifted she cried 'Sam,' and her spirit flew with him and other loved ones back to God who gave it. It was certainly a happy and victorious going. I mention this to comfort her children and friends. She went with absolute confidence in our Lord and Savior Jesus Christ, and I feel satisfied today that she is enjoying that bliss, unspeakable and eternal in the mansion which the Lord went to prepare for her and all the redeemed of earth."

Jake then stated that it was his custom not to dwell long eulogizing the departed one, when he was called on to preach a funeral. He said that however peaceful and hopeful the parting might be when it became necessary to lay away the mortal remains, he always considered it an opportune time to impress some good scripture lessons, that the living might benefit thereby.

"No one knew better than the Apostle Paul," he continued, "how a person should live to meet the hour that has recently come to Mother Sally. He knew his departure was near at hand. He was willing and ready to go and as it is the common lot of all mankind to come to the hour he was so near approaching, his heart went out to the Christians at Ephesus and he wrote to them, among other good things, this sixth chapter, which is a general admonition, commencing with the children and ending with the heads of households. Paul knew that all well regulated homes had children, parents, servants, and one master over all; and the first verse of my text is his admonition to the servants, and reads: 'Servants be obedient to them that are your masters, according to the flesh.'

"These are trying days on the servants of this community. Men who never had a servant are nightly coming to our quarters, are urging us to violate the sacred scriptures, and are trying to induce us to break up and tear down the homes we have labored so long to build. I see before me all the masters and servants of Old Cane Springs. If there is any place on the footstool of our Creator where more freedom, peace, and happiness reigns than here, I do not know of it. I am certain there is contentment here and no desire for a change to a better lot, and all these nightly visits only disturb our rest."

Then Jake emphasized Aunt Sally's obedience to the scripture he had just read, and expressed the opinion that her faithfulness was responsible for the presence of so many who had come to pay their last tribute of love and respect for her. He concluded this part of his discourse by saying, "Mother Sally was a true and faithful servant; thus her happy life and peaceful end. My colored brethren, let her life be a lesson to you."

Jake continued by directing his words especially to the whites. "My friends, I also deem it right and proper that I should on this occasion make a few remarks in relation to Paul's admonition in the 9th verse which reads: 'And ye masters, do the same things unto them, forbearing threatenings: knowing that your Master also is in heaven; neither is there respect of persons with him.' These are trying days with the masters as well as with the servants. I know that your patience is heavily taxed, and some of you threaten your servants for allowing these designing persons around the quarters. But you must not be forgetful of the scriptures and threaten your servants; we must work harmoniously in these trying days. I know that neither master nor servant in this community wants any change in the present state of affairs. It may be, however, that the Great Ruler of the Universe has a hand in it all and may bring about a change, as some believe will happen; but we all agree, both masters and servants, that all this effort to bring about discontentment and strife among us is the work of the evil one. May the Lord bring his efforts to confusion and naught and may we live in peace until it pleases Him to give us a better dwelling place, eternal in the heavens!

"Next to the children of Mother Sally, I will miss her most. She took me when a child in old Virginia and nursed and cared for me as if I were her own. She never gave me one word of bad advice; she always admonished me to do right. We have served Marse Cabell for forty years together, and I want to say here for him that he has been just as good and faithful a master as Mother Sally was a servant, both filling well the stations assigned them by our Lord. And now may we all, both master and servant, consign to its last resting place our true and loved one's body. Amen."

Then as the whippoorwills were beginning their evening calls and while the shadows were lengthening fast as the sun neared the western horizon, loving hands laid Aunt Creech Sally to rest by the side of Sam in the orchard on the hill. Her spirit had finally answered its mate's call to join him in the Great Beyond.

I was too young to take in the whole purport of Jake's sermon but I could see that it came from his heart, and that all his white hearers were well pleased. "By blood," exclaimed Captain Noland, "I wish some of the Home Guards who are nightly around our homes could have heard that. I'm glad all the Negroes heard it. It'll take Lincoln and his cohorts a long time to make the Negroes of this community believe that he is trying to get a better thing for them than they already have."

CHAPTER XXIII

A FAITHFUL NEGRO OVERSEER

SUMMER was almost gone, and still Bragg had not come. Many had been expecting him in Kentucky ever since early spring. All manner of rumors of his coming were afloat, but spring had come and gone and summer was nearing the end and still he had not arrived. The woods, the Rock House, and many other places were filled with men who were anxious to join the Confederate army, but they could not get to it. Through the grape-vine route we could hear of Bragg's approach, but the Confederates still appeared about as far away as in the early spring.

Late in August, Mary Ann came by one morning and requested me to ride over to her grandfather's with her. I could see she was greatly elated over something. I knew from the way she ran to Aunt Jose that she had good news. Presently we were on the road and I learned that General Bragg was certainly in Kentucky. She also told me that her father had come home the night before and was then supposed to be at the Rock House.

"He came in about midnight," she said, "and aimed to let no one know it but mother and me, but Pike demanded of him who he was and why he did not hollo before he came to the house. When he recognized father, it was like the meeting of two long-separated brothers."

After Mary Ann had attended to certain matters at Colonel Noland's, she said that I should return home with her. I felt anxious to have a talk with Pike to learn how he happened to be up late enough to catch Mr. Oldham as he came in. I had been about the place and with him so often that I felt free to talk with him and believed he would tell me, so I asked him pointedly how he happened to be up at midnight or later.

He looked at me in a quizzical way and said, "How'd you know 'bout Marse Othniel bein' heah? You're guessin', chile. I don't know nothin' 'bout 'im. I hain't seen 'im no mo' since him an' de boys rode 'way dat dark night months ago."

"Now Pike," I replied, "you must not fib to me. I have heard all about his coming and his effort to get in without anyone's knowing it except Mrs. Oldham and Mary Ann, and I also know about your catching him at the door before he got in. I am aware that you work and are on the go all the time during the day, and I want to know if you sit up and guard the house all night."

"No, chile," he answered, "I don't set up all night ebery night, but I did las' night, an' I'll allus be glad dat I did. W'en Marse Othniel an' James an' Kie make up der minds to leabe home, Marse Oth, he tuck me ovah yander in dat bunch ov cedars on de hill an' had me set down by 'im. Den he said, 'Pike, I've got to go 'way. I hates to do it, but de Home Guards ar' 'roun' de qua'ters, ez you know, nearly ebery night, an' dey insult me an' my sons ebery time dey meet us 'way frum home. Dey ar' 'restin' ebery one dat talks back to 'em, an' dey ar' shootin' an' 'restin' men in ebery part ov de county. I know dat dey ar' tryin' to cause niggers eber'whar to leabe der marsters. I feel jis like I wuz gwine to prison er death to stay, an' it's terrible to t'ink ov goin'. I brought you heah to ax you a question an' git frum you a promise. Ef we go, yo' missus an' de chillun'll haf no white man to look atter 'em, so I must leabe 'em in yo' care. Will you promise me dat you'll stay at home an' look atter 'em? My father, yo' ole marster, he give you to me w'en we wuz bofe chillun. We've grow'd up togedder. You've bin faithful to me an' allus tole me de truf, an' ef you promise to carry on while I'm gone I'll leabe, knowin' dat dey'll be safe in yo' keepin', jis ez ef I wuz at home. Do you promise?'"

Then Pike went on to say that he promised his master that he would do as he wished, and that Mr. Oldham and his sons soon rode away. He took charge of everything just as he would have done had his master been there.

"I've tried to pertect ebert'ing," Pike related. "Night 'fo' las' dar wuz a big rain an' a heap ov win'. I wuz 'fraid de fence might be blowed down 'tween us an' Dr. Moberly's an' let his big cattle in our corn, so ez soon ez I gits breadfas' I goes ovah dar to zamine de fence. At de head ov de holler whar de groun' is too rough to plow is a big thicket. I wuz zaminin' de fence close to dis thicket w'en I hears a noise like stock trompin', an' I sez to myse'f, 'dar's cattle in dar, sho', an' I'll git 'em out.' So I creeps into dat thicket an' w'at do you t'ink? Dar stood Marse Oth's bay mare dat he rode 'way mont's an' mont's b'fo', an' 'is bridle an' saddle!

"I 'most screamed fur joy," Pike went on to say, "but hit struck me dat dat wouldn't do, fur it wuz plain he wuz aimin' to hide de hoss. I hollered low-like, but no answer. De mare wuz wa'm, showin' she hadn't bin hitched dar long. I know'd he must be close. Den I runs to sev'ral places an' calls 'is name, but no answer. Den I went to annuder field an' to de woods, but nowhar could I find 'im. At dinnah I went home an' thought I'd tell Missus Oldham, but finally 'cided I wouldn't, but 'ud look fur 'im agin atter dinnah. I went back to de mare an' foun' dat someone had bin to 'er atter I left, an' had cut corn an' carried it to 'er, so I looked an' looked agin, fur I wuz 'termined I'd be de fust un to see 'im."

Pike stated that after searching in vain all afternoon, he decided that Mr. Oldham would make his appearance after dark. He was right, and in due time he saw him approaching the house very cautiously. "I saw 'is head duckin' dis way an' dat way, like a wild turkey," he continued, "An' den he'd take a few light steps an' duck agin. I wuz so glad to see 'im I wuz 'bout to speak to 'im 'fo' he got to de do'. Den I sez to myse'f, 'I'll show 'im I's guardin' Missus an' de chillun jis ez I promised,' an' den's w'en I halted 'im. At dat he throwed 'is arms 'round me an' said, 'I know'd I could trust you, Pike.'

"Dat suttinly sounded good to me," Pike exclaimed joyfully; but his countenance changed suddenly and he said. "I'm mighty 'fraid dat sumpin' gwine to happen heah tonight. W'en Marse Oldham come into de house he tole me dat he'd be up 'bout fo' in de mo'nin' an' he wanted me to meet 'im at de barn. So I goes on back to de qua'ters an' 'zactly on de hour we met at de barn. He said he wanted some ole corn fur de mare, an' I got 'im a good armful an' we walked off togedder.

"Finally Ole Marse, he say, 'Pike, you'd better go back to de house an' be 'roun' ez usual w'en de folks begin to stir. Atter while you can come to me. I'll move de mare into dat clump ov timber on de hill 'bove de creek dar, an' you'll fin' me close 'roun' w'en you come. My wife 'll prepare me sumpin to eat an' you can bring it to me.'"

Then Pike related how he put everybody to work as usual and then made some excuse to look over the plantation. He soon found his master, with whom he remained until noon. In the afternoon he saw that everyone went to work, and, pretending that the fence near Dr. Moberly's still needed mending, he was soon with Mr. Oldham again.

"We got a little mo' bold atter dinnah," he continued, "an' Marse Oldham come out ov de woods agin. He wanted to see de corn in de big bottom. We looked at it an' wuz talkin' away w'en suddenly we seen one ov dem Home Guards lookin' right square at us."

"Marse Oldham made out like he didn't see 'im an' said low-like, 'Pike, you stand heah 'til I come back.'

"I pretended not to see de Home Guard, but I kep' an eye on 'im all de time. Marse Oldham soon rode up whar I wuz an' spoke loud 'nough fur dat feller to heah: 'Pike, I must go now; continue to look atter things jis ez you've bin doin'. I hope to be back some day.'

"Jis 'fo' startin' he say low-like, 'You git back in de bushes an' watch dat feller. I may see you agin tonight.' Den he rode off lookin' brave an' ebery inch a solger, an' soon he wuz out ov sight in de big woods.

"I crept in some bushes on de hill 'bove de creek," Pike concluded. "By de time I got to a place whar I could peep out I seen de Home Guard git on 'is hoss an' go in a run towards Boxankle.[74] I know dar's a company ov guards up dar, an' I knows dey'll be in de big woods by dark er a little later an' how I wish I could tell Ole Marse. I walked all 'roun' up dar, but I couldn't see er heah nothin' ov 'im. I'm mighty 'fraid dey'll catch 'im tonight. I do wish I knowed how to tell 'im to stay 'way frum here tonight."

Pike was not alone in his anxiety over Mr. Oldham's fate. I felt that Mary Ann should be told of the facts I had just learned, so I left Pike and joined her at once. I told her all I had learned and Pike's great anxiety to have her father informed.

"You must go to the Rock House at once," she said hurriedly, "and tell him all. There is an unbroken forest between our big woods and the cedars and father must be there now, but it is late and as soon as it is dark he may ride off. So you must go and lose no time before he gets away."

I mounted Whizaker at once and started down the creek in a gallop. I hitched the mule securely at the foot of the hill and began to climb cautiously through the cedars toward the Rock House and at the proper distance began to whistle as usual. I recognized the short laugh of Nath Deatherage and heard him say, "It's Hart. Wonder why he is coming?"

I was greatly surprised when I went into the house. There were many more men present than I had even seen there before. They were preparing to eat supper and I was astonished at the great quantity of provisions. I thought I had been furnishing all the food, but evidently I had not brought in my weekly trips one-tenth of what was on hand.

My surprise at the number of men and the large supply of provisions did not detain me long. I inquired of Nath if Mr. Oldham was there, and was told that he was; but said he, "He is taking a snooze and I hate to wake him unless it is very important."

"I have been sent here by Mary Ann to tell him certain things at once."

"What are they?" he inquired. "I am as willing to serve her as I am to serve her father; maybe I can attend to it."

"I obey orders," I replied. "I was sent here to tell him certain things that Mary Ann said he must know at once."

Nath hurried away and soon returned with Mr. Oldham.

"Mr. Oldham," I began, "I have just come from your home. I am here by your daughter's command. I had a talk with Pike this afternoon and when I told Mary Ann certain things that he had related to me, she said that you must know them as soon as I could find you."

"Nath, you must hear this," Mr. Oldham said, and ordered me to go ahead.

I told him as near as I could in Pike's words the conduct of the Home Guard they had seen on the creek earlier in the day, what Pike thought we should do that night, and how anxious he was for him to know it so he would not come around home. After I had finished Mr. Oldham was silent for some time.

Finally he spoke, "Nath, you, Gustin, and I must go to my home as soon as possible."

"Mr. Oldham," I remonstrated, "I am riding Whizaker and if we should pass in a hundred yards of anybody around here, it would be a give-away; that spotted mule is known by everybody."

"There is no telling what those fellows may do," he said. "There are good men among the Home Guards, but many of them are murderers, thieves, and robbers, and some of them are likely to commit a worse crime than the three mentioned. We must be off at once. Don't be bothered about the mule. You will not be on the road after we arrive at General Jackson's and we shall hitch long before we get to my home. You go on and if you arrive at Mr. Jackson's before we do, wait till we come. If we get there first, we shall wait for you."

We arrived at General Jackson's almost at the same time,[75] and, without exchanging words, Mr. Oldham turned to the right into the forest. We traveled single file through the undergrowth and over precipitous hills and across deep and dark ravines. The night had become very dark, and I could see neither one of them and was able to follow only by the noise of their horses' feet.

Finally after climbing a considerable hill, Mr. Oldham spoke rather low, as if he only intended for Nath to hear. "We will go out here to the end of the devil's backbone and hitch and walk across through the big bottom and get in the orchard near the house."

Soon we were trudging through the corn and were about to get into the orchard when we heard the keen tenor voice of Pike say, "I tells you all, he's not in de house. Dar's nobody in dar but de Missus an' de chillun an' Marse Kie, an' you all knows de Yankees has done shot 'im."

Nath slipped a large pistol into my hands and whispered, "You may have to use it, and if you do, take good aim and shoot low."

We concluded to crawl through the orchard and get nearer the house, which we did as speedily as possible. We heard the voice of Pike cry out: "Don't break down dat do'. I tells you all he's not in dar, but ef you all'll let me wake de Missus an' git a light so you won't scare de little chillun, you all can search de house."

It was evident that there were several of the Guards who did not believe that Mr. Oldham was in the house. We overheard one say, "He's not in the house and it's useless to disturb the women and children, but the d—— nigger knows where he is. We'll make him tell, so we can go and get him, or we'll lie here for him until he comes in."

This suggestion must not have been agreed to for we heard again the voice of Pike: "Ef you all go in dis house befo' I wake up de Missus an' git a light, you'll go ovah my dead body."

We heard another voice say, "I don't believe he is in the house. The d—— nigger knows where he is. Let's make him tell or hang him."

"Take him down to the big cherry tree and make him tell, or hang him," came from several voices.

We were lying in weeds and underbrush about fifty feet from the big cherry. Mr. Oldham whispered, "They won't hang him. It's a big bluff. Pike can't tell, for he has no idea where I am."

Presently a number of men came leading the Negro to the tree. The Guard who had been seen on the creek spoke: "Now, Pike, you know where Mr. Oldham is or when he will be back and you ought to tell us. We are all working for you Negroes, and instead of your helping us, you help the people who will keep you in slavery. Now tell us where he is, or when he will be back."

"I've not seen 'im or had a word wid 'im since yo' all saw him today," Pike answered. "I don't know whar he is, er w'en he'll be back."

Someone said, "Hang the d—— nigger. That's the way to make him talk."

Then a chorus of voices cried, "Hang him!"

As we lay low on the ground we could see them putting one end of a rope around Pike's neck and throwing the other end over a projecting limb. At the same time we heard someone say, "The nigger don't know and that won't do any good."

Pike was pulled up, but in an instant he was let down and commanded to tell where Mr. Oldham was. He as firmly as at first denied any knowledge of his whereabouts.

"Hang him sure enough. Make an example of him," cried several voices; and he was again pulled up. He began to kick frantically and we three with pistols ready were just about to shoot, for we had resolved to die if necessary in an attempt to save him, when he was lowered again.

Pike fell limp to the ground and was unable to rise. I believe Mr. Oldham and Nath would have rushed forward in another second and sold their lives as dearly as possible had the captain not said, "Boys, you came near holding him up too long that time, but he is all right now and you must not torture him any more."

They released Pike as soon as he could stand up and told him to go to the quarters. We saw him limp off to the big house and sit down on the porch.

Presently we heard the captain's voice again: "Boys, I knew you were too anxious to make an arrest tonight. We should have slipped in here without telling anyone or letting anyone know. We shall now quietly disperse and return tomorrow night and the next and next, if need be, until we get him. He is lying out somewhere around here and will be slipping in again."

After they had dispersed, we went back to the Rock House. There I learned from Mr. Oldham that General Kirby Smith was then on the Big Hill and a fight was expected the next day. I secreted Whizaker in the cedars and spent my first night, or rather part of a night, on the straw in the Rock House.

Chapter XXIV

THE BATTLE OF RICHMOND

EARLY the next morning, we were awakened by the boom of cannon in the direction of Big Hill.[76] Excitement was soon at high pitch. To go at once and help kill and clean out the invading Yankees was the general acclaim. Mr. Oldham, who had actually seen some fighting, said such a move at this time would only be to go to certain death or capture.

"There is nothing to do but listen and wait," he advised. "If the Confederates whip or push back the Yankees, you will have no trouble in joining their forces. I feel confident that early in the afternoon we can go into Richmond in a body, if we so desire; we must by no means even try to do so now."

His advice was heeded, and no further mention of going was made. The cannonading grew more frequent and it was evident the battle was on in earnest. Hardly a word was spoken. It was, "Listen, Listen." Soon the musketry was plainly heard. Hours passed without any cessation, so far as I could tell, in either the noise of cannon or small arms. I noticed Mr. Oldham ascend a small eminence near the entrance to the Rock House and beckon in every direction to the men scattered about. They quickly assembled around him.

"Gentlemen," he said, "we will soon be leaving here. I must give you a few words of counsel before we go. We want this place to remain unknown, except to those who come here by direction, as you have come. That direction must be from the same parties that directed you. No one knows what the fortunes of war may be. For some time now this place will not be needed, but later it may be; therefore, nothing must be done that will particularly attract anyone to this place. You must slip away from here as you came. However, we must have a meeting place. That will be in Kavanaugh's woods on the Irvine pike. Those who do not know how to get to that point, learn from someone here before you start. It is not near time to go yet, but you can begin to get ready. I know that the Union forces have fallen back at least five miles from where the battle opened early this morning, and by four o'clock or a little sooner we can be with one wing of the Confederates close to the place I have designated."

He then spoke directly to me: "Gustin, will you go to my house and tell them that I'll be there for dinner?"

I scurried away and was soon at the Oldham residence. On my way I saw several Home Guards. They paid no attention to me and appeared to be troubled, but they were all going towards Richmond. At the Oldham home, I found almost the same people that were present when Kie and James came home.

A look of anxiety was on every face. The rattle of small arms and the roar of cannon could be plainly heard, but no one appeared to know how the battle was going. I announced to Mrs. Oldham that Mr. Oldham had sent me to tell her that he would be there soon and would eat dinner with her. There was handclapping by the children, but in a few minutes all faces were again turned in the direction of the roar and noise of the battle. About eleven o'clock Mr. Oldham and Nath Deatherage came riding up as boldly as if there were no war.

"Look yonder," said William Covington; "they know how the battle is going. The Rebels are certainly whipping the Yankees and they know it or they wouldn't be riding that way"; and then he threw his hat high in the air and shouted, "Hurrah for Kirby Smith! Hurrah for the Confederacy!"

At the mention of the approach of the two riders all faces were turned toward them. They alighted and walked up to the crowd. At one side stood Pike. Mr. Oldham went to him first and shook both of his hands heartily. Next Mrs. Oldham was in his arms and the smaller children were clinging to him in every way.

It was several minutes before the visitors, who were eager for news of the battle, could get in one word or handshake. Mr. Oldham soon assured them that the Yankees were being defeated and were falling back and had been since an hour after the battle began. He said further that the Confederate army would be in Richmond long before night.

Again William Covington pitched his hat high in the air and yelled, "Hurrah for Jeff Davis and the Confederacy!" Nearly everyone joined in the demonstration. Just then I felt my sleeve touched and looking around I saw Pike, his face shining and a look of delight on every feature. He spoke rather low: "Marse

Gustin, did you see I wuz de fust un Ole Marse shook han's wid?"[77]

There was much general rejoicing at the return of Mr. Oldham. Nothing was done that day except what was necessary. The Negroes, as well as the whites, turned the day into a general holiday and the Negroes were as happy as the whites. It was evident that the Union army was falling back, and as soon as dinner was over, Mr. Oldham and Nath started toward Richmond.

Just as they were leaving the front yard two Home Guards whom I recalled having seen the night before, came riding by from the direction of Richmond. I expected a clash. I thought possibly they would try to arrest Mr. Oldham and Nath, but to my surprise they spoke as cheerily as if they had not been on a hunt for them the night before. We heard in response to an inquiry, that the Union forces were not faring well and were retreating rapidly. By morning it was generally known that Kirby Smith with about sixteen thousand men had defeated General Nelson with a smaller force and had captured almost his entire army. The Southern sympathizers, who had either been hiding out or had kept their mouths sealed for more than a year, now spoke their sentiments boldly. The impression was that if the Union army could not prevent the coming of the Confederates, it would never be able to make them leave.

Everybody desired to go to the battlefield. I went with Mary Ann, whom I had not seen so happy for a year. In a short time after our arrival we met Mr. Oldham and Nath, and I saw I was no longer needed as company or escort. After Nath came up, I dropped behind with Mr. Oldham and watched him and Mary Ann as they rode over the ground where the battle had raged. I had never seen so handsome a couple. Both rode Kentucky thoroughbred saddle horses, and wherever the two went they attracted attention. If they passed close to Southern soldiers there were cheers, and if near captured Yankees, there were salutes.

The battle had been rather sanguinary.[78] The dead numbered about three hundred and twenty-five and the wounded more than one thousand. The Madison Female Institute, the Court House in Richmond, and Mount Zion Church on the Big Hill pike were converted into hospitals, and homes everywhere offered

The Thomas Palmer House, partly destroyed during the Battle of Richmond. Where Gen. John Miller died, September 5, 1862.

Mount Zion Church, built 1852. The south wall was struck by a cannon ball during the Battle of Richmond, August 30, 1862. The Palmer House, mentioned above, stands only a short distance from the rear of the church. See county map.

The Madison County Courthouse, built in 1849, as it looks today. Part of it was used as a hospital for a time after the Battle of Richmond, August 30, 1862.

Madison Female Institute, used as a hospital for a time after the Battle of Richmond in 1862.

to receive the wounded.[79] Limbs were being amputated and the dead buried in sundry places. By early in the afternoon mule and ox teams were coming in on every road with wagon and cart beds well filled with straw and quilts. Most everyone wanted wounded of both armies, and the Blue and the Gray were soon being moved in every direction to their temporary abodes.[80] Every home for miles along the Big Hill pike and its tributary roads rendered aid to the wounded and dying. General John Miller (born on Muddy Creek in Old Cane Springs), of Richmond, who had fallen while trying to rally a disordered column of Union soldiers near Mount Zion Church, was taken to the farm home of Thomas Palmer, where he died six days later.[81]

When Pike had five wounded men comfortably arranged in his wagon and other farmers' wagons were filled with as many or more, we all started for Old Cane Springs. On our return not a Home Guard was to be seen. Willis Hisle declared that they had all fled to the mountains of Estill County.

The main army of General Smith had pressed on to Lexington and had easily captured that town. A general recruiting station was established at Richmond and all who desired were enrolled for the Confederate service. Nath Deatherage could easily have become captain of a company, but on account of his youth he preferred to be a private and joined Captain Joseph Chenault's company in Colonel David Waller Chenault's Eleventh Kentucky Cavalry, C. S. A. This regiment was soon attached to General John Hunt Morgan's brigade.[82]

The Confederates were for more than two months in full and complete control of the county and retaliation was expected. For more than a year the Home Guards had been arresting everyone they could find who sympathized with the South, and causing those whom they were unable to catch to hide out. Now they themselves were on the run, but they soon learned that it was not pleasant to spend their days lying around in unfrequented places. Some of the neighbors who had received kindnesses at the hands of Captain Adams, sought him out and assured him protection. Strange to say no arrests of Home Guards were made during the occupancy of the county by the Confederates.

Those in sympathy with the South realized, after the battle of Perryville, on October 8, that General Bragg and his army would have to leave Kentucky and consequently they feared the recurrence of annoyances from the Home Guards; but there was a pleasant surprise in store for those who before had been terrorized. Soon the Union army was back in Richmond in greater numbers than ever, but kindness had discouraged further activities of the Home Guards. They ceased for a time to come around the Negro quarters or do anything to estrange master and servant. Peace and good will seemed to have returned to Old Cane Springs. Services at the church were renewed and largely attended with apparent good fellowship.

Chapter XXV

TWO OLDHAMS CONDEMNED AS SPIES

PRESIDENT LINCOLN'S proclamation in January, 1863, freeing the slaves in the states and smaller areas then in rebellion did not, of course, apply to Kentucky, and, although there were many Union soldiers in Madison County, the Negroes of Old Cane Springs remained for a time unaffected by the apparent tendency toward universal emancipation. The grape-vine route had again been regularly established and Joe Jackson carried mail going South to Fluty's every other night, as did Henry Barnes to Cunningham's; and many an escaped Confederate prisoner was guided over that route to the South and many a Southern spy was conducted through the Union lines by this means.

There appeared to be nothing to move the peace and tranquility of Old Cane Springs except the news from the South now and then of the death of some one of the boys who had gone out with the Confederate army. One day sadness came to every home in the community, when news was received of the death of young Cabell Chenault at Monticello, Kentucky.[83] A little later the community was startled by information that Othniel Oldham[84] and his cousin, Thomas Oldham, had been captured and tried as spies by a court-martial. Both had been found guilty and sentenced to be hanged. The letter came from Miss Juan Phillips, of Monticello, Kentucky. Miss Phillips informed Mrs. Oldham that she had interested her father in their behalf and hoped that execution would be stayed until the conviction could be set aside. She assured Mrs. Oldham that they were not spies and that every effort must be made quickly to save their lives.[85]

On the day this information was received Mary Ann came for me to go with her and her mother to Richmond. I accompanied her home, and by dawn of the day following Pike had a span of mules to the carriage and Mrs. Oldham, Mary Ann, Susan, and myself, with Pike as driver, were on the road to Richmond. We were halted several times by Union pickets, who, after learning who we were, permitted us to pass. On arriving in Richmond, we drove directly to the home of Major Curtis F. Burnam.[86] Major Burnam and his partner, Colonel J. W. Caperton,[87] were a firm of prominent attorneys, who were known as staunch Union men, and Mrs. Oldham had been advised by her brother, Captain Nathan Noland, to engage them to save the lives of her husband and his cousin.

Major Burnam knew Mrs. Oldham and her daughters quite well and received them very graciously. He asked the cause of their early ride, and in a very few minutes Mrs. Oldham explained her business.

"Madam," he said, after he had heard her request, "many are the times I have received the hospitality of your father, Colonel John Noland, and your brother, Captain Nathan Noland, and nothing would please me more than to be able to do a deed of kindness for the daughter and sister of those two men. I gather from Miss Phillips' letter that the court-martial was by order of General Burbridge now stationed at Danville.[88] I will telegraph him at once to stay the execution if the judgment has not been carried out, and I will go to Danville today to intercede for your husband and cousin, if they are yet alive. You and your daughters and this young man may wait in the parlor while I have your man drive me to the telegraph office. On my return I will let you know whether or not the sentence has been executed. If it has not been executed, I think I can help you. Mrs. Burnam doesn't get up as early as I do and she is not astir yet. You just walk in and make yourselves at home, and if Mrs. Burnam happens to come in you can explain the cause of my absence and your presence."

He then ordered Pike to take him down town as speedily as possible.

The talk with Major Burnam had depressed us all very much. It had never occurred to us that possibly the sentence had been executed. Mrs. Oldham and her two daughters began weeping as soon as he left us and nothing I could say appeared to console them.

Major Burnam was gone for an hour or longer. In the meantime Mrs. Burnam was up and astir about the house. We made sufficient noise to apprise her of our presence. She knew Mrs. Oldham very well, having met her at the Old Cane Spring Church. Of course, she received us very graciously and on learning of our mission, manifested sincere sympathy. Mrs. Burnam was a very attractive and intelligent woman, who possessed the charming attributes of feminine culture and refinement. She used all the art of optimism to encourage Mrs. Oldham to hope for her husband's good fortune, and by the time Major Burnam returned, her visitor's spirit was much revived.

I felt sure when I saw Major Burnam hand Mrs. Oldham a telegram that the sentence had not been executed. Mrs. Oldham read all or a part of the telegram, and, letting it drop to the floor, swooned and started to fall.

"I am mistaken," I thought, as I sprang forward to catch her. She recovered almost instantly, as Mrs. Burnam picked up the telegram and read aloud: "C. F. Burnam, Richmond, Kentucky. The two Oldham spies were to have been hung at high noon today. Sentence at your request stayed for five days, in which time you may file petition for rehearing. Burbridge, General Cumberland Division."

Words are inadequate to express the joy exhibited by mother and daughters when they took in the full meaning of the telegram. Major Burnam assured them that the sentence would probably not be carried out for a month or longer, even if he was unable to have it set aside. He promised to drive to Danville that day and

From a steel engraving used by Cassius M. Clay in his *Memoirs, Writings, and Speeches*, 1886.

The Cassius M. Clay Battalion. Citizens Defending the White House in April, 1861. Lincoln and his Cabinet are in the center. Mrs. Lincoln is in third second-story window at the left. (See pages 62, 180.)

file his petition for a rehearing and also obtain what evidence he could to prove to the court-martial that the men were not spies. Mrs. Oldham was to return on the second day following when he would inform her of the chances of having the court set aside its order of conviction. At the appointed time, we all returned to Richmond and arranged also for Captain Noland to be present for the purpose of arranging the fee.

Major Burnam showed at the start that he was somewhat worried about the two cases. He explained that General Burbridge had entered an order declaring that persons enlisted in the Confederate army who, dressed in civilian clothes, were captured in parts of Kentucky in possession of the Union forces, were to be treated as spies and punished according to the usages of war.

"Now, Mrs. Oldham," he said, "your husband and cousin both admit that they were dressed in civilian garb. General Burbridge says that his order is necessary to protect his men and to conceal the movements of his army. He stated further that he felt satisfied that the real object of these two men was to slip into their homes and slip out again and rejoin their comrades. He believes they did not really come as spies, but as a matter of fact, had they by chance learned anything that would have been of service to the Confederacy, they would have revealed it on their return.

"The order, therefore," he continued, "was drawn broad enough to prevent any Rebel soldiers from coming into our lines in civilian garb. Whether the intention was to spy into the position or arrangement of the Union army was not the question. The question for investigation was: 'Are these men regularly enlisted in the Confederate army? Were they caught within the Union lines, and at the time of their capture were they dressed in civilian garb?' They admit they are regularly enlisted men and that they were between Somerset and Stanford when arrested. Their dress spoke for itself.

"The court was bound to convict, Mrs. Oldham, and I see no chance to get around the conviction, unless it be to show clearly that they lied when they admitted they were regularly enlisted in the Confederate service. I told the General that I doubted very much if they were regularly enlisted men but that I had been informed that your husband had charge of General Morgan's wagon train. At any rate, I was permitted to file a petition for rehearing and have had the hearing postponed for twenty days. That will give us time to do something that I hope will save their lives.

"I am unable to understand why," he continued, "but both of them refuse to take the oath of allegiance to the United States and declare they will hang before they will do so. Why they will not take the oath is a puzzle to me. They both have families that need them at home. I can easily procure a pardon from President Lincoln if they will take the oath, but I have grave doubts of securing it unless they do.

"Now, Mrs. Oldham, you see the dilemma I am in. The only chance I have before the court is to prove that they are not regularly enlisted men in the Confederate army. They claim they are. They must now prove that the assertion was a mistake. I suppose you both believe they are just what they claim to be, namely, Rebel soldiers. I conclude, therefore, that no time is to be lost in trying to hunt up testimony to prove the contrary, but that we must try to induce them to take the oath. If they refuse, we must try to obtain their pardons without the oath."

"Did Othniel positively tell you that he would not take the oath?" inquired Captain Noland.

"Yes," Major Burnam replied, "he said that he had sworn allegiance to the Confederacy and that he had regularly enlisted in Captain Thomas Collins' company of D. Waller Chenault's regiment. He also stated that he knew nothing of Burbridge's order under which they had been convicted, or they would never have taken the risk. The order had never been published in the Confederate lines and he thought it cruel and ironical to take a man's life for violation of an order never published where either Thomas or he could have known of it.

" 'We were both anxious to see our families,' Mr. Oldham told me. 'It was mid-winter and there was no fighting, so we both thought we would run the risk of capture for the pleasure of seeing our families. As for our clothing, we wore the only ones we had, since no regulation uniforms had ever been furnished us. We had been furloughed by our commander and thought if we were captured we would simply be prisoners of war. I say to you frankly, Major Burnam, as much as I would like to live and be at home with my family, I will die before I will forswear the oath I have taken to the Confederacy. I hope to see the boys I enlisted with come home some day. I want them to greet me as a man. I don't want them to shun me as a deserter. It is just as honorable to die sometimes in the hands of the enemy as to fall facing him in deadly conflict. If you can save my life without sacrifice of honor, I shall certainly be happy, but if not, let me pay the penalty of my mistake. My execution will doubtless acquaint the Southern army of Burbridge's order and may save the lives of many others.'"

"By blood," said Captain Noland, "I imagined he would talk just that way. It's useless to lose any time on him along that line, but is there no other way?"

"One only," Major Burnam answered. "That is to go to Washington and lay their cases plainly before President Lincoln. He is resourceful and may suggest some way out."

"Well, Major Burnam," Captain Noland explained, "I came with my sister to arrange for your fee. She is unable to secure it, and her husband is not here to make the promise. I want you to go to Washington at once and get the pardons, if possible."

"Don't bother about the fee, Captain," Mr. Burnam said, assuringly. "I will look to Othniel and Thomas[89] for fees if I am able to save their lives. If not, I will charge only my expenses, and the two Mrs. Oldhams will see to that."

CHAPTER XXVI

PRESIDENT LINCOLN'S CLEMENCY

MAJOR BURNAM promised to start on the morrow for Washington, and we were to return to his office in eight days to learn whether the President had granted the pardons. We were soon on our way home, feeling proud of Mr. Oldham's refusal to take the oath.

The excitement created in Old Cane Springs over the arrest and conviction of Mr. Oldham and his cousin as spies was intense. The information was hardly known until our return from Richmond. Nothing was talked of but this for several days after our return. Many thought the men ought to be glad of the opportunity to take the oath to save their lives, while others believed it a glorious thing to die for a principle.

During this exciting time, news came that Captain Robert Covington had died at Monticello.[90] He was well known in Old Cane Springs, as was also his attractive young wife, who was a Miss Thorpe before her marriage. For a while this sad news diverted the conversation from Mr. Oldham and his cousin, but in a short time they were the subject of conversation again. It became generally known that Major Burnam had gone to Washington for the purpose of securing pardons, and speculation was rife as to whether or not he could secure them. The general opinion was that no pardons would be granted unless the men would take the oath of allegiance, and it was generally believed both would accept death before they would renounce their allegiance to the Confederacy.

On one occasion I found Mary Ann very despondent over her father's condition. I expressed surprise at finding her so discouraged. She had usually been light-hearted and happy. Even in our night rides to the Rock House she was cheerful and would make a joke of it, appearing to be a stranger to fear. But it was becoming evident that anxiety over her father's misfortune was affecting her.

"How could I be otherwise?" she asked. "I know father—I know he will never take Lincoln's oath, and then he will die. You cannot imagine how I hate to give him up. It makes the world look dark and meaningless. Everything has always been so bright and promising to me. Father taught me to ride horseback almost as soon as I could walk. I rode with him over the plantation. I have ridden horseback with him in driving mules to the market in South Carolina. We have been companions as well as father and child. To think it will never occur again appears almost unbearable."

"Perhaps he should take the oath," I suggested.

"Well, that would be one way out of the difficulty," Mary Ann replied, "and sometimes I feel like going to him in prison and imploring him to forswear his allegiance to the Confederacy and live for the sake of his loved ones—live for mother, myself, and his other children. Then I think how selfish that would be. I wonder what the proud boys who rode to war with him would think of him if he were to take the oath. I wonder if they would not say he was weak and a coward who went back on the Confederacy before he ever fired a gun at the enemy. And then I conclude the people who remained true to their convictions would think of his children as being like their father, weak and wavering when under trial."

"Let's look on the bright side of it all, Mary Ann," I said reassuringly. "You seem to forget that we expect Major Burnam to secure pardons. President Lincoln, you know, is believed by some people to be very considerate when difficult cases of human conduct are submitted to him."[91]

"Oh, all these horrible thoughts are enough to distract anyone," she continued, without appearing to have heard me. "I know father, I know he will never bring disgrace on himself or his children. He will die if not pardoned without the oath, and I hardly see how he and Cousin Thomas can be pardoned if they refuse to take the oath. It certainly looks gloomy to me, but I am proud he has taken the stand he has. I would much rather remember him as I know him now, than to have him at home, dishonored, and have to apologize for him with my head bowed."

Nothing I said appeared to revive Mary Ann's hope for her father, and as we parted near her home she looked more disconsolate than I had ever seen her before. Naturally I felt rather unhappy too, and I wondered if a certain gallant trooper among Morgan's men could not have succeeded in dispelling the gloom which had settled over the heroine of Old Cane Springs.[92]

The seventh day was almost gone, and I was at the Oldham home to accompany Mrs. Oldham and her two older daughters to the office of Major Burnam on the morrow. I felt almost like one of the family, since everyone received me so cordially. Little Nettie, certainly the prettiest child I had ever seen, crawled over me just as she did over her brothers, Charles and Thomas; and strange to say, I found myself actually in love with her, dreaming of her, and in my wakeful hours, actually wanting to see her grown up, believing that she would then love me as I loved her. With her, even as a child, I was happy, contented, satisfied, dreaded to leave her and longed to return to where she was. Just to look at her and be with her made me very happy. Then I would wonder why I had this fancy for one so young and I would conclude that all of the family were most charming to me, and since they were so foolish over the baby girl, I had simply gotten the family admiration for the child and did not love her as I sometimes thought.

At any rate, while the entire family appeared to be depressed, except the two little girls who were too young to take in the situation, I could not help but be optimistic and as happy as if about to go on a picnic. We were not so anxious to start as on the first trip, but shortly after breakfast Pike was at the front door with the carriage and two large sorrel mules, and we were on our way to Richmond.

We found Captain Noland waiting for us when we arrived at Major Burnam's office. He had ridden a nearer way on horseback. In a short time Major Burnam, accompanied by Mrs. Burnam, drove up to his office. Mrs. Burnam preceded the Major and most cordially greeted Mrs. Oldham and her two daughters and then Captain Noland. Turning to me she said, "I suppose this is your son. He was with you on your visit last week, but was not introduced."

By this time the Major was in the office extending a hearty handshake to everyone, and as he reached Mrs. Oldham, she, speaking to Mrs. Burnam, said, "No, not my son. He is Master Gustin Hart, a nephew of Mrs. Robert Chenault. He appears to be fond of my sons and has been about our home often and we take him with us frequently."

"Why, sir," said Major Burnam, "you are a son of my friend, Professor Thomas Hart, a most estimable gentleman. I am glad to know his son. But I imagine he would not be pleased if he knew you were riding around with the wife and daughters of a Rebel."

He made this remark with a twinkle in his eye towards Captain Noland.

"Pardon me, Major Burnam, what success did you have at Washington?" Mrs. Oldham asked anxiously.

"Well, Mrs. Oldham, I will say at once I had more success than I dared hope I would have. I found the President to be a man with a big heart and very sympathetic. Instead of being displeased when I told him that your husband would not take the oath of allegiance to the United States but would rather die, he said, 'He must be made of the proper stuff. I consider a man who, in order to live, will do an act that tends to lower his manhood, is not much of a man. I feel more like pardoning these men for not taking the oath than I would if you were here begging for two cringing cowards who were willing to surrender all principle and right, simply that they might live. I will pardon them,' he said promptly, 'from the death sentence, but they will still be prisoners of war, and they may have to go to prison until exchanged.' The pardons were then ordered and I have them both here in my pocket."

This explanation caused Mrs. Oldham to utter a sigh of relief.

"While the secretary was making out the pardons," Major Burnam continued, "I explained to the President that both of the gentlemen were near fifty years of age, and that I feared prison life would be very hard on them as they were both active farmers. The President, to my surprise, said, 'I will recommend that they be paroled if you think they will observe it.' I assured him that not one jot or tittle of their parole would be broken and I doubted very much if either one of them would make much of an effort for an exchange. So I have the pardons. They will be respected, and your husband will not be hanged. I have the recommendation for parole. I think the President's recommendation will be followed. I will go to Danville tomorrow to lay both matters before General Burbridge and I hope the following day your husband will be at home."

There was much rejoicing on the part of Mrs. Oldham and her daughters. Mrs. Burnam said, "The Major told me the good news, when he returned, and I came down to rejoice with you."

Captain Noland, who had sat in silence all the while, at last said, "Well, Major, I sent my sister to you and I'm glad I did. By blood, you are a whole team!"

A happier party never left Richmond than those in our carriage that afternoon. I had never heard the President spoken of before except as "Old Abe" by any of the Oldham family, and, in fact, by most of the families in Old Cane Springs. Mary Ann remarked, "Mother, we have certainly been mistaken in our opinion of President Lincoln. If he talked the way Major Burnam says he did—and I don't doubt that he did—he is a much greater man than we have been led to believe."

In two days Mr. Oldham arrived. He said it was a great surprise to him to be at home. He could hardly realize how it had all been accomplished, but some time he hoped to know whom to thank for saving his life. "Old Burbridge appeared so anxious to hang us," he said, "that I thought we would be executed before anyone who might save us would know of our danger."

Mr. Oldham's pardon and return had a good effect on the community. The Negroes had been almost as bitter towards President Lincoln as the whites. The soldiers for months had been around everywhere explaining to them that they were free and trying to induce them to join the army, but every such approach was met with scorn. The soldiers from the North were astonished that the Negroes did not quit their unwilling servitude, as they had been taught to consider it. I heard a Union soldier say one day that he believed Cabell Chenault's Negroes were more attached to his plantation than his old gray mares. He had seen them tried and knew they could not be driven off the pasture.

The pardon granted Mr. Oldham appeared to draw the Negroes toward President Lincoln. They did not know how to appreciate his Emancipation Proclamation or his offer to make soldiers of them, but when one in their midst for whom they had the highest regard was sentenced to die, and Mr. Lincoln said, "No, he must live," it caught them. It put them to thinking of and talking more about Mr. Lincoln than anything else he had ever said or done. Most all of the Negroes in Old Cane Springs were of a highly sympathetic nature, and the President's act of kindness in this instance drew them to him.

MAJOR CURTIS F. BURNAM
Voted for Bell in 1860, but supported Lincoln thereafter.

COLONEL JAMES W. CAPERTON
Voted for Lincoln in 1860, and supported him throughout the war.

GENERAL JOHN MILLER
Mortally wounded in the Battle of Richmond.

CAPTAIN P. P. BALLARD
Provost Marshal at Richmond during the war.

Merritt Jones's Tavern as it looks today. In February, 1864, General Grant was entertained here, while on his way from East Tennessee to Washington, D. C. Jones had four sons in the Confederate service. (See county map and Big Hill view facing page 129.)

White Hall, the home of Cassius M. Clay, as it looks today. Gen. Green Clay built the rear of this mansion before 1800. (See page 3 and county map.)

Shortly after Mr. Oldham's return, Mr. James Golden, a known Union man, went to Monticello and brought home the remains of young Cabell Chenault for interment in the family burying ground in Old Cane Springs. Nearly everyone in the entire community, white and black, was present at the burial. Union soldiers were on picket duty every half mile on the public road that went by the Chenault home, but they did not deter anyone from attending the funeral and burial. Good will seemed prevalent and the people of Old Cane Springs appeared on this occasion to be on as good terms with each other as before the war.

CHAPTER XXVII

THE DRAFT

FINALLY one thing occurred that stirred the entire community, both whites and blacks. President Lincoln, in the fall of 1863, issued a proclamation calling on the States not in rebellion to furnish enough men to surpress the Rebellion, and if men suitable for service failed to volunteer there would be a draft.[98]

Not long before this order, General John H. Morgan had gone into the state of Ohio with his command and he, with his entire army, had been captured. Most all of the young men of Old Cane Springs and surrounding country had been captured with him and placed in military prisons. There was little fear that any of them would be shot, and anxiety on that account was about quieted when the draft was announced, and men everywhere were being drafted into the Federal service. Many who felt they could not leave home were drafted and had to go or furnish substitutes. White substitutes were so hard to find that the Federal authorities announced that anyone drafted into the service could furnish a sound, able-bodied Negro of proper age to enlist in his stead.

My Uncle Robert, who owned a very likely man named Humphrey, had a brother-in-law named John Huguely. Mr. Huguely owned a fine Negro by the name of Matthew. Uncle Robert wanted Matthew as a foreman and had often tried to get him from Mr. Huguely, but had never succeeded. Matthew was under size and a little beyond the age for military service. To the surprise of my uncle, Mr. Huguely came one day and offered to exchange Matthew for Humphrey. The trade was soon arranged and after the exchange had been legally closed Mr. Huguely informed my uncle that he had been drafted, had passed the medical examination, and had to go to the army or furnish a substitute. He stated further that he had made the exchange for the purpose of using Humphrey as his substitute.[94]

The exchange and its object were soon known throughout the entire community. There was much indignation among the Negroes. One could hear them on all sides complaining that the white folks had not permitted them to go earlier with their young masters to fight the Yankees and now they were going to force them to join the Yankees and shoot their young masters. It looked as if there would be open revolt. The colored people were never the same after this episode. Humphrey was the first of their race to become a Union soldier from Old Cane Springs. He was a son of Alfred and Jennie, who were owned by Cabell Chenault, and a grandson of Aunt Creech Sally. There was much complaint in the quarters when he went away to take the place of his master in the service. Many reasons were given why he should not have been forced to go, but the objections were of no avail. Mr. Huguely declared that he could not afford to go and that his man must substitute for him.

Other drafted men throughout the county furnished Negro substitutes and the whole colored population of the county became aroused. These substitutions at first influenced the Negroes to object to joining the Federal army, notwithstanding the fact that the Union soldiers treated them with the greatest consideration. While none of them could write, letters came promptly every week to their parents. The Negroes seemed pleased with their new surroundings. They usually sent their monthly pay to their folks at home, and they always closed their letters with an appeal to their relatives to visit them in camp. This permission was finally given by the masters, and the greatest kindnesses and favors were shown these visitors.

By January, 1864, sentiment among the Negroes toward joining the Union army had entirely changed, a condition which those who had been the first to be forced into the service helped to bring about. It might be said, therefore, of the many white Southern sympathizers who had remained at home and who had been drafted into the Union army, that they, by their substitutions, contributed to the influences which caused the Negroes to enlist in the Federal service. On one occasion Alfred returned from visiting Humphrey and notified his master that he could not bear to be away from his son, whom he had promised to visit again in a week. In fact, he stated that he expected to join the army, and he did, making another Negro from Old Cane Springs to enlist. He told his master that there was likely to be a second draft and that he might become a substitute, and if he did, he would not fare as well, so he had been told in camp, as he would as a volunteer. This information must have been given generally to the Negroes, judging from the fact that the younger men began disappearing from every plantation. By early spring all of the able-bodied Negroes of proper age had joined the Union army. Gloomy indeed was the outlook for farming in 1864.

Chapter XXVIII

THE LOST CAUSE AND ANTICIPATIONS OF
THE FUTURE

NEARLY ALL of the Rebel boys from Old Cane Springs who were captured with Morgan were imprisoned at Camp Douglas, in the environs of Chicago, Illinois.[95] David and Anderson Chenault had made their escape from this prison and it was learned through the grape-vine route that they, with other

Rebels, were trying to make their way South. Finally Anderson got as far as the Rock House and informed us that his brother had contracted a fever and was then sick near Bloomington, Illinois. Mr. Cabell Chenault became very anxious over the condition of his sons when he learned that one was near but afraid to come home and the other was far away and sick. He was informed that David was known at the place where he was ill as David Hunter, and that if he sent anything to him it must be in that name and in care of James Jackson, Bloomington, Illinois.[96]

The Rock House was well filled with men, hoping for some chance to go farther South, but the Kentucky mountains were so closely guarded that it was almost certain death to make the effort. Getting them provisioned without detection was becoming more difficult every day. The risk of working through to the South became so hazardous that most all who arrived at the Rock House turned back, thinking their chance of evading arrest much better north of the Ohio River.

The departure of all of the able-bodied Negroes and the report of the Rebel boys from prison or a word from the escaped ones hiding under assumed names made the homes around Old Cane Springs look desolate and their occupants appear grave and depressed. There was no life or buoyance anywhere. I rode a great deal with Mary Ann, and while she was glad to have her father home she was worried because her brother James and Nath Deatherage were cooped up in prison.

"Oh, such distressing tales of misery and death come from up there! If they were only out and free to fight!" she would often exclaim. But her head was bowed and her countenance indicated that she was depressed. It was easy to see that one brave spirit was about to surrender and say, "The cause is lost."

Wherever I went I found the plantations growing up with weeds and briars. Many homes looked as though they had been deserted as the year 1864 dragged slowly by. There was no regular preaching at the old church;[97] no singing at night in the quarters; no corn shucking and no wood gathering in the old way; and no preparations for Christmas as the end of the year drew near.

I remarked to Mary Ann on Christmas eve, as I escorted her home after we had ridden together, that I could hardly believe so great a change could come over a community in so short a time. "When I came here," I said, "as a mere lad a little over three years ago, I felt as if I were in a fairyland. I was charmed wherever I went. Prosperity, love, and hope appeared to be everywhere; but now how changed! And I never feel very comfortable any more unless I am with my aunt or with you or at your home. Do you suppose, Mary Ann, the good old days will ever return?"

"I fear neither you nor anyone else will ever see again what you saw here when you came," she replied.

Mary Ann paused and appeared to be looking far away, causing me to feel that she had not said all she wanted to say. Apparently she was holding communion with one then languishing in a northern prison.

Finally she spoke: "Yes, a change has come—a change that I never dreamed of until shortly before the night you and I stopped on the hill yonder and heard the Negroes singing up here at home and down at Mr. Deatherage's.[98] I went into the war with a light heart, Gustin, and you joined me; and we have fought a good fight. We have satisfied the hunger of many a poor boy away from home and afraid to ask for a crust of bread and a cup of water. We have borne messages of love and words of information to others; we have made many homes happy by reason of our efforts; and we may have saved the lives of many by timely warnings. Our friends will never complain of our work or the part we took in this war. We have done the task assigned us and to that extent tried to have Old Cane Springs remain what it was, but there has been a failure somewhere and things have gone differently from what I hoped and expected.

"I know now that the cause of the South is doomed," she sighed. "Its efforts are a failure. There will be no Confederate States of America, and with their failure everything will change. No, you will never see again the happy homes you then saw. Mourning is now in nearly every home and it will take a new generation to forget the acts and causes that brought on that mourning. No, you will never see it again. You will never hear again the Negroes sing as you heard them when you first came and for two years thereafter. The change has already come; when it will end I am unable to say.

"The war is almost over," she continued. "I hope it will close before all our boys die in prison. When they do come home, a new life will begin, but it will never be the life that was here before this cruel war. You were too young to know, Gustin, but here lived the highest type of manhood and womanhood, and by reason of their surroundings they could exhibit their exalted characters. Such homes as you found and saw were responsible for the well-known saying, 'Kentucky hospitality.'"

Then after a pause, she said with a look of horror on her fair face: "I often dread—I shudder sometimes at what might happen and that quickly in this immediate community. There are not many more than a hundred white people here, and there are seven or eight hundred Negroes. The whites and Negroes now in the army who survive will soon return. I wonder—oh, how often I wonder whether they will come home the gentle, kind spirits they were when they went away. My conclusion is, however, that they will return with much the same spirit they possessed when they went away, and, consequently, I don't expect much trouble with them. That is the conclusion I have reached.

"My fear," she continued, "is that trouble will develop later. Negroes not reared with gentle, kind, Christian white people never develop properly. They must be reared with white people to become men like our Pike or Mr. Deatherage's Henry, or Mr. Cabell Chenault's Amos, William, and Jerry, or grandfather's Harrison, and your Uncle Robert's Matthew, and many other grand and good Negroes we both know; but when they pass away you will never see their equals again. All will be changed."

She had become grave, and for the first time since I had known her I felt as if I were a mere child in the presence of a mature and learned woman. We alighted at the Oldham stile, where we were met by Tempie and little Nettie, who claimed Christmas gifts from both of us.

Save when I was at home with my aunt or at Mr. Oldham's the Christmas of 1864 was a dreary one for me. In fact, it appeared to be a dreary one for almost everyone I saw. I recall that towards the latter part of Christmas week I went with my aunt to dine at the Deatherage home. Many of the mothers of the neighborhood had been invited, but the meeting had none of the life and enjoyment of former gatherings of this kind. Everyone had some sad news from the war or from the prisons to relate. Aunt Jose reported, with much feeling, that Humphrey, who had cared for her first three children while they were very young, had been killed in battle, and it was plain that the women were sorry, for they all knew the likely Negro.

Mrs. Deatherage read a letter from her son, Nath, who was still in Camp Douglas. He said he wondered what they had to eat on Christmas day, and wished he could have been with them to help eat it. He said that he knew they had a good dinner. "All I had," he wrote, "was fat bacon and pone bread with black coffee." The letter made all the women present weep.

Spring came and with it the surrender at Appomattox, and soon the boys began to come home, first the Rebels and later the Union soldiers. There was rejoicing in every home over those who came back. They were a hungry, lean, lank-looking lot, but all were received with open arms by both whites and blacks. David and Anderson Chenault, having escaped from prison, had arrived early in 1865. Their father engaged the law firm of Burnam and Caperton to persuade the Federal authorities to allow them to take the oath of allegiance to avoid arrest and reimprisonment. Both were sick and unable to report at Richmond to take the oath, so Captain Ballard, the provost judge, who had authority in the county, was asked to come to their home and administer it. He came, and when Mr. Chenault called for his bill he said it had cost him two dollars to get a horse to ride out there and if he wanted to he could pay that amount and nothing more. The lawyers, of course, were paid for their services.[99]

David Chenault had been nursed in his sickness by a Miss Mary Bullock in Illinois,[100] and as soon as he was able and before the return of the Negroes from the war he went to her home and brought back a charming young Yankee girl as his wife. In a very short time one of her cousins, Miss Bettie Fogg, of Woodford County, Kentucky, was captured by Anderson Chenault, though she was not a Yankee.[101] Marriage appeared to be the bent of the soldier boys as soon as they returned. James B. Ellison, who lived near Speedwell, a comrade in arms of the boys of Old Cane Springs, visited the community shortly after his return and in one week acted as best man at four such weddings.[102]

Nathan Deatherage returned home in May, 1865, having walked all the way from Richmond, Virginia, where he had gone from Camp Douglas in February to be exchanged. How different was his coming from his going! In 1862 he had ridden away as a young, brave, and handsome trooper on an uncle's fine coal-black stallion, which carried him even through the Ohio raid! Now two and a half years later he returns like a pilgrim, tired and footsore from a distant and inhospitable land, a "sadder, older, and wiser man." I should hasten to qualify the word "sadder," for Nath Deatherage never let disappointment overcome him to any extent. He would have been the first to join an optimist club.

Mary Ann was happier than she had been for a long time, even though her hero had not returned a conqueror. Apparently she and Nath saw much of each other during the following months, for I often saw them riding together over the country. In November cards were received announcing their coming marriage at the home of her parents. On the evening of the wedding, hundreds of white guests and many Negroes assembled to enjoy the festivities. Joy and happiness appeared to reign once more, as the handsomest couple I had ever seen stepped before the minister of the gospel and were made one in the holy bonds of matrimony.[103]

The infare at the Deatherage home the following day was equally enjoyable. Thus was begun in the seasons immediately following the close of the war what was expected to restore Old Cane Springs to its former splendor and glory—if such prosperity could ever possibly be attained again.[104]

FINIS

MR. AND MRS. NATHAN BIRD DEATHERAGE
Soon after their marriage in 1865.

Big Hill view, looking toward Richmond: (1) The Palisades; (2) Madison-Jackson County Highway; (3) Jones Tavern, where Gen. U. S. Grant spent a night in 1864; (4) The Boone Trail; (5) Pilot Knob. (See Map of Madison County. Along this highway came General Kirby Smith's army in August, 1862. (See pages 106-110, 190-198.)

NOTES AND REFERENCES

NOTES AND REFERENCES

CHAPTER I

1. MADISON COUNTY AND RICHMOND.

"The Virginia law passed in 1785, creating Madison County, the fifth county in what is now the State of Kentucky, did not go into effect until August 22, 1786, when the new county was duly organized at the home of George Adams at a settlement called Milford, on Taylor's Fork of Silver Creek, about four miles southwest of the present town of Richmond. The commissioners' choice of a county-seat was confirmed by the Virginia legislature in 1789.

"At Milford a temporary place to hold court was prepared in 1787 at a cost of 880 pounds of tobacco, and a year later a stone and frame courthouse was built, where the business of the county was conducted until 1798, when the seat of government was moved to a more favorable site, later called Richmond. It appears that the removal was confirmed by a fistic encounter between representatives of the two communities, the Milfordites losing. The county authorities later compensated certain citizens of Milford to the amount of $1,600 for the depreciation of the value of their property due to the change of the seat of government. In the formation of other counties Madison was reduced in size from time to time until it now contains about 490 square miles. It was named for James Madison, who later became President." Madison County plans to celebrate the sesquicentennial of its organization in 1937.

"The first settlement at Richmond was made in 1784 by Colonel John Miller, who was a Revoluntionary captain with Washington at Yorktown. It appears that Miller purchased four hundred acres of land from William Hoy, who had pre-empted one thousand acres where Richmond now stands. The order removing the county seat from Milford in 1798 stated that 'the ridge near John Miller's barn and brick kiln is appointed and fixed on for the permanent seat of justice for this county.' The records show that Miller's barn served as the courthouse until

1799, when another house was built, which served the county government until the present courthouse was erected in 1849.

"Richmond was not incorporated until 1809, and as late as 1818 it was referred to in print as a 'manufacturing little log village.' The present courthouse, though built eighty-seven years ago, presents a very substantial and attractive appearance. Its massive classic architecture is both impressive and beautiful. The records therein date back to August, 1786, and contain valuable information relating to the early history of Kentucky and Madison County. Richmond was named for Richmond, Virginia, which had been named by Colonel William Byrd, 'probably because of the similarity of its site to that of Richmond on the Thames.' The town now has about 7,000 inhabitants, exclusive of non-resident college students. It is replete in historic lore and includes houses which have stood for more than a hundred years. In many homes are interesting antiques, old manuscripts and books, and valuable paintings, many of which intrigue the imagination and stir the emotions."—J. T. Dorris, *A Glimpse at Historic Madison County and Richmond, Kentucky,* pp. 21-22.

2. "Robert Chenault: married Josephine Prewitt Cavins, of Fayette County, Ky., in 1854; she died in 1872 and he married his second wife, Sallie Prewitt, of Jessamine County, Ky. In 1861 he went South and joined the Confederate army."—W. H. Miller, *History and Genealogies,* p. 450. This monumental work of 855 pages pertaining to families of Madison County, Kentucky, will be used often in this book. Mr. Miller's equally valuable manuscripts in seven bound volumes, now in the library of the Eastern Kentucky State Teachers College, Richmond, will also be used. Both are indispensable in writing on Madison County history.

3. The reader will appreciate the narrative more after a careful study of the accompanying maps.

4. Sycamores are indigenous to Kentucky and grow in great profusion, especially along streams. Sometimes they become very large and often they develop very interesting groves, as in Sycamore Hollow at Boonesborough, a few miles below Old Cane Springs on the Kentucky River. This grove of more than a hundred trees is one of the largest in the United States. Three

huge sycamores on this spot became famous during the sieges of Fort Boone in 1776-1778. The last of these giant trees to die was removed to Richmond late in 1932 to be preserved for posterity. The sycamore, because of its whiteness, might well be called the "ghost tree." See J. T. Dorris, *A Glimpse of Historic Madison County and Richmond, Kentucky,* pp. 13-14.

5. About 1847, it appears, one Phil. A. Huffman came to the community now called Waco and bought a pottery from Mathew D. Grinstead. Apparently sometime later, according to French Tipton, "Huffman named the place Waco because he liked Waco, Texas." The superior clay of this place was awarded a centennial medal at Philadelphia in 1876.—The French Tipton Papers, Vol. L., p. 131.

Mr. Tipton, a lawyer and journalist of Richmond, worked on a history of Madison County for ten years or longer until his death in 1901. His valuable manuscripts are now in the possession of the writer.

Waco, Texas, was settled in 1849. "It was named for the Hueco Indians, who had a large village here until 1830, when they were exterminated by the Cherokees."—*Encyclopedia Britannica,* 14th edition, Vol. 23, p. 264.

6. The name Texas was given to this community because Abner Oldham, on being pulled from his horse by briars while riding in the region, "got up and said he 'wouldn't have all this d—— Texas country as a gift.'" Oldham's provocation happened while riding over the land as one of a commission appointed by the executors of William Lipscomb to divide his estate after his death in 1811.—French Tipton Papers, Vol. L, pp. 129, 202; Madison County Will Book A, p. 577.

The village kept the name Texas until after the War between the States, when the postal authorities allowed another community in Washington County to retain the name Texas and assigned the name College Hill to the community in Madison County. This name was used because a school was established there in the late 1860's and conducted by J. J. Johnson. A "Student's Certificate" of grades issued June 30, 1871, to A. W. Williams and signed by J. J. Johnson, Principal, is in the writer's possession. At that time the school was called Texas Seminary.

By 1876 it was called College Hill Seminary. The school, however, was often called Ayres Seminary, because Dr. J. Ayres, who lived nearby, apparently was the school's chief benefactor.

7. The elm is also indigenous to Kentucky and has figured largely in the history of the State. It was under a giant elm at Boonesborough, about fifty yards from the south bank of the Kentucky River, that the first legislative body and constituent assembly ever to meet in the State assembled on May 23, 1775. Judge Richard Henderson, the chief promoter of the Transylvania Colony, presided, and Daniel Boone, James Harrod, and fifteen others sat as delegates. Under this tree the first recorded religious service in Kentucky was also held on the following Sunday (May 28), which was the day after the close of the session of the law-making body. This elm was cut down in 1828. George W. Ranck, in his *Boonesborough* (1901), page 236, says of this tree: "It was the most unique and precious historical monument in the whole domain of Kentucky, and was invested with a charm that the loftiest sculptured column could possess." Also see R. H. Collins, *History of Kentucky*, p. 500.

8. Colonel John Noland is said to have been one of the first men in Madison County to be given the honorary title of colonel. His fine old home, built more than a hundred years ago, still stands on an eminence overlooking the Kentucky River. See illustration facing page 5.

9. The foundation ruins of Captain John Chambers' home may still be seen on the right as the road approaches the Red River ferry. See map of Old Cane Springs.

10. A large brick house (eleven rooms) now stands on the earlier site of the Jack Martin home near the Red River ferry. The present owner (1936), W. C. Brandenburg, believes this house was begun in 1861 and finished in 1863. Careful inquiry indicates it was under construction about 1860 or 1861. The great spring near this house deserves mention. See illustration facing page 12.

11. Captain Nathan Noland lived on the west bank of Muddy Creek. He was the son of Colonel John Noland, mentioned above, and the father of Green Noland and J. B. Noland now

living in Madison, and the grandfather of Mr. John Noland, an attorney of Richmond.

12. The John Black Noland farm now belongs to Mr. C. C. Wallace, an attorney of Richmond.

Chapter II

13. Only the foundation of Bogie's old stone mill on Silver Creek remains. It was built in 1810, as indicated in the Tipton Papers, Memorandum Book, p. 186.

The home here referred to is still used as a residence. It is a two-story stone house, which was built in 1796 by Andrew Bogie, as a cornerstone shows. Another larger stone house farther up Silver Creek, built in 1811 by James Bogie, a brother of Andrew, is also used as a residence today. Three other such houses, built more than a century ago and still used as residences, stand along Silver Creek.

14. SILVER CREEK, THE MADISON COUNTY RHINE.

Silver Creek might well be called the Madison County Rhine. Rising among the picturesque knobs of the southern part of the county near the unique College of Berea, whose very name is reminiscent of the struggle against slavery, of the progress of human liberty, of the unifying spiritual power of Christianity, of the glorification of honest labor, and of the worthy ambitions of youth, the silver thread of this stream follows a winding course to empty its crystal waters into the historic Kentucky. Fortunately, the romantic student can leisurely follow its entire length in nearly any way he chooses and appreciate its scenic beauty and interesting history.

The ancient Indian mounds and forts along either bank suggest the fact that an aboriginal race also appreciated the grandeur of this stream and its immediate primeval environment. Most certainly the pioneer was attracted by its allurements and built his home along its meandering pathway.

Very early Silver Creek's productivity justified in another way one of the connotations of its name, and the prosperity of its dwellers was manifested by numerous commodious homes, some built entirely out of native stone and others constructed from brick burned on the premises. Nearly all of these picturesque old residences built prior to the War between the States are still standing to intrigue the imagination and stir the emotions of the visitor.

Furthermore, during the first half of the last century there were erected along the banks of Silver Creek rustic stone water mills, whose varied allurements contributed to the enchantment of the region through which the stream flowed. Numerous other industrial establishments—hemp mills, cloth mills, sawmills, and even distilleries, built in the same period—also gave evidence of the resourcefulness and prosperity of that part of Madison County. The ruins of many of these industries may be seen today.

Through all these enchanting and picturesque human institutions flowed Silver Creek in that glorious era of Kentucky history, when the Harry of the West was conciliating the discordant sections of the Union, while the Lion of White Hall was hurling his damaging phillipics at the citadel of slavery through the columns of his *True American,* while the sister of the famous Beechers was evolving her *Uncle Tom's Cabin* out of human ebony in an adjoining county, and while the Bard of Federal Hill was composing the songs that have made Kentucky famous the world over. Here, enclosed by verdant hills and fertile fields and fed by many babbling brooks and pebbled licks, Silver Creek, with its many noisy rapids and deep, clear pools of crystal water, still retains much of its earlier splendor.

15. The census for 1870 shows that there were fewer Negroes in Poosey precinct than in any other of the nine precincts of Madison County. Only 118 is given for Poosey, while 714 is given for Union precinct, in which Old Cane Springs was. Million precinct, just east of Silver Creek and joining Poosey, had 403, while Elliston precinct, just south of Union, with Waco as the center, had 624. Yet the area of Union and Elliston was considerably larger than the combined areas of Poosey and Million.—Map of Madison County, Kentucky, published by D. G. Beers and Co., Philadelphia, 1876. Dr. Ivan E. McDougle, *Slavery in Kentucky, 1792-1865,* a reprint from the *Journal of Negro History,* Vol. III, p. 8, gives 10,684 free Negroes in Kentucky in 1860.

Bogie's Mill, on Silver Creek, built in 1810—as it looked in the 1890's. (From a photograph in the French Tipton Papers.) The mill race is shown in the foreground.

Cascades of a small brook near its union with Silver Creek along the Barnes Mill pike. (From a photograph in the French Tipton Papers.)

The Andrew Bogie House, built in 1796 on Silver Creek. (From a painting by Algin Reeves.) The house is still a residence.

The Gen. Samuel Estill House, built in the 1840's, on Silver Creek. Now the residence of Mr. and Mrs. J. B. Noland.

Chapter III

16. The minutes of the Republican Baptist Church, 1798-1865, and the Old Cane Spring Church, 1803-1865, of Madison County, do not contain the word slave in referring to Negro members. Such members are referred to as "Lydia, a black woman," and "Caesar, a black man."—Copies of the minutes of the first-named church and the minutes of Old Cane Spring Church are in the possession of the writer.

17. Dr. McDougle's *Slavery in Kentucky, 1792-1865,* pp. 75-76, states: "Legally, there were no marriages among the slaves. They were not citizens, but property. The men were urged to take their wives from among the women of the home estate, if a suitable companion could be found. But if not they eventually secured one in the neighborhood and the master usually allowed the slave a pass to see his wife every night in the week.

"It was the economic as well as the humanitarian interest of the master to have sympathy with the peace and contentment of his servant. Thus most of them took care that the family relationships of the slaves should not be disturbed. Oftentimes when the owner of either a husband or a wife was on the point of moving out of the county the masters would get together and make a trade which would obviate any disruption of the slave family. Under such conditions a man would part with a servant who otherwise could not have been bought at any price. . . ."

18. Thomas M. Hart, said to have been a cousin of the famous sculptor, Joel T. Hart, was a teacher and preacher. As a teacher he seems to have been associated for a time with John Augustus Williams, President of Daughters College, Harrodsburg, Kentucky, and author of the *Life of Elder John Smith* (better known as Raccoon John Smith).

The widow Bogie was Hart's third wife, in whose old stone house, built by Andrew Bogie in 1796, he lived after this marriage until his death some time after the war. The likeness of Thomas M. Hart facing page 36 was reproduced from a fine old portrait now in the possession of a grandson, Eugene Barnes, near Richmond.

19. Provisions in the wills of David Chenault (died 1851) and Colonel John Noland (died 1865), of Old Cane Springs, indicate the kind consideration that slave owners in Kentucky often gave their slaves. Chenault's will provided: "I wish my executors at my decease to sell all my slaves and personalty not included in my wife's third . . . In selling the slaves no one is to purchase except one of my children or grandchildren who live in the State of Kentucky, as it is my desire that none of my slaves should be taken or held out of my family residing in Kentucky, but this is not to prohibit such as hereafter remove from Kentucky from taking such with them any of said slaves he or she may own. . . . My servants Harrison and Jenny are not to be sold but are to live with any of my family at discretion, and be supported, if necessary, out of my estate."—Madison County Will Book J, pp. 579-581, David Chenault's will.

Colonel John Noland's will, which was probated and recorded as of May 1, 1865, after allotting certain slaves to members of the family provides: "I now say how the remainder of my slaves shall be disposed of. . . . It is my will that a Negro woman named Fanny and the youngest child she may have on the day of my sale be sold to the highest bidder to give the owner of her husband a chance to buy her and her child. It is my will that the remainder of my Negroes be sold one at a time among my heirs to the highest bidder, my heirs to be the only purchasers."—Madison County Will Book R, pp. 163-165.

20. THE ETHNOLOGICAL JUSTIFICATION OF SLAVERY.

Dr. William Sumner Jenkins' *Pro-Slavery Thought in the Old South,* pp. 243-246, has these paragraphs in a chapter on this topic:

". . . . Jefferson, the great theoretical equalitarian, had early insisted that the ultimate decision of the abolition question would depend upon the results of research in the field of ethnology, the science that investigates the mental and physical differences of mankind. Jefferson believed that the Negro lacked native ability for the higher pursuits of civilization. From the Colonial period on, the inferiority of the Negro was an assumption made by the slaveholder for which he required little or no demonstration. Accepting this premise without question, to the mind of the

Southerner there could be no alternative to a system of slavery, except a condition of race conflict which would, after horrible experiences, eventuate in the extermination of the inferior race. The entire pro-slavery thought was imbued with the belief of Negro inferiority. . . .

"The problem in constructing the ethnological defense, therefore, was a problem of verification and substantiation of the inferiority belief. It was necessary to demonstrate that the faculties of the Negro, as compared with those of the Saxon, qualified him for a state of servitude and made him unfit for the enjoyment of freedom. The ethnologist argued that slavery needed no other justification, excuse, or apology than the proof that the Negro race was weak and imperfectly developed in mind and body and, therefore, belonged to a lower order of man. One of them freely admitted that 'if this be not true, American slavery is a monstrous wickedness.'

"THE ARGUMENT OF DIVERSITY OF RACES"

"Let us then review the arguments brought forth by Southern ethnologists to establish the physical and mental difference between the races to the slave relationship. These may be divided into two types, historical and physiological. From a comparative study of the races throughout the course of history certain conclusions were drawn significant to a proper understanding of race relationship. In the records of the earliest civilization discovered at that time, the monuments of the Egyptians, the Negro was pictured as occupying a servile position in human society; and, as the history of the race was traced through succeeding civilizations, the Negro was found to have remained the subject of continued enslavement. Moreover, when left alone in his native land, he had never of his own initiative advanced from a state of barbarism to develop a civilization of his own. This fact was considered as strong proof of his lack of capacity to advance. Moreover, the large continent of Africa stood in plain view as an ever-present reminder, a rank wilderness, where the various tribes engaged in incessant attempts to subject each other to slavery. . . .

"As a further link in the chain of the historical argument, the slaveholder pointed out that on every occasion on which the servile race had gained freedom, after once having been held in bondage, that it had inevitably within a time lapsed into barbarism. A most vivid illustration of this tendency was found in the history of Santo Domingo and Haiti. The results of emancipation in this island were a powerful object lesson, a timely and salutary warning to the Southerner. Closely scrutinizing the situation, an official representative of the United States in Haiti wrote it was a conviction forced upon him by his observations that 'Negroes only cease to be children when they degenerate into savages.' He was convinced that a short residence there would cause 'the most determined philanthropist to entertain serious doubts of the possibility of their ever attaining the full stature of intellectual and civilized manhood.'"

21. THE SCRIPTURAL ARGUMENT FOR SLAVERY.

Dr. Jenkins also says, pp. 203-206, in his chapter on "The Moral Philosophy of Slavery": "Arguments drawn from the New Testament, or the Christian dispensation, strengthened the scriptural justification of slavery. Christ came to fulfill and not to destroy. Therefore, He sanctioned the institutions and relationships existing at His time which He did not expressly condemn. Notwithstanding the fact that slavery flourished in every known part of the world and that Christ and the Apostles were continually coming into contact with it, He did not condemn it in the Sermon on the Mount or in any other formal enumeration of sins given by Him or the Apostles. . . . On the other hand, Christ tacitly approved it on the occasion when he healed the slave of the Roman centurion while he spoke no word of freedom (Luke VII: 2-10). Finally, in the precepts of the New Testament, the Apostles taught submission of the slave to his master, and by so doing recognized the relation as being compatible with Christianity. The example made most use of was taken from the epistle of St. Paul where he tells the story of sending back the runaway slave, Onesimus, to his master, Philemon. On many other occasions the Apostles exhorted the slave to be obedient and abide peacefully by his lot. . . .

"THE THEORY OF THE CHURCH'S RELATION TO SLAVERY"

Dr. Jenkins also in the same chapter, pp. 208-209, says: "Although the church had no authority to interfere with slavery as a political institution, yet it did have a definite duty to perform in regard to the personal relationship of master and slave. In carrying out its ministerial duties the church had certain obligations enjoined upon it by its constitution. Accepting the Biblical argument in its entirety, the theory of the church taught that there were duties of both master and servant, which were just as definitely commanded as the right of slaveholding was sanctioned. The commission of the church should be given a free hand to carry out its work. The duties of both master and slave were recorded in the Bible and when followed the relation became a mutual benefit. As the servant was directed to 'obey in all things your masters' so the master was commanded 'to give unto your slaves that which is just and equal.' The instant, however, the moral duties were neglected then the scriptural argument lost its force, for God approved of slavery in that manner alone."

It might be well in closing this note to give Henry Clay's estimate in 1829 of the condition of "free" Negroes, as quoted by Asa Earl Martin in his *Anti-Slavery Movement in Kentucky Prior to 1850*, p. 49: " 'Of all the descriptions of our population, and of either portion of the African race, the free people of color are, by far, as a class, the most corrupt, depraved, and abandoned. . . . They are not slaves, and yet they are not free. The laws, it is true, proclaim them free; but prejudices, more powerful than any law, deny them the privileges of freemen. They occupy a middle station between the free white population and the slaves of the United States, and the tendency of their habits is to corrupt both.' "

Mr. Martin follows this quotation by saying: "In the North as well as in the South, the free Negro was deemed an undesirable member of society, and many slaveholders who recognized slavery as a great evil were convinced that general emancipation without a removal of the freed slaves would be yet worse, and must result in insurrection, murder, and every form of outrage."

22. JOHN G. FEE MOBBED NEAR OLD CANE SPRINGS.

John G. Fee (1816-1901), a native of Bracken County, Kentucky, attended college at Augusta, Kentucky, and Oxford, Ohio, and studied theology "at Lane Seminary, Ohio, where he became convinced of the great evil and sinfulness of American slavery." After failing to persuade his father to emancipate his slaves he "carried the gospel [of freedom] to others," for which his father "disowned and disinherited him, giving him one dollar in his will."

"In Lewis and Bracken counties he labored eight years and organized three anti-slavery churches. At the request of Cassius M. Clay he sent a box of anti-slavery manuals, which were scattered through Madison County. The result was, the people invited him here, where, after preaching nine sermons, he organized a church in 1853 which refused fellowship with slaveholders, and after one year he became its pastor. . . .

"In 1856 Mr. Fee experienced a series of mobs in this region. He had before this been mobbed in Lewis, Mason, and Bracken counties. The first of this series was at Dripping Springs, in Garrard County; the next near Mt. Vernon, in Rock Castle County; the third and most violent was near Texas, in Madison County. Mr. Fee was preaching on the subject of Christian union, and was accompanied by Robert Jones, a native of the county, who was acting as a colporteur of the American Missionary Association. He was also encouraged by the two Messrs. Field and Marsh, residents in that vicinity. There was apprehension of danger, and Mr. Fee had been consulted as to the propriety of carrying arms. He said: 'No; if I am disturbed I will appeal to the courts.' He believed in the right of self-defense, but opposed the practice of carrying arms, and believed they were oftener a source of danger than a means of safety."—See E. H. Fairchild, *Berea College, An Interesting History*, pp. 6-9.

Mr. Fee gives the following account of his experience with this mob in his *Autobiography of John G. Fee* (Chicago, 1891), pp. 112-122:

"In the years 1857-8 I had appointments for preaching at Lewis Chapel in this county, in the region known as Big Bend of the Kentucky River. In this region Bro. Robert Jones had also traveled as a colporteur, selling the publications of the American Tract Society, and also distributing anti-slavery documents—tracts written by myself and others.

"In the month of February, 1858, I went to the house of a Mr. Fields, an excellent man, a substantial farmer; and on Friday evening preached at his house.

"I had been warned not to come again into that region; but my covenant was upon me to preach the Gospel of Christ in this my native State. . . .

"Saturday morning was one of comparative comfort for that month of the year. After breakfast I retired to an adjacent forest for prayer and reflection. On returning to the house, Mr. Fields said to me, 'Mr. C——, an ex-member of the Legislature, has been here, and advises me not to go to the chapel; "for," said he, "there will be trouble there today." '

"Just at this moment a man rode by, carrying before him three double-barreled shot-guns. 'There,' said Mr. Fields, 'do you see that half-Injun? He lives at old C—— O——'s; there is something up.' Turning to me and looking gravely he said, 'Shall we take guns? I have one rifle, and my brother has two.' I replied, 'No, I carry no weapons but the gospel of truth; and then, three rifles will only provoke greater violence. If we shall be disturbed I will make my appeal to the Civil Courts, as I always have done.' He assented. In due season we took our horses and started for the chapel—the place for preaching.

"When we arrived, Mr. Marsh, a friend who was outside waiting for us, advancing, said, in a very subdued tone, 'We shall have trouble here today.' I replied, 'Let us do our duty, and leave the results with God'; and passed on into the house; for when duty is clear, it is not wise to counsel with fears. Mr. Marsh followed in, and seated himself near to the desk where I stood. He seemed to desire to be near to me. Exactly on time, eleven o'clock, we commenced the service of the morning. I had advanced about half way in my sermon when I noticed restiveness in the congregation, and some young men left the house. I knew the occasion, for I was so situated that I, too, could see the crowds of men, on horseback, with guns on their shoulders, riding rapidly toward the chapel.

"In a moment the house was surrounded with armed men. I said to the congregation, 'Sit still'; and I preached on. Soon Mr. C—— came in, and seated himself by Mr. Marsh. C—— commenced whispering to Marsh. Marsh shook his head, and

C——got up and retired from the house. I continued preaching as though all was right. Soon C——came in, and advancing to me said, 'Mr. Fee, there are men here who want you to stop and come out.' I said, 'Mr. Covington, I am engaged in a religious duty and in the exercise of a constitutional right; please sit down and do not interrupt.' He turned on his heel, and went out. Soon three men entered the doorway, with guns in their hands, and with horrible oaths cried out, 'Stop, G—d D—n you, and come out here.' I preached on. Marsh, Fields, and others—men and women—remained, still apparently listening. Soon the men referred to rushed forward, and, seizing me by the collar of my coat and by my arms, dragged me to the door. There a stout man, S——, stepped up, and pulling a new rope from his pocket, swore he would hang me to the first limb if I did not then promise to leave the county and never come back again. . . . With violence they pulled me out into the highway—the county road. The captain of the company, coming up, said, 'I am captain of this company; leave him in my hands.' They surrendered. The captain led me aside, and with the concurring entreaty of Mr. C——, advised me to promise these men that I would leave the county and not come back again assuring me if I would do so they would not hurt me. I replied, '. . . I cannot pledge myself to leave where I believe duty calls.'

"They then brought my horse and demanded that I mount. I did so. They then went back into the chapel and brought out Bro. Jones; and the captain of the company took him behind him on his horse, and they started with us for the Kentucky River, distant, perhaps, two miles, swearing they would duck me as long as life was in me. . . .

"When the crowd had advanced about half the distance to the river, the captain called a halt, and again demanded that I promise to leave the county and not return again; and added, 'You have said that the men engaged in mobs are generally poor and irresponsible men; but we will have you understand that the men in this crowd are men of property and standing.' I replied, 'So much the greater peril to society, when men of property and standing will consent to disregard law and order.' I again said, 'I can make no pledges to leave.' They then started again for the river.

REV. JOHN A. R. ROGERS
One of the founders of Berea College.

REV. JOHN G. FEE
One of the founders of Berea College.

REV. LINDSAY HUGHES BLANTON
Chancellor Central University,
1880-1901.

REV. ROBERT L. BRECK
Chancellor Central University,
1874-1880.

Main Building of Central University, built in 1874. Now used by the Model High School of the Eastern Kentucky State Teachers College.

John G. Fee Memorial Union Church, center of the religious life of the student body and staff of Berea College.

"I had been in the hands of several organized mobs before. I had been in the midst of infuriated crowds not organized, who seemed ready to rush upon me, but were in some way hindered. I had been often waylaid and suddenly assaulted. I had been stoned on the highway; but this was the most formidable of all, and, apparently, 'meant business.' The mob took us near to the bank of the river. There the leaders left me in the care of others, and turned off to counsel with men who were for some reason already on the ground.

"The men left to guard me were manifestly poor men, with some young men. These seemed to enter into sympathy with me, and in an undertone one said to me, 'Just promise these men to leave, and they will not hurt you.' I replied, 'It is not fitting that I, a native citizen, pledge to these men that I leave my home and the work to which I believe God has called.' I said, 'You cannot see my motives now; you will at the Judgment Day.' By this time the leaders had returned, and men were around me in circles three deep, and heard these last words. One cried out, 'We did not come here to hear a sermon, let us do our work.' They then took Bro. Jones and myself nearer to the bank of the river and ordered Bro. Jones to strip himself. He took off his coat. The captain cried out, 'Take off your jacket.' He did so. 'Now your shirt—strip to the red.' Jones hesitated. The captain stripped him to the bare back, bent the man down, and with three sycamore rods, heavy and thick, struck the unoffending man many severe blows, leaving the marks on his body as distinct as the fingers on a man's hand. The suffering man groaned and fell forward.

"The captain then turned to me, and, with an oath, said, 'I will give you five hundred times as much if you do not promise to leave this county and not come back again.' I said to him, 'I will take my suffering first,' and knelt down. One of the crowd, whom I then knew not—who 'held the clothes'—now an official in the county, and a very estimable citizen, cried out, 'Don't strike him.' Then another cried out, 'Don't strike him.' O—— said, 'I feel that I ought to, but don't like to go against my party; get up and go home.'

"I got on my horse, and took Bro. Jones behind me, for he was so disabled by the whipping that he could not walk.

"The retreat of these men of 'property and standing,' from their work at the Big Bend of the Kentucky River, was ludicrously orderly. . . .

"The procession marched in this manner for some two or three miles. On coming to Covington's factory, the command was given, 'Right about, wheel.' This was meant for those who had enlisted for the previously described 'service.' Bro. Jones and I had not thus enlisted; hence we kept the straightforward road, as all then desired us to do.

"After a ride of . . . quite a number of miles [we came] to the house of a relative of Bro. Jones. There we stopped for the night.

"In the morning Bro. Jones was not able to travel. That portion of his body . . . which had been bruised by the whipping was purple because of the bruising and stagnated blood. I left him, only sorrowing that I had not shared some of his suffering, and thus been brought more fully into sympathy with our once suffering Lord and his then suffering poor. Of this experience I was conscious.

"Alone I started for my home, some ten or twelve miles distant. Terror had spread its pall over all the country. No glad faces greeted [me], until I came to my little home. Wife and children were glad to see me—wife not apparently surprised nor dismayed. Violent persecution was to both of us no new thing; it had been of frequent occurrence during the past twelve years. . . .

"We remained at our home in great quietude for two days. I then took my horse and rode to Richmond, the county seat, and engaged the services of two lawyers to aid Bro. Jones in the prosecution of the leaders of the mob. I chose to make the prosecution in his behalf rather than in my own. He was regarded as a Republican, and I as a 'Radical.' I also thought that in this way I would secure Mr. Clay's co-operation, and addressed a letter to him, requesting his aid in behalf of Bro. Jones. He declined, saying, 'To do so would be only "robbing Peter to pay Paul," ' and then advised me to leave the county. He kindly offered to take care of my family and property.

"I returned home. Speedily large numbers of the mob came to Richmond, and, as I was informed, swore they would give five hundred lashes to the lawyer who would dare to defend Fee or Jones. As a matter of fact, no prosecution was made. The Circuit Judge, a kind man, afterward a Republican, witnessed the bravado of the threatening mob; the Grand Jury took no notice of the occurrence; the civil arm was paralyzed by the slave power."

23. Berea College and Central University

Berea College is "a monument to the anti-slavery sentiment of the South." The selection of its location was due to Cassius M. Clay, who, in 1853, encouraged Reverend John G. Fee, another ardent Kentucky opponent of slavery, to establish an anti-slavery Union Church in Madison County. Two years later, at the same place and for a similar purpose, a district school was established and a student from Oberlin College "became the first principal, a constitution was adopted, and the collegiate and preparatory departments were planned." From these early efforts grew the college and the town of Berea.

"The school prospered, notwithstanding its opposition to slavery, until December, 1859, when, soon after the John Brown episode, Rogers and nine other men of Berea and their families were driven from the community. This act of violence stopped instruction at Berea until 1865, when the school opened again. Soon thereafter it began to admit Negroes to its classes, which it continued to do until prevented by a general state law in 1904.

"Under the prosperous administrations of Reverend John A. R. Rogers, E. H. Fairchild, William Goodell Frost, and the present incumbent, Dr. William J. Hutchins, Berea has become a great institution, varied in its activities, and possessing properties and endowments worth several millions. Apparently much of its inspiration has come from Oberlin College, but it has always received support from some of the great leaders of America, including Henry Ward Beecher, Gerrit Smith, Carl Schurz, Andrew Carnegie, Theodore Roosevelt, President Eliot of Harvard, William E. Barton (an alumnus), and a host of others equally prominent. The general aim of the college is to contribute 'to the spiritual and material welfare of the mountain region of the South, affording to young people of character and promise a thorough Christian education, elementary, industrial, secondary, normal, and collegiate, with opportunities for manual labor as an assistant in self-support.' "—J. T. Dorris, *A Glimpse at Historic Madison County*, etc., pp. 40-41.

While the actual founding of Berea College dates back to the ante-bellum period during the bitter controversy over slavery, Central University was in reality a sequel of the War between the States; for its establishment was the result of certain social, political, and ecclesiastical developments prior to and during that conflict. In 1861 a separation in the Presbyterian Church occurred in those states forming the Confederacy. Though serious differences existed among Presbyterians in Kentucky during the war, a division did not occur until 1866. Immediately a controversy arose between the two synods over the ownership and use of their property before separation. The Kentucky Appellate Court eventually gave Centre College at Danville to the Northern synod and consequently the Southern synod established Central University at Richmond.

The school was planned on a large scale, and came to include a liberal arts college, a preparatory department and a college of law in Richmond; medical and dental colleges in Louisville; and preparatory schools in Jackson, Middlesboro, and Elizabethtown. The institution opened on September 22, 1874, and continued until 1901, when, owing to financial difficulties, competition, and an increasing spirit of conciliation among Presbyterians in the State, Central University united with Centre College. Reverend Lindsey Hughes Blanton was the able chancellor of the University from 1880 to 1901.

It is significant indeed that two colleges growing out of the controversy over slavery—one sympathetic with the North, the other with the South—were established in Madison County. Stately University Hall, built in 1874, stands today on the campus of the Eastern Kentucky State Teachers College as a monument to the issues and struggles of the War between the States.—See the writer's long account of "Central University, Richmond, Kentucky," in the *Register* of the Kentucky State Historical Society, Volume 32 (April, 1934); also his chapter on "Central University" in *Three Decades of Progress, Eastern Kentucky State Teachers College*, J. T. Dorris, Editor.

24. CASSIUS M. CLAY.

"General Cassius Marcellus Clay, son of General Green Clay, was born in Madison County, October 19, 1810. He graduated with distinction from Yale University in 1832, having the singular honor, on invitation, of giving the Washington Centennial address in New Haven, on February 22, 1832, then and there delivering his 'first anti-slavery speech.' In 1845, he founded at Lexington, Kentucky, an anti-slavery paper called 'The True American,' which he published for more than a year at the peril of his life. Though opposed to slavery and to the annexation of Texas, he served as captain in the Mexican War, and so endeared himself to his company of Kentuckians that, on his return, Lexington gave him a public reception, and Madison County presented him with a beautiful sword. The sword is on display in the Berea College library. By this time Horace Greeley, of the New York Tribune, so appreciated Mr. Clay that, in 1848, he edited and published 'The Writings, Speeches, and Addresses of Cassius Marcellus Clay.'

"General Clay served several terms in the Kentucky Legislature; he gave land and money to the movement which produced Berea College; and he was a candidate for the Vice-Presidency before the Republican convention in 1860. He was minister to Russia during Lincoln's and Johnson's administrations. In 1862 he was made Major-General of Volunteers by President Lincoln. He always claimed the credit for the purchase of Alaska in 1867. He was one of the earliest emancipationists, and no man of prominence in the United States manifested greater courage in fearlessly asserting his constitutional rights in assailing the institution of slavery. In 1886 he published the first volume of 'The Life, Memoirs, Writings, and Speeches of Cassius M. Clay.' The second volume was never finished. Mr. Clay escaped death by violence many times and survived his bitterest and greatest enemies. He died July 22, 1903, near the age of ninety-three." The grave of this picturesque and prominent son and citizen of Madison County is in the Richmond Cemetery.—J. T. Dorris, *A Glimpse at Historic Madison County,* etc., pp. 24-25.

25. THE EXPULSION OF THE BEREANS.

Perhaps the most interesting event in the early history of Berea College was the expulsion of the Bereans in December, 1859. The Reverend John A. R. Rogers, the school's first principal, gives the following graphic account of this unfortunate affair in his *Birth of Berea College, A Story of Providence:*

"In October, 1859, John Brown made his famous raid into Virginia and took the arsenal at Harper's Ferry. Berea had been known from the first as a school in favor of liberty, and though it had equally stood for law and order, doing nothing rashly or contrary to the laws of the State, yet in the excitement of the times these characteristics were overlooked or disregarded. The stir in Madison and adjoining counties was greatly increased by false rumors, some of which were published in the newspapers as facts. It was said that boxes of Sharpe's rifles had been intercepted on the way to Berea. The situation of Berea, in the rear of the Blue Grass region, was pointed out as most admirably selected for strategic purposes and as a base for a raid, and this was regarded by those who were ready to believe the wildest tales as evidence of the warlike purposes of the Bereans.

"At this time Mr. Fee was at the East, raising money for the school, and said in a sermon at the church of Henry Ward Beecher that the country needed men with the courage and spirit of sacrifice of John Brown, not with his methods. It was reported in the papers of Kentucky that he was in the East and at Beecher's church, raising John Browns for Kentucky. All these things stirred the people to a perfect whirlwind of excitement. Public meetings of the citizens of Madison County were called that they might decide what should be done to rid the State of the Bereans. Finally, after many such gatherings, at a meeting at the Court House, sixty-two leading citizens of the county were appointed a committee to remove the most prominent Bereans from the State; peaceably if possible, forcibly if necessary, and John G. Fee and John A. R. Rogers were mentioned by name.

"At this meeting a paper addressed to the people of Kentucky was adopted, giving the reasons for their course; this paper when published filled several columns of the county newspaper. The substance of these reasons was that it had been settled that Kentucky was to be a slave State forever, and that the Berea school and the town were in opposition to a fundamental principle of the State, and they could not be tolerated any longer without the most serious results to the Commonwealth. It was said to be a case where necessity sets aside law. The document also said liberty and slavery could not dwell together, and that the school favored liberty.

"It was decided that the work of removal should be done without violence, if possible, and that ten days' notice to leave the State should be given to the obnoxious persons, and if they were in the State at the end of that time, they should suffer the consequences of their refusal. Though not a few prominent men in the county opposed this movement, their opposition did not avail.

"During all these weeks of excitement the Bereans went about their usual work quietly, though not without forebodings and fear. When rumors came that one or another was to be strung to a limb, it required all their faith and courage to go unmoved about their customary duties, but calling on the Lord for strength and wisdom, they preserved a good degree of composure. . . .

"While the meetings were going on in Richmond, the county seat, and elsewhere, the prominent Bereans took no special pains to find out what attempts were to be made to drive them away. . . .

"Whether the committee appointed to remove the Bereans took the utmost pains to conceal the time when they should in a body visit Berea is not known, but the first intimation of their approach was when they were drawn up before the house of Mr. Rogers, the first place they visited. His house was in a grove some distance from the road, and without a fence about the grounds. A slight snow had fallen and the men came up so quietly that their approach was not noticed by Mr. Rogers and family, who were at dinner, until someone announced:

" 'They have come.'

"Who 'they' were was known at once. Mr. Rogers went immediately to the front door, his three-year-old son clinging to his coat skirts, to find sixty mounted men drawn up in a regular wedge-shaped array, the point of the wedge at the front of the house. The leader dismounted from his white charger and stated the object of their visit, giving Mr. Rogers a printed document with the reasons for their course. Mr. Rogers replied that he was a quiet, law-abiding citizen, and had violated no law or done anything to disturb the peace or welfare of the Commonwealth, and was proceeding, when the leader, seeing some of his men restless, said they could not discuss the matter, and added that if Mr. Rogers and his friends did not leave in ten days they would return and complete their work. He then ordered his men to wheel and move on. They then went to the residence of Mr. Fee, who was at the time in the East, leaving a similar document with his family, and then on, serving the same notice to eight other prominent Berea citizens, Mr. Hanson among the number. In two hours the work was done and they rode away.

"After the committee had gone the question came up in earnest what should be done; whether those ordered away should remain and protect themselves as best they could in their houses, or whether they should leave within ten days.

"By common consent all met in the evening at the school building, which was the usual place for all public gatherings, to pray for wisdom. It was a remarkable prayer meeting. It was not a formal coming together to perform a duty, or to ask for general blessings, but to ask God, who they felt alone could make known to them their duty, to make plain whether they should go or stay.

"Those gathered for prayer had no clear vision of the Civil War, so soon to break out, or the evils that should ere long befall many of the men who had come that day to drive peaceful persons from their homes, but while they claimed no special goodness for themselves, because they were seeking to help God's poor, they felt confident of His help, and in the ultimate success of the work in which they had been engaged.

"The next day it was decided to appeal to the Governor of the State for protection, and Mr. Rogers drew up the following petition, which was signed by all those warned away, and Mr. Reed and Mr. Life, two of the number, took it to Frankfort and presented it in person to Governor Magoffin.

To His Excellency, the Governor of the State of Kentucky:

1. We have come from various parts of this and adjoining States to this county, with the intention of making it our home;

have supported ourselves and families by honest industry and endeavored to promote the interests of religion and education.

2. It is a principle with us to "submit to every ordinance of man for the Lord's sake, unto Governors as unto them that are sent by Him for the punishment of evil-doers and praise of them that do well," and in accordance with this principle we have been obedient in all respects to the laws of this State.

3. Within a few weeks, evil and false reports have been put into circulation, imputing to us motives, words, and conduct calculated to inflame the public mind, which imputations are utterly false and groundless. These imputations we have publicly denied and offered every facility for the fullest investigation, which we have earnestly but vainly sought.

4. On Friday, the twenty-third inst., a company of sixty-two men, claiming to have been appointed by a meeting of the citizens of our county, without any shadow of legal authority, and in violation of the constitution and laws of this State and the United States, called at our respective residences and places of business, and notified us to leave the county and State, and be without this county and State within ten days, and handed us the accompanying document, in which you will see that unless the said order be promptly complied with, there is expressed a fixed determination to remove us by force.

In view of these facts, which we can substantiate by the fullest evidence, we respectfully pray that you, in the exercise of the power vested in you by the constitution and made your duty to use, do protect us in our rights as loyal citizens of the State of Kentucky.

J. A. R. ROGERS	J. G. HANSON
J. D. REED	JAS. S. DAVIS
JOHN F. BOUGHTON	SWINGLEHURST LIFE
JOHN SMITH	E. T. HAYES
CHARLES E. GRIFFIN	A. G. W. PARKER
	W. H. TORRY

Berea, Madison County, Ky.,
December 24, 1859.

"The Governor received the bearers of the petition respectfully, but said it was impossible for him to do anything for their protection.

"When they returned and reported the Governor's answer, and what condition of the public mind they had seen on their journey to and from the Capital, the feeling strengthened that it was the part of wisdom for those ordered away to quietly depart. . . .

"Mourning and sorrow were rather the portion of those who were permitted to remain. They were to lose, at least for a time, their leaders, and the school on which their hopes were set was to be closed, when to be reopened they knew not.

"Finally the day on which they were to leave arrived. The families departing met under the oaks in front of Mr. Roger's house, with a concourse of neighbors and friends gathered about them. Then with bared heads under the vault of heaven they lifted up their hearts to God, while the Rev. George Candee, of Jackson County, led them in prayer as they committed themselves to the guidance of the Lord God Almighty. Then the farewells were uttered and the exiles mounted their various vehicles to begin their march. They formed a motley but not dangerous procession, these 'people who were a menace to Kentucky.' Patriarch and babes in arms, a bride and groom, men and women in the prime of life, young people and children of all ages, all moved slowly away from the hill.

"This band of the exiles spent the night in Richmond, the county seat of Madison County, in which Berea is situated, and next day went by public conveyance to Cincinnati. While in Richmond Mr. Rogers called on Mr. Hathaway [William Holloway, Major and Paymaster, Union army, February, 1863, to November, 1865], its leading merchant, to see about his account, and made the request that he would give him a few weeks in which to pay it. Colonel Hathaway's [Holloway's] reply was:

" 'Most certainly, and I will give you any amount of money you need.'

"Colonel Hathaway [Holloway] was a princely man, one of Kentucky's noblest sons. He, like a great number of Kentuckians, was opposed to disturbing peaceable men, seeking only the welfare of the State, and this little incident is mentioned to show the confidence which such men felt in Berea.

"The next morning after the exiles had arrived in Cincinnati the papers were filled with glaring headlines, giving the story of the banishment of the Kentuckians accused of no misdemeanor whatever, and these accounts were telegraphed to every part of the land.

"The next few days public meetings were held in churches and public halls in Cincinnati, where the exiles were invited to tell their own story. Ministers, jurists, and other prominent men pronounced this act an unparalleled outrage.

"Soon the various families driven from their homes made their way to the homes of their friends. Mr. Fee and family went to relatives in Bracken County, Kentucky, from which place he was soon ordered away. Rev. James Scott Davis was also compelled to leave Lewis County, where he had been a faithful minister for many years. The whole slave power of Kentucky was aroused, partly through fear because of the John Brown raid, and partly because it seemed an opportune time to stamp out all anti-slavery feeling in the State. So man proposed; how God soon disposed is known to all. Later, when Mr. Fee went back to Kentucky on a peaceful errand, to put up some stones at the grave of his son, he was again driven out of the State.

"In March, 1860, Mr. John G. Hanson returned to Berea to look after his business, when he was hunted like a wild beast. His sawmill was destroyed and his pursuers broke into a house where they thought he might be concealed and conducted themselves in such a way that several men armed themselves to put a stop to the outrages, and a number of shots were fired by both parties. The excitement was such that cannon were brought from Frankfort, the capital of the State, and for a time a warfare similar to that previously in Kansas seemed imminent."

26. CASSIUS M. CLAY VS. JOHN G. FEE.

Cassius M. Clay had made clear his disagreement with the course pursued by Mr. Fee and his followers at a Fourth of July celebration in 1856, at Slate Lick Springs on the west branch of

Brushy Fork, a little above Berea in Madison County. Fee, who spoke first and who accepted the doctrine of the "higher law" with regard to the legality of slavery, concluded his speech by saying, " 'A law confessedly contrary to the will of God ought not by the human courts to be enforced,' " and then, referring to the Fugitive Slave Law, said that he " 'would refuse to obey [it and] then suffer the penalty.' "

Mr. Clay spoke next and warned his hearers that " 'Mr. Fee's position is revolutionary, insurrectionary, and dangerous.' He continued by saying, 'As long as a law is on the statute book, it is to be respected and obeyed until repealed by the Republican majority.' " Though Fee charged Clay with inconsistency for saying, "When he [Clay] came to the Fugitive Slave Law . . . , 'So far as this is concerned, I would not obey it myself; it is contrary to natural right, and I would not degrade myself by obeying it,' " Clay maintained always thereafter that Fee and his followers taught disobedience to law and were, therefore, radicals and revolutionaries, while he advocated opposition to slavery through regular constituted channels, which meant repeal by "Republican" (representative) legislation. Thus Clay was an emancipationist and Fee an abolitionist, just as were Lincoln and Garrison, respectively.

This difference of procedure against slavery caused Clay not to defend Fee's course of action, which precipitated mob violence in Madison County and finally, late in December, 1859, caused Fee and other Bereans to be expelled from the county. In this wise, Clay ceased to champion the cause of Berea College and consequently he might be denied the honor, in the truest sense, of being one of its founders, even though he gave land and money to start the institution and invited Mr. Fee to come to Madison to continue his program against slavery.—John G. Fee, *Autobiography*, pp. 101-105. Also Cassius Marcellus Clay's *Memoirs, Writings, and Speeches*, pp. 241-247.

Chapter IV

27. The Economic Evils of Slavery.

Dr. McDougle, in his *Slavery in Kentucky, 1792-1865*, pp. 26-27, makes this interesting statement: "Was slavery profitable to the Kentucky Planters? In the many debates on the slavery question which took place after 1830 no one ever stood out in the affirmative. The only ones to discuss the economic side of the issue were those in opposition to slavery. As has often been said of the Kentucky situation, 'the program was to use Negroes to raise corn to feed hogs to feed Negroes, who raised more corn to feed more hogs.' Tobacco was the largest crop raised in the State and corn came next. Neither proved to be peculiarly adapted to slave labor. There were few large plantations in the State where it could be made advantageous. What Negro work there was to be done was never confined to any particular kind of cultivation but was used in the manner of farm labor today in the State. Squire Turner, of Madison County, in the Constitutional Convention of 1849 made a careful summary of the existing economic problems of slavery. 'There are,' said he, 'about $61,000,000 worth of slave property in the State which produces less than three per cent profit on the capital invested, or about half as much as the moneyed capital would yield. There are about 200,000 slaves in Kentucky. Of these about seventy-five per cent are superannuated, sick, women in unfit condition for labor, and infants unable to work, who yield no profit. Show me a man that has forty or fifty slaves on his estate, and if there are ten out of that number who are available and valuable, it is as much as you can expect. But my calculation allows you to have seventy-five per cent who are barely able to maintain themselves, to pay for their own clothing, fuel, house room, and doctors' bills. Is there any gentleman who has a large number of slaves who will say that they are any more profitable than that?'

"No one in the convention answered the last question put by Squire Turner. But regardless of such an economic condition, not a single piece of remedial legislation was passed and the members of the Constitutional Convention added a provision to the Bill of Rights which rooted the slavery system firmer than ever. That most admirable of all southern characters, and at the same time the most difficult to understand, the Kentucky master, took little heed of a question of dollars and cents when it interfered with his moral and humanitarian sentiments. He had inherited, in most cases, the slaves that were his. He knew well enough that the system did not pay, but supposing that he should turn his slaves loose, what would become of them? What could they do for a living? The experience of later years proved that his apparently obstinate temperament was mixed with a good deal of wisdom, for once the slaves were set free their status was not to any great extent ameliorated if they went abroad from the plantation where they had lived from childhood."

Dr. W. D. Wetherford in *The Negro from Africa to America,* p. 223, says: "Slavery absorbed all free capital and thus made it impossible for the South to accumulate enough surplus wealth to enter largely into manufacturing. The result was that her own cotton must be sent north or to England and then manufactured into cloth and sold back to her with the added cost of transportation and profits for those who acted as the middle men. 'Outside of the plantation buildings and moderate accumulation of buildings and stocks of goods in a few cities, the South knew but two forms of wealth, land and slaves.' Traveling through Virginia, Olmsted was amazed at the lack of industrial plants, for he observed plenty of water power, he saw the raw material about him, and he knew the great expense of transportation from the North. Of this importation he writes: 'No man can form an adequate idea of the extent of this trade unless he travel through the southern states. Scarcely a broom, a clock, a boot, or shoe, or anything of the kind is used in the South that is not manufactured by northern industry; and yet all articles used can be readily manufactured here as well as there, and, if taken hold of by some enterprising men, would be found most profitable.' "

In this respect Kentucky differed little from the cotton states. She had much water power (Madison County has sixty-five miles frontage on the Kentucky River) but slave labor confined her interest to agriculture. There never could be much capital; yet the wills of slave-owning Madisonians show that many of them had managed to put aside several thousand dollars in cash.

Chapter V

28. The widow Bogie was evidently the second wife (Polly Hughes) of James Bogie, who died in 1832 and was buried in the old Indian Fort Cemetery not far from the stone home which Andrew Bogie (1768-1823) built in 1796. Her first husband

left her considerable property, and Thomas M. Hart, her second husband, went to live with her in the old stone house.—"Bogie Record," a manuscript genealogy of the Bogie family in the possession of Jessie Bogie, on Silver Creek.

29. BOONESBOROUGH.

"The arrival of Daniel Boone and his party at the Kentucky River on April 1, 1775, was the beginning of the town of Boonesborough, which thus became the second settlement in Kentucky. Harrodstown, or Harrodsburg, as the place was later called, had been settled in June, 1774, by James Harrod and a party of Virginians, who abandoned the place late in July, 1774, because of Indian hostilities. They returned, however, March, 1775, and made Harrodsburg a permanent settlement, thus antedating the settlement at Boonesborough by seventeen days.

"Boonesborough played an important part in the early history of Kentucky. By the time of its incorporation in October, 1779, a town plat of twenty acres had been laid off into streets and 119 lots. It was estimated that fifty acres more would soon be needed for the same purpose. The remainder (570 acres) of the section of land allotted the town was to be used as 'commons' by the townspeople. The act of incorporation named Daniel Boone, Richard Calloway, James Estill, and seven others as trustees. They declined to serve, however, and in 1787 a supplementary law vested the government in ten other men, including Green Clay, William Irvine, and Robert Rodes.

"The town may be said to have had an auspicious beginning. It was established by the Transylvania Company, whose purpose was to found a colony west of the Allegheny Mountains. It had the first considerable fortification, and it was the first seat of government in what later became Kentucky. One of its citizens, Richard Calloway, obtained the first ferry right (October, 1779) in Kentucky at Boonesborough, and it was the first in Kentucky to be incorporated (October, 1779). The town was also first in other particulars, but it was doomed to oblivion as an urban community.

"It appears that in 1789 Boonesborough had 'upwards of a hundred and twenty houses,' and in 1792 it was conspicuous for its shipments of tobacco in barges down the Kentucky River. In

1792, Green Clay, William Calk, William Irvine, and thirty other Kentuckians offered the State 18,550 acres of land and 2,630 pounds sterling to locate its capital at Boonesborough. The town's prosperity, however, continued to wane. The census of 1810 gives its population as sixty-eight, and other government records show that it was intermittently a United States postoffice until December 4, 1866, when, it appears, postal service was discontinued and not resumed until the time of rural free delivery.

"The place today has not even a country store, and there remains no vestige of the old cemetery which had its beginning within the walls of the fort. Even the last of the three giant sycamores, which witnessed many important stirring events in the first decade of Kentucky's history, was removed to Richmond late in 1932.

"This abortive colonial enterprise, however, was a great asset to the expansive revolutionary program of the Americans. It encouraged a considerable emigration to Kentucky, and the fort at Boonesborough rendered the greatest protection to the settlements south of the Ohio. Had the fort not withstood the long siege of September, 1778, the Indians and British would most likely have wiped out the other settlements in Kentucky and frustrated Clark in his attempt to hold the Illinois Country.

"This singular service in itself justifies the recognition of the colonial efforts of Henderson and his colleagues in founding Boonesborough as a major service in the building of our Nation. Had there been no Transylvania Company, there would have been no Boonesborough, and that might have meant the defeat of George Rogers Clark and the probable loss of the Northwest Territory in the Treaty of 1783."—J. T. Dorris, *A Glimpse at Historic Madison County*, etc., pp. 11-18.

CHAPTER VI

30. It appears that Abner Oldham (1783-1852), who had considerable land on Muddy Creek and the Kentucky River and who shipped bacon and tobacco to New Orleans and even to Cuba (going to the latter place himself once), brought George Weddle (1794-1863) from New Orleans to build a water mill on Muddy Creek. French Tipton states that Alf Williams told him that a

man named Jones built the mill and sold it to Weddle and that the place later burned "with 100 barrels of whiskey" in it, and that Weddle rebuilt it.

The mill stood about a hundred yards west of the creek and was run by a race which entered the building and passed over a huge wheel that is falling apart today in the wet ground room of the structure. The big hewed timbers and the stone foundation indicate that the old mill will stand many more decades.

Weddle was followed by a man named Walden, who was succeeded by W. C. Ogg about 1870. Ogg ran the mill until near 1890 and then Sam Griggs obtained the management. Its operation was discontinued soon after the opening of the twentieth century. The distillery was closed much earlier, and only a pile of stones indicates its site near the mill.—Miller's *History and Genealogies,* p. 514; The Tipton Papers, Memorandum Book, pp. 181-191.

Alf Williams was a builder of water mill wheels.—Tipton Papers, Book O, p. 95.

31. This was before Jerry (J. B.), another son who now lives in the fine old brick Samuel Estill home (built in 1840's) on Silver Creek, was born. Green, who is now along in the eighties, lives not far from Union.

32. The bear in this story, it appears, had escaped from captivity and remained at large for a time in the community. Old Caesar was a most estimable Negro, who for many years was a member of Old Cane Spring Church, for which he was janitor until relieved by the trustees in December, 1870, as shown by Volume II of the church's minutes.

33. On May 29, 1857, Edward W. Hawkins was hanged at Irvine, Estill County, Kentucky, for the murder of a sheriff and his deputy, who had him in custody for stealing a horse from Hezekiah Oldham, of Old Cane Springs. Thus ended the varied, startling, and revolting criminal career of a handsome, intelligent young man (not yet twenty-one), whose crimes began at a very early age in Kentucky, were continued in Kansas Territory, Missouri, Ohio, and finally resulted in his execution in his native county. His public execution was a momentous event that

was attended by people from near and far. "The Hanging of Hawkins" is still a subject of conversation in Estill and Madison counties. See Estill County, Kentucky, *Circuit Court Records* for 1857, and *The Confessions of Edward W. Hawkins,* published by the Irvine, Kentucky, *Tribune* in 1906. Mrs. Chas. L. Searcy, who lives near Waco, states that her father, William Q. Covington, attended this hanging with his little son Robert, who often said thereafter in his sister's presence that he wished he had not seen the man hanged. For years the scaffold was allowed to remain, and even today the place is pointed out to the visitor.

Chapter VII

34. The time Aunt Sally and her Sam were sold into Kentucky was evidently about 1820. The 1798 slave code of the State had forbidden the importation of slaves and fixed the penalty at $300, unless the importer brought them in "for his own use. . . .", or unless "persons emigrating to this State" brought "their own slaves with them." This law was later amended, as Dr. McDougle states, so as to "show that the whole theory of non-importation is summed up in the word *intent*. It was the intent with which the slaves were introduced, and to this alone the penalty attached . . . . Once these slaves were within the State there was no penalty provided if they were sold." Thus the slave population of Kentucky increased through importation, notwithstanding laws which were purposely intended to discourage such increase. In 1833, however, a law was enacted forbidding the importation of slaves for even personal use. Opposition to this measure increased until 1849, when it was amended to allow persons to bring slaves into the State "for their own use."—William Littell, *The Statute Law of Kentucky,* Vol. II, pp. 119, 293; McDougle, *Slavery in Kentucky,* pp. 43-49.

35. McDougle, in his *Slavery in Kentucky,* pp. 22-23, says: "It would appear from all the evidence at hand that while Kentucky furnished many slaves for the southern market there was no general internal slave trade, as a commercial enterprise. There were in Louisville, however, a few heartless business men who took advantage of the decreasing value of slave labor in

Kentucky and the rising prices of slaves in the far South. In this respect, Kentucky became a field of supply for the slave markets of the lower South. . . . The author of *Slavery and Internal Slave Trade in the United States* estimated that 80,000 slaves were annually exported from seven states to the South. He gave no figures that were not his own estimates. He ranked the seven states, however, in the order of the number of slaves which he thought they furnished as follows: Virginia, Maryland, North Carolina, Kentucky, Tennessee, Missouri, and Delaware.

"Martin estimates that Kentucky sent on the average about 5,000 slaves to the southern market. Again this must be considered purely conjectural. It is reasonable to suppose that during the last two decades of the slavery era there were few slaves imported into Kentucky that were intended for the purely Kentucky market. What Negroes came into Kentucky were for the most part on their way to the more profitable southern trade." —Also see W. H. Townsend's graphic account of the slave trade in Kentucky in his *Lincoln and His Wife's Home Town*, pp. 88-111, 216-222.

36. THE AFRICAN BACKGROUND OF AMERICAN NEGRO SUPERSTITIONS.

Dr. Wetherford, in his *The Negro from Africa to America*, pp. 45-46, says: "It thus arises that the second constituent element in African religion is spirits. These are of three kinds. First, spirits conterminous with God, having always existed, but never considered quite equal to God. Second, spirits created by God, but seemingly playing a very small part in the thinking or religion of the African. And third, spirits which are the souls of departed men. Speaking of these spirits, Mary Kingsley says: 'Their number is infinite and their powers varied as human imagination can make them.' 'Individual spirits of the same class vary in power; some are strong of their sort, some weak.'

"*Each Person Has Two Spirits.* Each human being has two spirits, one the soul spirit, the other the body spirit. The spirit which corresponds to our conception of the soul lives after death, but the body spirit died with the body. Dr. Nassau thinks this false conception of a double spirit has caused not a few Africans to be buried before they are dead, and only the body spirit is there shaking and troubling the body. He tells of such supposedly dead persons coming to consciousness on the way to the grave, and others having roused themselves in their death struggle to sitting postures in their shallow graves where they have barely been covered by a thin layer of dirt. There seems also to be a belief in a dream soul which can wander at will even while the person is alive.

"*Placating the Spirits.* When a man dies his spirit adds itself to that innumerable company of spirits which fill the world about us. The spirit needs food and care just as it did in its human incarnation, save that it now only consumes the essence of the food, leaving the visible or material food, which is eaten by the natives. A hut is built for the spirit of the departed man and food is regularly taken and left by the relatives. 'I have seen in these sacred huts a dish of boiled plantain or a plate of fish. This food is generally not removed until spoiled. Sometimes, where the gift is a very large one, a feast is made; people and spirit are supposed to join in the festival, and nothing is left to spoil. That it is of use to the spirit is fully believed.' 'Among the Ivani it was formerly customary, and no doubt still is, on the death of a chief or big person, to pour a couple of casks of rum or palm wine on the ground or over his grave, the idea being to provide the departed soul with a sufficient supply of spirits for the entertainment of his ghostly visitors.' In Nigeria, 'It is also customary to bury implements, weapons, insignia of office, ornaments, and other articles, such as cloth, wearing apparel, plates, furniture, powder, pottery, wooden or clay images, in addition to the sacrificial victims, human and animal. The reason given in explanation of this custom is, as has already been pointed out, that while the former are for the use of the departed soul in spirit-land, the latter are his personal attendants.' Among the Inaku of the Niger valley it is customary to bury the chiefs inside the village, to build a hut over the grave, 'which is always swept and kept clean, and offerings of food and medicines are regularly placed in two holes which are made in front of the mound.'

"*American Survivals.* The writer has found a survival of this old custom in America. Wandering through a country cemetery in Hale County, Alabama, he noticed a number of fresh graves in the Negro section of the cemetery, and stuck into the fresh dirt of each grave mound were the half-emptied bottles of medicine which the deceased had evidently been using before death. On investigation it was found that every Negro grave in the cemetery had had some such remains left on it. Doubtless this custom is a lineal descendant from the African custom, but, of course, has lost its significance and probably no Negro now following it has any definite idea why he does so. Thus does a custom far outlive its original purpose."

CHAPTER VIII

37. Sometimes, as in the case of Mr. Jackson, Kentucky parents name their sons General, Colonel, or Captain, and even Governor. A few years ago the college in Richmond graduated a young man named Colonel Hammonds, who is now County Superintendent of Schools of Garrard County.

38. "Amos M. Deatherage, son of Bird Deatherage, married Susannah J. Lipscomb, daughter of Nathan Lipscomb and Nancy Gentry, his wife, of Madison County, Kentucky, December 20, 1838. Nathan Lipscomb's heirs.... deeded 320 acres of land lying on both sides of Muddy Creek.... to Amos M. Deatherage and his wife, who established their home upon the land allotted to them and there lived and died."—W. H. Miller, Mss. Vol. II, p. 256.

39. This hill is near the elevation where Gustin Hart beheld Old Cane Springs on the day of his arrival, as told in the first chapter.

40. NATHAN B. DEATHERAGE.

"Nathan Bird Deatherage was born in Madison County, Kentucky, December 17, 1843, and was reared on a farm. He received a common English education. On September 10, 1862, he enlisted in Company B, Kentucky Confederate Cavalry," in Col. D. Waller Chenault's regiment of Gen. John H. Morgan's command. He was in all subsequent engagements of that army until captured in Ohio.

"After being confined in Camp Chase one month Mr. Deatherage was taken with other prisoners to Camp Douglas where he was imprisoned nearly nineteen months, suffering and enduring all the hardships of that Federal prison. When exchanged and sent to Richmond, Virginia, he was one day late in reaching that point for the exchange and was sworn not to take up arms again. Before another exchange Gen. Robert E. Lee had surrendered all his forces, after which event Mr. Deatherage walked from Richmond, Virginia, to Mount Sterling, Kentucky, and from there to his home in Madison, where he resumed farming.

"In 1876 Mr. Deatherage was elected sheriff of his county commencing the duties of his office January 1, 1877. He was re-elected in 1878, but after his second term he returned to farming. In 1884 he made another successful race for the same office and was again re-elected in 1886. . . ."—W. H. Miller, Mss. Vol. II, p. 257.

Mr. Deatherage, in the *Confederate Veteran,* Vol. XXXVI (August, 1928), p. 305, tells the following about his war experiences: "We joined the Confederate army at Richmond, Kentucky, and were under Colonel Chenault in the 11th Kentucky Cavalry, Morgan's command. We started on that famous raid from Tennessee about July 1, 1863, through Kentucky, Ohio, Indiana, about a thousand-mile ride. My colonel was killed July 4, 1863, and also my captain, Alex Tribble, and several of my company and regiment at Green River Bridge, near Columbia, Kentucky.

" 'Comrade John Fox [a friend of Mr. Deatherage, then living in Marion, Kansas] was not on the noted Morgan raid, he having been made manager of the wagon train. We had fights nearly every day, one at Lebanon, Kentucky; crossed the Ohio River at Brandenburg. We rode night and day, and never dreamed once that Morgan would be captured. We were ahead of the Yankees and thought we could ride faster than they could. Most of the command was captured at Buffington Island, Ohio, but I was captured at Cheshire, Ohio. We were first sent to Columbus, Ohio, and then to Camp Douglas, about the 20th of August, 1863, and we were kept on about as little food the last year as men could live on, and when we started on our journey for exchange, heaven will not be any sweeter to me than the day we left prison. We went through Grant's army on the Potomac River, and saw what looked like

50,000 blue coats. The Yankees looked fat and their horses were fat; and when we crossed over into the Confederate lines, the few soldiers we saw were thin in flesh, their clothes worn out, their horses thin. We landed at Richmond, Virginia, on March 2, 1865, and I saw more men on the streets of that city than I saw in the army, their heads and arms and legs all wrapped up, all disabled.

" 'The war did not last long after we got to Richmond, as General Lee surrendered on the 9th of April. When the soldiers started home in every direction, it was sad to meet them. No one knew what would be his fate after he got home. I had not seen Fox for twenty months, but we came together at Mount Sterling, Kentucky. He was riding, and he never let me ride one step. I got used to walking and could keep ahead of the cavalry, about 750 old soldiers in the gang. The day after we got to Mount Sterling, we were put on horses bareback, and about one hundred and fifty men who had been in prison were sent to Lexington, guarded by a company of Negroes, and then discharged. We got to Lexington about the 1st of May, 1865, and that ended the last day of our service for the Confederacy.

" 'Now I am hale and hearty at the age of eighty-four, and do all I want to do in the way of farming; have been to thirty-five of the thirty-eight reunions of the U. C. V., and don't want to miss one in the future.' "

Mr. Deatherage's first wife, Mary Ann Oldham, died in June, 1869, and was buried in the Noland-Chambers family graveyard in the clump of trees shown in the rear of Colonel John Noland's old home overlooking the magnificent panorama of the Kentucky River, which she loved so dearly (see picture facing page 5). From this place she was removed to the beautiful Richmond cemetery after the death in 1927 of Mr. Deatherage's second wife, Mary Noland, who was her cousin and the daughter of Captain Nathan Noland. On his death in 1932, Mr. Deatherage was buried between these two Marys. In 1929 he married Mrs. Nanny May McCord, who survives him.

Nathan Deatherage was a successful farmer and business man. His ability and integrity were indicated by long terms of service as a bank director, as trustee of the Madison Female Institute, as a member of the board of directors of the Confederate Home at Pewee Valley, as an elder in the First Christian Church in Richmond, and as commander of the Kentucky Branch of the Veterans of the Confederacy. He was kind-hearted and philanthropic, and the latchstring of his home was always out. His dining room was probably more crowded with guests than that of any other citizen of Madison County in his lifetime. J. W. Deatherage, his nephew, who lived with him for fifteen or twenty years, counted the different guests during one average month and found that ninety-six persons thus enjoyed his hospitality.

Mr. Deatherage's sympathetic interest in Berea College while he was sheriff in the 1870's and 1880's won him friends among the college authorities there. He and John G. Fee were particularly friendly. Even in later years this friendship appeared to be manifested toward the Deatherage family.

In 1929 Mr. Deatherage was defeated as a Democratic candidate for membership in the lower house of the General Assembly. Apparently his advanced age caused many in his party to decline to support his candidacy.

Mr. Deatherage often exhibited rare humor, and his terse and witty expressions frequently elicited admiration. The range of his long and useful life may be indicated by repeating a statement he made to a niece a little while after his third marriage. "Well, Nettie," he said, "your Aunt Mary and I went honeymooning on horseback; your cousin Mary and I went honeymooning in a buggy; my present wife and I went honeymooning in an automobile. The next time I go mooning I am going in an airplane." He passed this life May 23, 1932, in his eighty-ninth year, retaining his remarkable health, his good nature, and subtle wit to the end.

41. In the autumn of 1927 the national fox hunt was held in Madison County with headquarters at Richmond. The region west of Muddy Creek was the scene of one of the "trials" at this time. In 1932, when the national organization had its headquarters in Lexington, one of the "trials" was started at Boonesborough in Madison County. The State Association held its hunts in Madison County in 1926 and 1933.

Chapter IX

42. In 1935-36 farmers along Muddy Creek and vicinity sold their cedar rail fences, many of which were built more than a century ago, to pencil, tub, bucket, and souvenir manufacturers. Often the purchasers compensated the farmers by building first-class wire fences with cedar posts along the entire length of the rail fences removed. Old cedar log houses were also purchased for the same purpose. In 1936 a saw mill was located in Richmond to prepare lumber from cedars growing in Madison and surrounding counties.

43. The present owner of this place, W. C. Brandenberg, uses a hydraulic system to convey the water from this spring to his house.

44. The minutes of the church for May, 1866, state that "the church agrees that there shall be no more schools taut in their meting house." For September of the same year this entry appears in the minutes: ". . . the church agrees to let a school house be bilt on their lot with restriction not to injuary the church property." The house built on this property was moved away after a few years.

45. Susan Oldham died in the late 1860's. Temperance became the second wife of David G. Martin, and Nettie, whose real name was Eleanor Bird, eventually married John Cabell Chenault, the author of the original manuscript of *Old Cane Springs*. She died in August, 1916. Nettie has always been a popular name in the Oldham family, and in this instance the girl was called Nettie, even though she had been christened Eleanor Bird. The little Nettie of this narrative became a very beautiful woman, as the story indicates. She and her husband were a devoted couple. Having married Mary Ann's sister, Judge Chenault, in speaking for his cousin, Augustine Hart, naturally praises Nathan Bird Deatherage and Mary Ann Oldham.

46. William Q. Covington was a prominent farmer who lived a short distance down the creek from Othniel Oldham. He had a brother, Coleman, who served a term in the State Legislature (1855-57) and was the Covington referred to by John G.

Fee in his account of the mob episode at Lewis Chapel (The Big Bend schoolhouse). The Covingtons were strong in their opposition to the abolitionists. Their father, William Covington (1783-1869), was the son of Robert Covington (1760-1841), a Revolutionary soldier, who settled on Muddy Creek near the village of Elliston in 1792. It is said that Coleman never recovered from the severe financial loss occasioned by the freeing of his slaves after the war. His flour and carding mill was at Waco.

Chapter X

47. The reader should remember that 1860 was the day of the "Little Brown Jug" and that drinking was much more general than it has been since. There was not likely to be a social gathering of the nature of a corn shucking in those days without the host's serving whiskey. Even in the Union army an effort was made to provide liquor for the soldiers in the camps, just as in the World War the soldiers were provided with cigarettes. The fact that liquor was forbidden during the recent war shows how much human conduct has improved since the War between the States, a condition that is indeed encouraging.

48. Mr. Green Noland (see Chapter VI) remembers attending, as a very small boy, a moonlight corn shucking at Walter Norris' and hearing the wonderful singing of the Negroes on that occasion. He said rather indignantly, however, that all the Negroes got for their labor was whiskey and a good supper.

49. Robert Turpin's Reminiscences.

Robert Turpin, the son of Haden Turpin and now eighty-two years old, remembers many interesting things pertaining to life in Old Cane Springs. He knew Aunt Creech Sally as a fine old Negress, whose Jake, "a yellow darkie," took care of Cabell Chenault's farm down on Muddy Creek, and also Aunt Millie, whose cabin was placed at a distance from the regular slave quarters at Robert Chenault's.

Mr. Turpin (as do many others) calls the Rock House "Camp Boone Hollow," thereby associating it with Daniel Boone's life in that part of Madison. He has always known of the place as having been a Confederate hide-out. Union soldiers, he states, were often seen along the road through Texas. He never attended a moonlight corn shucking but he heard the Negroes singing from a distance on such occasions. His belief is that the miller Weddle was called Si or Silas instead of George.

Whizaker left an indelible impression on Mr. Turpin. He told an amusing incident when the old spotted mule was suddenly appropriated by young Harvey Chenault to carry him "a-courtin'." The young man walked to church one Sunday at Cane Spring, where he met some interesting young women, whom he concluded to accompany home. They were riding horses, which made it necessary for him to go home for a horse. As he ran toward his father's house he met a Negro on Whizaker, and, deciding that a mule in hand was worth a horse in the barn, he breathlessly and unceremoniously jerked the Negro off the mule, mounted it, and proceeded as fast as the animal would go to overtake the girls.

As "Old Spot" went galloping down the road the church people wondered what Harvey was about, and when they saw him approach the young women, whose horses were frightened at the sudden advent of the fine knight on his wheezing, whizzing spotted mule, their sense of humor and appreciation of the ridiculous were stimulated to expressions of amusement. Old Whizaker thereafter meant more to them than Cabell Chenault's Cuff's Old Spot.

Mr. Turpin knew old Caesar well and sold him a horse once. Pike, he says, became a wagoner after the war.—Interview with Robert Turpin, near Red House, August 9, 1936.

AUNT ANN BRADLEY'S REMINISCENCES.

This fine old Negro woman was born in June, 1854, the slave of Jake Huguely, who lived near Red House in Madison County. Her father belonged to a Mr. Richardson, who lived four or five miles away in Madison, toward Lexington. Her father usually came to see her mother and the children on Wednesday and Saturday nights, often remaining until Sunday evening on the latter visit.

Mr. Huguely owned about twenty slaves, but he was not a hard master. He allowed his Negroes to make money in various ways, but he objected to their paying any of it to his young sons, whom he found teaching them to read for pay. The boys wanted more spending money than their father would give them and engaged themselves to teach the slaves to read. Their teaching, of course, was done in secret, and even when their father had forbidden it, the lads were tempted to disobey, causing their parent to lock the doors at night to keep them in.

Aunt Ann understood that Negroes who sought to learn to read would be sold down South. In fact, she says that masters often threatened to sell slaves down South who were hard to discipline, believing that such threats would cause the disobedient slaves to improve their conduct. She remembers her master's selling a slave "to Dick Harris, the father of Dr. John Harris," of Richmond. She recalls seeing the Negro taken away on a mule with his hands tied behind him. It is her belief that the slave was to be sent to the South.

Salt, Aunt Ann says, was often taken to Africa to exchange for slaves. Harvey Cobb, whose descendants live in Madison County, traded salt for Negroes, and at least one such slave was brought to Madison. (Salt was certainly more desirable as a medium of exchange in such commerce than rum, which New England Puritans used as slave traders in Colonial days.)

When news of freedom came to Red House, Mr. Huguely called his slaves together and told them that they were as free as he was. Aunt Ann remembers the strange feeling which came over her—a feeling of fear, for her mother and father were both dead by that time and she wondered what would become of her. She says the slaves generally did not welcome their freedom.

Aunt Ann often heard her first husband tell of his mother's being sold down South from Bath County, Kentucky. To keep from being punished the woman hid out for two weeks, slipping in at night to nurse her baby. (The man referred to above was then a big boy.) Finally the master got word to the slave that he had sold her and that she should come in to be delivered to her new master.

When the woman came in, her first master insisted on whipping her, as he had intended when she began hiding out, her new master being willing. Thereupon the slave displayed a knife when thus approached and declared that she would kill herself before submitting to a whipping. This threat caused the punishment to be dispensed with, and the mother with a wave of her hand bade farewell to her children and went away "down South" with her new master.—Interview with Aunt Ann Bradley, near Red House, August 10, 1936.

Chapter XI

50. The books referred to are evidently the scientific treatises of Alfred Russell Wallace, Sir Charles Lyell, and Charles Darwin, which appeared in the 1850's. Darwin's *Origin of Species by Means of Natural Selection* was published in 1859.

51. OLD CANE SPRING CHURCH.

"We the Baptis Church of Christ Cane Spring Meting house on the waters of Muddy Creek, Madison County, was constituted, 24 August, 1803, our number [of members being] 39, by our Reverent Brethern James Quisenberry and James Hagerd, on believing the word of God contained in the old and new testament is the only infalible rule of faith and practice, on believing in the finel preciance [perseverance] of the Saints through grace to glory and on believing in baptism by immersion." With this simple statement of faith and with a brief "Constitution and covenant" and a "decorum," Old Cane Spring Church began its interesting history. It joined the North District Association and after "traveling" awhile for a preacher unanimously chose David Chenault, who at the time was pastor of the Flat Woods Church near Waco.

Elder Chenault was a prosperous farmer, on whose land the church was located. He and his wife were received into the church by letter on the first Saturday in June, 1806, and his long ministry there was formally begun. He served several other churches too during his fifty years in the ministry, but never charged anything for his services. It was his belief that " 'A man who preaches for money is a gospel peddler' "; nevertheless he cunningly remarked: the " 'Gospel's as free as the water that runs in the branch, but if you've got any poor calves or colts run 'em down to my farm.' " He appears to have been relieved of his pastoral duties at Old Cane Spring Church about 1830 to preach at White Oak.

After Elder Chenault's ministry Cane Spring was served by William Hickey, Henry H. Rennels, and G. M. Thompson. In May, 1856, William Rupard, of Clark County, was chosen minister. This pious gentleman served the church for forty years or longer. He was generally beloved by both whites and blacks. One communicant, Mrs. Shelby Jett, who is now in her seventy-sixth year, relates having seen him wash the feet of Gabriel Slaughter, the Negro janitor of the church, in the footwashing part of the service, as a tribute to the Master whose will on earth he zealously endeavored to do.

In July, 1807, the church chose William White as deacon. It had already (in 1803) formulated a "decorum" for the government of the church, had chosen trustees to look after the property, and had also determined to keep a "Record" of its proceedings. The first house of worship was evidently a wooden structure. The minutes indicate that the existing brick building was erected in 1812-13 on land belonging to Elder David Chenault, who in 1816 gave the church a title to an acre of ground around the house.

A committee "appropriated two seats [pews] on the northwest side of the meeting house for the black people" in July, 1816, and ultimately (1856) a special door convenient to these seats was provided. This entrance was discontinued when the Negroes came to worship elsewhere. In earlier days the pulpit was near the main entrance but later it was placed in the rear.

The records indicate that the church was not only a religious body but that it was also a governing institution. The members were subject to disciplinary measures which tended to discourage evil-doing. During the first thirty or forty years of the life of the church the congregation held court, as it were, at its regular Saturday monthly meetings. In this wise charges of irregular conduct against members might be considered and disposed of. Cases of immorality, drunkenness, profanity, Sabbath-breaking, stealing, libel, fighting, and the like were solemnly adjudicated. Frequently committees were appointed to remonstrate with the accused to cause such persons to improve their conduct. Sometimes a refusal "to hear the church" caused the recalcitrant to be "excluded" from fellowship. Often the verdict was exclusion when the accused could not or did not "satisfy the church." Instances are on record where the person excluded subsequently did "satisfy the church" and was readmitted to membership.

In August, 1817, the congregation determined that "all verbal contracts should be [regarded as] valid in the church." At that particular time John Henderson complained by letter that "Br. William Noland had penned him up so that he could not get to meting nor to mill and that his stock could not get home without being drove round Br. John Noland and [also] for failing to comply with his contract about a road." The church "took the matter on motion" and after some consideration appointed a committee to visit the "premises . . . and take any testimony in writing which they think cannot be got on the church floor . . ." At the September meeting the committee "reported that Br. Henderson was not injured and the church exonerated Br. Noland from the charges."

But the friction between Henderson and Noland got another brother into trouble. At the January, 1818, meeting, "Br. William Noland laid in a complaint against Br. Jonathan Floyd for saying that Br. and Sister Henderson had tryed all ways for satisfaction with Br. Noland and all the satisfaction that Br. Noland would give them was 'there is a bar; take me to it.' The church took up the matter," but continued the case to the February meeting, and at the March session "Br. Floyd contradicting himself in his statements and failing to give the church satisfaction was excluded."

In this manner the Old Cane Spring Church of Christ was a strong leavening force for good in the community. Its sphere of activity suggests earlier times when the church often functioned in the capacity of the modern state. It is interesting to note the appearing infrequency of such disciplinary cases in the records of the church after the first three or four decades. Evidently as the community became less primitive, the moral standards of the people improved, the power of the civil law became more evident, and the spiritual influence of the church became more fruitful.

But the records reveal other difficulties which tried the souls of the church members. Even though six full pages of the minutes for the period from October, 1829, to April, 1831, inclusive, were cut from the record book and apparently destroyed, there remains enough in the minutes and in other sources to indicate that the teachings of Alexander Campbell and other kindred spirits disturbed Old Cane Springs. As early as July, 1827, the North District Association had convened in the church there with Elder David Chenault presiding as moderator. The renowned Elder John Smith, often called "Raccoon John," was present and was arraigned by the brethren for preferring the *Holy Spirit* to the *Holy Ghost* in the baptismal ritual, for preferring actually to break the bread when taking the sacrament, and for preferring a more recent translation of the Bible to the King James version. Chenault and a big majority were strongly against him and such innovations.

Elders Chenault and Smith crossed swords again in the summer of 1828, and in February, 1829, Smith arrived at Chenault's home with Josiah Collins, a prominent member of the Flat Woods Church near Waco. Smith announced that they had come to stay all night with Chenault and that he (Smith) would preach in the Cane Spring Church on the morrow, making it clear that if the church could not be entered the services would be held in Elder Chenault's home!

On Saturday the people assembled at the church but could not enter. Whereupon, Elder Smith sent word to Chenault that if he did not send a key to unlock the building, he and the congregation would forthwith go to his home to hold services. "A key was sent, the doors were quickly opened, and the house was soon made warm, and John Smith went in and sowed the seeds of an abundant harvest that day from the pulpit of Elder Chenault!"—See John Augustus Williams, *Life of Elder John Smith,* pp. 180-190, 281-285.

In brief, dissension soon split the church, but not beyond reparation. A second volume of the minutes shows that in April, 1830, "The United Baptist Church of Christ at Cane Spring" came into being. A new decorum was formulated and David Chenault was "continued" as pastor. The other element continued as the Cane Spring Church of Christ, but joined the Tates Creek Association (September, 1831) and recognized Allen Embree as pastor in February, 1832.

Fortunately the two congregations agreed to use the same building and thus left the way open for ultimate reunion. An entry in the first minute book, however, stating that a committee request "David Chenault to return the Bible and hymn books to the table drawer [in the church] and let them remain there," suggests the existence of some friction in the use of common property.

The two congregations met on different Saturdays in the month until 1841, when it appears that they united for worship only. At any rate, the minutes of the Cane Spring Church of Christ give, on the final pages of the first record book of the old church, the lamentable circumstances of the separation on the first Saturday in April, 1830, and state at length the desirability of union with the other congregation for fellowship. Thereafter the minutes indicate that on a given Saturday in each month one or the other of the two bodies with the other present met at the church for services. Sometimes the record is for the "Baptist Church of Christ"; at other times for the "Cane Spring Church of Christ." No entries at all appear for some months, especially in the late 1840's.

The monthly meetings appear more regularly in the 1850's, and in May, 1854, the names Cane Spring Church of Christ and Baptist Church of Christ (the word "United" had been omitted for some time) cease altogether and the minutes are recorded under the heading "The Predestinarian Baptist Church of Christ at Cane Spring." Henceforth there seems to be only one organization, but no reason for such changes was recorded. The word "Predestinarian" was dropped in 1869, but no explanation for the omission was given in the minutes. In March, 1872, the word "Old" was added, and thereafter the Old Baptist Church of Christ at Cane Spring was the titular designation. Mr. W. C. Griggs, of Union, an older communicant, believes the changes in names came with changes in secretaries, and that no other significance need be given the use of different names. A union of the two divisions, then, may be said to have been effected in 1841.

Meetings during the last twenty-five years or longer have been less frequent than formerly and the church at present is less evident than ever before in its history. For a century, however, it exercised a considerable beneficent influence, especially on those who lived in the northeastern part of Madison County. The picture facing page 44 was taken on the occasion of an all-day meeting on Sunday, June 7, 1936, when several preachers spoke and a bountiful dinner was served on the grounds in the old-fashioned way.

The old spring nearby, after which the church was named, promises to flow on forever, even though this institution of man may cease to exist. The spring is like Tennyson's Brook: "Men may come and men may go, but I go on forever."

Chapter XII

52. Elbridge J. Broaddus (1835-1918) was the son of Andrew Broaddus, who made a trip from Missouri in 1826 to Santa Fe, Mexico, with Kit Carson, another native of Madison County. On this trip Andrew was accidentally shot through the hand and it became necessary to amputate his arm. This was done in the crudest and most heroic manner. "The instruments used were a razor, an old saw, and, to arrest the hemorrhage, the king bolt taken from one of the wagons was heated and applied to serve as an actual cautery." The man lived to a ripe old age and was buried in 1872 on his own farm, which is now the home of J. W. Deatherage on the Four Mile pike in Madison County.—Dewitt Peters, *Kit Carson's Wild West*, pp. 28-30; Tipton Papers, Memorandum Book, p. 216.

"Elbridge J. was admitted to the bar at Richmond, Ky., in March, 1858, where he practiced law until 1867, when he moved to Chillicothe, Missouri. In 1874 he was elected Circuit Court Judge of the 17th Judicial District of Missouri for six years and several times re-elected." Subsequently he served twelve years as Chief Justice of the Kansas City, Missouri, Court of Appeals. He was married three times, his first wife being "Ann Chambers, daughter of John Chambers and Temperance Noland," of Madison County, Ky.—W. H. Miller, Mss. Vol. II, p. 194. French Tipton states, Memorandum Book, p. 216, that Elbridge J. Broaddus served as a captain in the C. S. A.

53. General Basil W. Duke's *Reminiscences*, pp. 223-242, gives an excellent description of the good times the Negroes had

at hog-killing time, Christmas, and on other occasions in Kentucky in the ante-bellum days. The General also emphasizes the fact that slavery in Kentucky was much milder than in the far South.

Chapter XIII

54. Some controversy has existed concerning the number of slaves in various parts or precincts of Madison County. The census of 1870 gives the following numbers of Negroes for each of the nine precincts and the town of Richmond. These figures cannot be far different from those in 1860. Union had 714; Elliston, 624; Yates (southeastern Madison), 778; Foxtown, 739; Richmond, 1,509; Town of Richmond, 749; Glades (Berea in the center), 548; Million (between Tates Creek and Silver Creek), 403; Poosey (between Silver Creek and Paint Lick), 118; Kirksville, 839.

Chapter XIV

55. See note 51 under Chapter XI for an account of William Rupard.

56. BASKET DINNERS AT THE CHURCH AND THE NORRIS-HISLE FAMILY REUNION.

The custom of having basket dinners on the church grounds also developed at Old Cane Spring. These have often been enjoyed at least once a year, especially during the summer. Ministers and other worshipers come from a wide area and an all-day meeting is held. Such an occasion was enjoyed on Sunday, June 7, 1936. Several ministers were present and spoke, and a crowd gathered, which far more than filled the church house. The people, however, confined themselves to talking, singing, praying, and eating and omitted the footwashing service which used to be observed.

In 1929, under the leadership of Will Norris, part owner of the Union Stockyards in Cincinnati, the Norris-Hisle Family Reunion was instituted. This social event is an annual affair that is enjoyed by hundreds of members of the two families and their friends on the last Saturday in July.

Thus far every reunion has been held on the old Hamilton Norris Homestead in a grove just across the road from the place where the magnificent view of the Kentucky River, shown in the illustration facing page 4, can be seen. Will Norris, who is now in the late seventies, is a grandson of Hamilton Norris and the son of Walter Norris referred to in Chapter X.

Formal morning and afternoon programs are planned for these reunions and delicious dinners are served on improvised tables. Suffice it to say that the gatherings are most enjoyable and beneficial. In this manner the kinsfolk who constitute these two pioneer families of Old Cane Springs renew the ties that blood relationship alone can bind, and then, as the shadows begin to lengthen, they return to their respective homes, strengthened in soul and body from communion with those most dear to them.

The writer enjoyed the coveted privilege of attending the last reunion (July, 1936). He was also present at the June, 1936, meeting at Old Cane Spring Church, when the picture opposite page 44 was taken.

57. THE CLAY BATTALION.

There was much excitement in Washington during the siege of Fort Sumter and immediately after the surrender of the fort on April 14, 1861. Among those in the Capital who believed that the defense of the city was inadequate and that Washington was in danger of being seized by the Secessionists and perhaps the President assassinated were Cassius M. Clay, of Madison County, Kentucky, and Senator James H. Lane, of Kansas. These men (apparently on Mr. Clay's initiative) organized and armed with weapons from the War Department a battalion of volunteer citizen soldiers to defend the Capital and especially the White House.

The two men operated independently until April 24th, when they were ordered to unite their forces and "take post at the United States Navy Yard for its protection." Mr. Clay wrote many years later: "When the two commands met, Lane desired the joint command to which I objected, as my force was much larger than his; and referring it to the soldiers themselves, I was made the commander of the battalion...." Vice-President Henry Wilson also wrote in his *History of the Rise and Fall of the Slave Power in America,* Vol. III, p. 171: "Cassius M. Clay was chosen leader, and the body was known as the Cassius M. Clay battalion. They patrolled the city that night [April 18], while a body, a division of the battalion, went to the White House, encamped in the East Room, and prepared to protect the President."

The battalion was dissolved soon after regiments arrived from northern states; and Mr. Clay also wrote: "Lincoln issued an order thanking me for my services; and presented me with a Colt's revolver, as a testimony of his regard." Late in life Mr. Clay gave this weapon to his friend, Col. J. W. Caperton, whose grandson, Rollins Burnam, of Richmond, now has it.

The illustration facing page 113 shows a part of the Clay battalion drawn up in front of the White House. President Lincoln and his cabinet are in the center of the group and Mrs. Lincoln is at an upper window. Mr. Clay is believed to be the man at the left in light trousers. It appears that this is the first time this picture has ever been published. See Mr. Clay's own work, *The Life of Cassius Marcellus Clay, Memoirs, Writings, and Speeches,* pp. 259-264.

58. Rev. William Rupard was a Republican and loyal to the Union. Captain Noland was a Democrat and more nearly a Southern sympathizer. His magnanimous act in inviting Major Burnam and Rev. Rupard to his home for dinner on this occasion did much to harmonize the two factions in Cane Spring Church. Especially did the Captain's diplomacy and common sense cause Rupard to retain his standing in the community.—Interview with Green Noland, a son of Captain Noland, on August 2, 1936.

W. H. Miller, Mss. Vol. II, p. 194, says: "Captain Nathan Noland was a successful farmer of Madison County—a man of very strong intellect and fine judgment. He was much beloved by all who knew him, and left a good name to his children and died a member of and in full fellowship of the Baptist Church at Cane Spring." He received the title of captain while commanding a company of local militia.

59. Frank Moore, *The Rebellion Record, A Diary of American Events,* Vol. IV, p. 56, gives: "A Negro's Account of the Wild Cat Retreat."

"A gentleman whose slave accompanied a young Confederate officer on the Wild Cat expedition asked the darky on his return to Nashville how long the army was on the march from its encampment to the battlefield. "About four days," was the reply. "Well, how long were they in marching back?" "About two days, massa." "Why, how is that, Joe? Could the men travel any faster back, when they were broken down with four days' march and a severe fight, than they traveled forward after a good rest in camp?" "Oh! I'll tell you what made the difference, massa," said old Joe; "it was the music. They marched toward Wild Cat to the tune of Dixie. When they marched back, the tune was: 'Fire in the mountains—run, boys, run!'"

The same author in his *Anecdotes, Poetry, and Incidents of the War North and South,* pp. 84-85, gives some interesting "Incidents in the Battle of Wild Cat."

60. The place called the Cedars in which the Rock House was located is now part of the large farm of Mrs. Nancy Harris. This hide-out of Confederate sympathizers looks as if it had been more nearly a considerable shelter in earlier times than it is now. It is from this locality especially that old cedar rail fences have recently been removed by pencil, tub, and bucket manufacturers.—See note 42 in Chapter IX.

Chapter XV

61. HOME GUARDS AND STATE GUARDS.

The Home Guards were preceded in Kentucky by the State Guards, which Simon Bolivar Buckner had organized under a law passed in March, 1860, and which were some sixty-one companies strong early in 1861. Apparently the State Guards were under the control of those who were in sympathy with the South and although these troops existed ostensibly to maintain the neutrality of the State in the armed controversy, there was abundant evidence that they were likely to cast their lot with the Confederacy.

This danger caused the Unionists of the State to cast about for a military force to offset the presence of the State Guards. The result was that the two opposing factions obtained the creation of a military board of five men (law of May 24, 1861) to control the armed forces of the State. This compromise allowed two distinct bodies of soldiers in Kentucky "to be placed on an equality and . . . to participate equally in an initial fund of $750,000."

"The Home Guards, in many respects, were a peculiar organization. They were not organized militia and were, therefore, not recognized as State troops and, hence, could not be called out of the county. As their name implied, they were to be strictly home guards. They were to receive their arms after the county judge should certify their organization, and they could hold them in their possession for five years, unless they were called in earlier. The distinct danger here arose of placing arms in the hands of irresponsible groups at a most critical time. The legislature carefully specified that none of the State armament should be used either against the North or the South, unless Kentucky were invaded . . ."

Naturally a competitive spirit developed immediately between the two factions in the process of obtaining arms. The Unionists appealed to the President, who adroitly and secretly sent arms to the Home Guards. Knowledge of this action naturally increased the bitterness between the two systems of guards. The Military Board, however, insisted on allowing the Home Guards to arm until their strength equaled that of the State Guards. "As time went on, the Unionists became more and more suspicious of the State Guards and sought to curb them." After certain other precautionary measures were applied the Military Board "proceeded against the State Guards by calling in all of their arms; but few guardsmen were so timid as to obey. As the crisis in Kentucky approached, the State Guards left in great numbers to join the Confederacy, and in September [1861] the legislature abolished that branch of the service altogether. . . . When Kentucky remade her military organization after actively joining the Federal side, she left the Home Guards as a sort of unorganized force; and because of their lack of restraint and responsibility they at times brought discredit upon themselves by their rash acts."—See E. Merton Coulter, *The Civil War and Readjustment in Kentucky*, pp. 82-91.

62. P. P. Ballard was also postmaster at Richmond during the period of the War between the States. According to the French Tipton Papers, Book X, p. 25, he was a member of the

legislature in 1849, which called the constitutional convention of that year. He was a Henry Clay Whig, who voted for Bell in 1860 and for Lincoln in 1864. He held several responsible positions in Madison County and was a highly esteemed citizen.

Chapter XVI

63. The Tipton Papers, Memorandum Book, p. 395, state that there was a company of Home Guards at Doylesville, which is far down Muddy Creek below Weddle's Mill. Companies are also listed at Richmond and Bear Wallow near Big Hill, but no information about the activities of the units is given. Boston Dillon was captain of the company at Bear Wallow until Major W. A. Coffey took charge.

64. An examination of a map of Kentucky will disclose the fact that the Rock House was on a direct line between Irvine in Estill County and Winchester in Clark. The Rock House was also on a direct line between Cumberland Gap and Cincinnati. Conditions along Muddy Creek, especially on the west side, were favorable to the passage of those whose movements were expected to be hidden from the Home Guards or any other Federal agency.

Chapter XVII

65. Prison camps were at Louisville, Kentucky; Columbus and Sandusky, Ohio; Baltimore and Point Lookout, Maryland; Chicago and Alton, Illinois; Boston, Massachusetts; New York Harbor; St. Louis, Missouri; Fort Delaware, Delaware; and Indianapolis, Indiana. Often prisoners became weary with such seclusion and on taking the oath of allegiance to the United States were given their freedom. Many times prisoners thus released re-entered the Confederate service. By May, 1863, the Federal authorities issued regulations for releases on oaths with the view of determining whether the applicants were really sincere in their desire to swear allegiance to the Union.

There were escapes from these prisons from time to time and those escaping were often apprehended and returned; but there were times when they succeeded in getting through the

Union lines to the South. The Rock House always stood ready to aid such escaped prisoners.

By the close of 1863 the Federal authorities adopted a rigid policy against permission to obtain freedom by taking the oath and they also became less willing to exchange prisoners, believing that such refusals would hasten the end of the war.

CHAPTER XVIII

66. Dr. Jeremiah Ayres lived near Texas, as the map of Old Cane Springs indicates. His residence, which is now owned and occupied by Mr. G. L. Edwards, is still an interesting place. There is an enchanting spring near the bottom of the hill on which the house stands, that flows continually with good drinking water.

67. Kentucky is famous for her specially cured "old hams" and "beaten biscuits."

CHAPTER XX

68. Camp Nelson, in Jessamine County, which is just across the Kentucky River from Madison, was a general recruiting place and rendezvous for Federal soldiers. The location was made a national cemetery soon after the war, and both Federals and Confederates are buried there. It is a beautiful and interesting place, and was named for General William Nelson, who commanded the Union forces at Richmond, August 29-30, 1862.

69. MILITARY ROADS IN KENTUCKY.

Collins' *History of Kentucky,* Vol. 1, page 110, says: "Aug. 24, 1862—Great excitement in Fayette and Madison counties [was] caused by a military notice served upon slave holders to furnish a specified number of able-bodied men 'for the use of the U. S. government as laborers'—the object being to repair the road between Mt. Vernon and Cumberland Gap. General Boyle says that if the government will furnish the iron and the rolling stock he will impress Negroes enough to build a railroad between Lexington and Cumberland Gap."

Coulter's, *The Civil War and Readjustment in Kentucky,* pages 157-158, states: "A network of wagon roads had to be constructed over which military supplies should go; fortifications had to be built; and even the construction of military roads was begun. Large numbers of slaves were early set to work on a road from Central Kentucky to Cumberland Gap; and by the middle of 1863, Boyle was calling for 6,000 slaves to extend the railway from Lexington to Danville.

"Threats of arrest and imprisonment besides the seizure of all slaves between 18 and 45 were made against masters failing to deliver slaves called for. . . . As to payment for the services of slaves, 'Those of loyal owners will be paid for, as other laborers in government employ—those of disloyal owners, referred to the Department at Washington for adjustment.' The actual result was that loyal owners had great difficulty in making collections and many failed altogether, while the disloyal were never able to secure a hearing."

70. SLAVERY IN THE CHURCH.

The apparent avoidance of the use of the word slave in Old Cane Springs is interesting. The absence of the term in the minutes of the Republican Baptist Church on the upper Boonesborough pike and the Cane Spring Church has already been noted. No cases involving slavery appear in these minutes, but this was not the condition among the Methodists of the county.

The minute book of the Quarterly Conference of Madison County, Kentucky, Methodists, from 1811 to 1845 gives much information concerning controversies of the sale and purchase of slaves by members of the churches of that conference. On February 27, 1813, the Quarterly Conference, meeting at New Providence, Madison County, adopted the *Ohio Rule* to regulate the sale and purchase of slaves. Thereafter many cases involving the application of this rule came before the county unit of the church for adjudication.

The provisions of the Ohio Annual Conference Rule were:

"No member of our Society shall purchase a slave except in cases of mercy or humanity to the slave purchased. And if he purchase a slave he shall state to the next ensuing Quarterly

Meeting Conference the number of years he thinks the slave should serve as a Compensation for the price paid, and if the Quarterly Meeting Conference think the time too long they shall proceed and fix the time, and the member who has purchased shall immediately after the determination execute a Legal Instrument of manumission of such slave at the expiration of the time determined by the Quarterly Meeting Conference, as the Laws of the State will admit. And in default of his executing such instrument of manumission or on his refusing to submit his case to the judgment of the Quarterly Meeting Conference he shall be excluded [from] the Society provided also that in case of a female slave it shall be inserted in the Instrument of manumission (if the Laws of the State will admit) that all her Children born during the time of her servitude shall be free at the age of twenty-one, if the Laws will admit so early a manumission and if not at such times as the laws will admit. And if any member of Society shall sell a slave except at the request of the slave to prevent a separation in families he shall be excluded [from] the Society. Provided nevertheless that if any member of our Society shall think it necessary on any other occasion to sell a slave he shall apply to the preacher who has the Charge of the Circuit whose duty it shall be to appoint a Committee of three members of our Society not slave holders to judge whether such sale be propper and the person applying shall abide by their determination or be excluded [from] the Society."

Two cases from the minutes concerning the application of these rules will suffice:

"January 14, 1815.

"The Committee that enquired into the case of bro. John Bennett respecting a slave are of opinion that it was a purchase and have reported the same to the Q. M. Conference and the Consideration of the said report is refered as unfinished business to the next Q. M. Conference."

"Again the report of the Comm'tee . . . refered from the last to the present Q. M. Conference in the case of bro. J. Bennett and the s'd Comm'tee report that he has purchased a Negro girl & the Conf has confirmed the report of the Committee. And in consequence of his refusing to comply with the Rule on slavery is expelled from the society. Bro J. Pace in behalf of J. Bennett means to appeal his case to the annual Conference"

"November 4, 1815.

"Question are there any Complaints or appeals.

"Answer Bro. Bennett who was expelled from Society for refusing to comply with the Rule on slavery submitted his case to the Q. M. Conference a Negro girl named Sarah of 18 years of age for which he gave 370 dollars he proposed that the said girl should serve 20 years and the Conference thinks the proposal reasonable, and in consequence of this compliance the Conference agrees to restore him his former privileges in the Church."

"February 1, 1817.

"This conference have concluded to readopt the Rules of the Ohio Conference respecting slavery until further directed by the Tennessee Conference.

"The case of Philip Prather's purchasing a Negro man came before the Conference, and the bro Prather stated to the Conference that he was to give five hundred dollars for a Negro man named George aged 40 years and proposed keeping him for life and the Conference are of opinion that 15 years Service will remunerate bro Prather."—These minutes are now in possession of Rev. W. E. Arnold, of Winchester, Kentucky. Two typed copies are in the possession of the writer.

Such cases involving slavery are not mentioned in the minutes after 1826.

The last quarterly meeting recorded in this minute book was held at Providence Church in Madison County, January 18, 19, 1845. This very significant entry appears for this date:

"There was a motion made and seconded that the stewards and class Leaders bring the subject of division of the Methodist Episcopal Church before the different Classes between this and next Quarterly meeting that the minds of the members of the Church be known on the Subject."

The split that occurred in the Methodist Church in 1845 promises to be healed before 1945.

Chapter XXI

71. W. H. Miller, *History and Genealogies*, p. 525, says: "Hezekiah Oldham ... enlisted in the Confederate states army, under the command of General Morgan, and was wounded in the fight at Pine Mountain, Sept. 8, 1862, when Captain Jesse, commanding two companies of Confederates, went into an ambuscade of Federal soldiers. He died shortly after retiring from the army service, having never been married." Miller, *Ibid.*, also gives an account of James Oldham's military experience after his enlistment after the Battle of Richmond. See notes 77 and 81.

72. In referring to laws against peaceful assembly in Kentucky, E. M. Coulter's *The Civil War and Readjustment in Kentucky*, p. 140, says: "... As an answer to the Provisional government's attempt to lead the state into the Southern Confederacy, a law was passed making it a crime punishable by imprisonment in the penitentiary from one to five years for anyone to hold any secret or public meeting of an organization or belong to one 'intended to effect, promote, or endanger the separation or secession of this State' from the Union ..." The Captain Adams referred to here appears to have been Peyton Adams, or P. K. Adams, who lived on the road just south of Texas.

Chapter XXII

73. "Thomas Shelton Moberly, a doctor of Medicine, had a successful practice of his profession for a number of years in Madison County, Ky., besides farming on a large scale ... After a time he retired from the practice and moved from his farm ... to Richmond where he and his wife resided till death. He married Nancy Lipscomb, March 5, 1844, daughter of Major Nathan Lipscomb and Nancy Gentry, his wife."—W. H. Miller, Mss., Vol. II, p. 470.

Chapter XXIII

74. Boxankle appears to have been the crossroads where what was called Noland's Creek road crossed a road running due north to Union. The place was about one and a half miles south of Union.—See county map.

75. See Old Cane Springs map for General Jackson's home.

Chapter XXIV

76. THE BATTLE OF RICHMOND.

"While General Robert E. Lee, in August, 1862, was pushing the Federals aside and making a way for his first invasion of the North, the Confederates were also planning to occupy Kentucky and carry the war north of the Ohio. A month earlier General John H. Morgan had made his first raid through Kentucky, returning via Richmond to Tennessee. It was evident, therefore, that Kentucky could be invaded. Accordingly, General Kirby Smith, with about 12,000 infantry and 4,000 cavalry, passed through the defiles west of Cumberland Gap, and avoiding the Federal troops guarding that passage, marched on in the direction of Lexington and Cincinnati.

"General William Nelson, whose headquarters were at Lexington, had about 16,000 troops to defend the Blue Grass Country. The Confederates met no opposition until they entered Madison County, where about 7,000 of Nelson's command, under General M. D. Manson, were located near Richmond. The first skirmish occurred August 29, near Rogersville, on the Big Hill pike. In this engagement the Confederates were repulsed, but early the next day they drove the Federals back to Richmond and beyond the Kentucky River. All day, with the temperature reaching ninety-six in the shade, the battle raged along the highway, over the meadows and cornfields, and even in the cemetery and on the streets of Richmond. The Federals made two or three desperate attempts to stop the enemy, but, being mostly raw troops just from their homes across the Ohio, and believing themselves greatly outnumbered, their efforts were in vain. General Nelson arrived from Lexington about 2:00 P. M., and vainly tried to stem the tide. The Federal army was entirely routed and Union soldiers who escaped fled across the Kentucky River to the North. The Confederates reported the Union loss as 206 officers and men killed, 844 wounded, 4,303 prisoners, besides the capture of '9 pieces of artillery, 10,000 stands of small arms, and large quantities of supplies.' Their own loss was probably 75 killed and 200 wounded. The Confederate Military History (Vol. VIII, p. 46) states that 'the attack was made and resisted with energy and vigor, so much so that Smith believed that he had encountered

10,000 men, and Manson was confident that he was beaten by an army of veterans 16,000 strong.'

"The Madison Female Institute in Richmond was converted into a hospital for the wounded, and the dead were buried in the Richmond cemetery, from which they were later removed to the National cemetery at Camp Nelson. The trustees of the Institute, in February, 1863, lodged a claim against the United States for damages done the school while it was used as a hospital and as late as May, 1915, received $5,200 from the Federal Government.

"General Smith recruited troops in Richmond and places near and was soon assisting General Bragg, who had invaded Kentucky farther west, in setting up a Confederate state government at Frankfort. The Confederates, however, after the Battle of Perryville, October 8, retired from the State. General Lee had already (September 17) been turned back at Antietam."—J. T. Dorris, *A Glimpse at Historic Madison County*, etc., pp. 27-29.

77. Old citizens of Cane Springs who knew Mr. Oldham and Pike state that Mr. Oldham always manifested the highest regard for Pike's faithful service during the war. Pike certainly was an unusual Negro.

78. REMINISCENCES OF THE BATTLE OF RICHMOND.

In the Madison County Order Book M (1859-1864), page 427, in large bold script is the following entry: "On Monday 1 day September, 1862, there was no County Court held for the County Court of Madison, the State having been invaded by the rebels, and the town of Richmond having been invested by a portion of their forces under the rebel General E. Kirby Smith, after having defeated the Union forces under Gen. Wm Nelson on the preceding Saturday in the Great battle of Richmond." The Court house was a hospital for a few days and court was not held until September 13.

Mt. Zion Church on the Big Hill pike was struck by a cannon ball during the battle but it was not seriously damaged. The brick home of Thomas Palmer nearby, however, did not fare so well, for it was struck several times and needed considerable repairing after the battle (see note 79). With a little effort this old home can be seen a few hundred yards back of the church. The forty or more soldiers who were buried in one grave near the church were soon reinterred in the Richmond cemetery, but, as stated, what remained of their bodies in each instance was removed in 1869 to the national cemetery at Camp Nelson.

Mr. S. D. Parrish, an attorney of Richmond, states that he and his mother rode one horse into town the next day after the battle. They passed into the cemetery as they came from their home on the Irvine pike and saw a number of dead men lying about. One handsome young fellow, whose gun appeared to have been made small to accommodate its owner, so impressed the little boy that he can still visualize the tragic scene of that warm August morning. Mr. Parrish states that his parents kept two wounded soldiers—a Federal and a Confederate—in their home until they were sufficiently recovered to go their respective ways. He saw the two shake hands on the day of their departure and turn their steps, one toward the North and the other toward the Southland.

Mrs. Margaret Jane (R. C.) Boggs, whose maiden name was Turley, who lived on the eastern outskirts of Richmond, in 1862, and who is now nearly ninety-two years old, has described to the writer the horrors of this battle, especially the suffering of the wounded and dying. She visited the Madison Female Institute on one of the exceedingly warm days when the building was crowded with disabled soldiers, whose groans rent the air as their limbs were being amputated, and whose cries for water were pitiful to hear.

Mrs. Boggs relates also having seen Confederates wearing the clothing of Union soldiers, whose dead bodies they had stripped. The garments had been turned inside out. She heard one Confederate say, "I'm Yank within but Reb without." Evidently Smith's men were poorly clad and were also thinking of the winter months ahead of them. She further states that her brother, Robert Turley, gave a Union soldier a suit of clothes in which to make his escape. The soldier's uniform then became a possession not to be coveted and was disposed of.

The home of Robert Cornelison which still stands, but remodeled, on Big Hill Avenue near the pond of the Richmond Ice Company was also used as a hospital for three weeks. Mrs. Margaret Ann Adams, a daughter of Mr. Cornelison, who is now in her eighty-fifth year, states that her parents and their children lived with a bachelor uncle named William Boggs until their home was vacated. When they returned there remained only one pillow of all their bedding. Bandages for the wounded and shrouds for the dead had depleted the entire supply. Their carpets had to be burned and the place was greatly disordered.

Mr. Cornelison was a Union sympathizer, however, and took his loss as his contribution to the cause, never lodging a claim against the government for damages, as did the Madison Female Institute. He soon found it necessary after returning home to rebury arms and legs which the dogs dug up near the fence around the place. It should be noted that the fine spring near Mr. Cornelison's home was a great boon to the soldiers on those warm September days.

It is interesting to know that the Federals gave the name Camp Boggs to the grounds which they occupied near Richmond. The place was near Woodlawn and its fine spring on the Big Hill pike. This old E. C. Boggs farm is now the home of County Clerk J. B. Arnett. It was in its vicinity that the Eleventh Kentucky Cavalry (David W. Chenault's regiment) was temporarily organized on September 10, 1862.

79. ANTE-BELLUM HOMES REMAINING ON THE BATTLEFIELD OF RICHMOND.

On the map of Madison County the line inclosing the battlefield of Richmond should extend nearly to Kingston. There are many fine old homes standing along the highway through this battlefield, near and around which the battle raged on that hot August day in 1862. The Kavanaugh Armstrong home, where G. W. Herd lived a little later and where Mrs. A. R. Gibbs now lives, was used as a hospital after the battle. Thomas Palmer's home, which is not far from Mt. Zion Church, was damaged considerably during the fight. The story is that a distillery then stood by a spring about a hundred yards from the house (the spring was flowing on August 20, 1936, when the writer visited it), and Union soldiers, on finding a quantity of liquor in the large basement of the residence, were making merry when the Confederates fired on the place. An east room was never restored because of the damage done, but the south portion was rebuilt with wood. General John Miller died in the large "front room" of this residence six days after the battle. J. B. Ellison later owned the farm, which is now the property of Dr. H. L. Donovan, President of the State College in Richmond.

The two-story brick home, built by Adam Rogers in 1811 and later occupied in turn by his son, Ben Rogers, by Socrates Maupin, by Daniel Maupin Terrill, and by Robert Dunn, was also used for a short time as a hospital. Classic "Cumberland View," built by Alexander Tribble about 1855 (some say nearer 1845) and after his death in 1888 the home of three generations of Chenaults, shared its hospitality with the wounded soldiers. Beautiful "Castlewood," built in 1825 by James Estill and now the property of Mrs. James W. Caperton, also witnessed the carnage of this battle.

"Woodstock," erected by Archibald Woods near the end of the 18th century and now the home of Wilson Brandenburg; the E. C. Boggs residence; and "Woodlawn," built in 1822 by William Rodes and now owned by Mrs. James W. Caperton, probably saw more of the battle of Richmond and experienced more numerous relations with the armies of both sides than any of the other houses mentioned. The residences of Robert B. Cornelison and William Holloway should be included in this list of houses still standing that figured in caring for the wounded after the battle. The Cornelison residence, which was later the home of Green Turley, has already been mentioned. The classic Ionic columns of the Holloway residence, facing the entrance to the Richmond cemetery, undoubtedly witnessed the passing of soldiers of both armies. Colonel William Holloway, the builder and owner of this mansion, was a benefactor of the Bereans, a staunch Union man, and major and paymaster in the Union army from February, 1863, to November, 1865, and certainly his home was always open, especially to those in sympathy with the Union.

Unfortunately there are no markers along the Dixie Highway going south from Richmond to indicate the stirring days of 1862, when "Boys in Blue" and "Boys in Gray" engaged in fratricidal warfare to determine the character of our government. These and a few other old homes and Mt. Zion Church, therefore, are left to stand alone in mute testimony to the heroism and suffering of both sides in the sanguinary Battle of Richmond. Surely the view of any one of them should intrigue the imagination and stir the emotions of those who are informed in this period of the history of Madison County.

80. AN ANTE-BELLUM AUTOGRAPH ALBUM RETURNS TO RICHMOND.

Early in 1856 Miss Clara B. Wherritt, of Richmond, Kentucky, received a beautiful autograph album, in which, during the ensuing months and years until the memorable August of 1862, many of her admirers wrote delightful expressions of admiration and friendly greetings in various styles of excellent chirography, as was the custom in those days. Shortly before the Battle of Richmond a friend took the album to the courthouse and that was the last Miss Wherritt ever heard of it until April, 1886. At that time she received a letter from L. A. Austin, of Granville, Ohio, "telling her of the album in his possession and asking her if she would like to regain possession of it."

Mr. Austin stated that after the battle a young paroled soldier named Robert Thrall, a member of the 95th Ohio Volunteer Infantry, was strolling about town and entered the courthouse, where he found the album. The book appealed to his fancy and he took it away to his home in Kirkersville, Ohio. "It remained in his possession until 1873, when it fell into the hands of his brother-in-law, Mr. L. A. Austin," who finally "conceived the idea of trying to find out if the original owner was living." He wrote a letter of inquiry to the postmaster at Richmond, Kentucky, who informed him that Miss Wherritt had married a Mr. T. W. Olds and was living in Lancaster, an adjoining county seat.

Mrs. Olds immediately wrote Mr. Austin expressing her joy at learning of the existence of the album. "I have wondered so often and so vaguely what had become of it," she said. "I treasured it very highly on account of mementos from attached friends . . ." She regretted depriving the Austins of it, "but I am so anxious to see it again and [to] treasure it for the sake of 'ye olden time,'" she wrote, "[that] I can scarcely wait to see it." She stated further that her only daughter, who was then nearly grown, "would value it greatly" for its contents and "for the wonderful way in which it has been restored."

Mrs. Olds asked Mr. Austin and others of his family to write something in the book before returning it, which he, his wife, and her sister, Miss Clara Thrall, each did. Mrs. Austin stated that the album had been one of her "household treasures." "We return it to you cheerfully," she wrote, "and wish it might tell its own story of its travels through the rebellion and its sojourn in the North. May the return to its owner bring her much pleasure is the wish of your new-found friend."

Mrs. Austin's sister, Miss Clara Thrall, closed her contribution thus: "We take great pleasure in returning to you the book you prize so highly as a memento of your happy girlhood, and hope you will treasure no ill feeling toward the 'Boy in Blue' who brought it to us. . . ."

About four years ago Mrs. Old's daughter, Mrs. John E. Stormes, of Lancaster, fearing that the album with its interesting history might be lost after her death, gave it to the writer to be preserved in Richmond for all time as a pleasant bit of sentiment linking together the daughters of the "Boys in Gray" of Kentucky with the daughters of the "Boys in Blue" of Ohio.

It is interesting to know that Mrs. Olds' father, Samuel H. Wherritt, allowed the lower floor of his three-story home, which stood where the government building now stands, to be used as a hospital after the Battle of Richmond. Miss Clara B., therefore, surely saw much to remember about Union and Confederate soldiers at that time.

81. GENERAL JOHN MILLER.

"General John Miller was born on Muddy Creek, near the mouth of its tributary, Hickory Lick, in Madison County, Kentucky, June 30, 1798 . . . His first introduction into military life, for which he ever had a fondness, came about in this way: During his young manhood, whilst living in Richmond, the young blood of the town and surrounding country organized a volunteer military company and uniformed it, which organization was equipped with guns and munitions of war by the State. John Miller was elected captain of the company. In the military system of the State all the officers were commissioned by the Governor; it was always the custom for each company to select by vote its own captain, and while the Governor was not bound by law to respect

"Castlewood," built by James Estill in 1825. (From a painting by Miss Adelaide Everharte, of Decatur, Georgia.)

"Cumberland View," built by Alexander Tribble about 1855 (perhaps nearer 1845). It stands across the Dixie Highway from Castlewood. (See county map.)

"Woodlawn," built by Colonel William Rodes in 1822. Near camping sites of Union and Confederate armies.

The Solomon Smith House, built more than a hundred years ago. At this house, which stands on the hill near the site of the old Madison Female Institute, many of the Union Soldiers captured in the Battle of Richmond were paroled.

such selection, yet he invariably commissioned the choice of the company. After receiving his commission as captain, John Miller rose by regular promotion to major, lieutenant-colonel, colonel, brigadier-general, and major-general. . . . At his death General Miller held a commission to raise a Brigade of Federal troops to be composed of four regiments of which he would be given the command, . . . but his death ended his endeavors in this direction.

"The Battle of Richmond, Kentucky, was fought August 30, 1862, between the Federal and Confederate forces, in which engagement the Federals were utterly routed. General Miller took an active part in this battle—he went into the battle as aid to General Schaoff (August 30, 1862)—and whilst trying to rally a disordered Union column near Mount Zion Meeting House on the Big Hill Road, fell mortally wounded; he was removed to the residence of Mr. Thomas Palmer nearby, where he breathed his last September 6, 1862. His remains were buried in the Richmond cemetery, the inscription on the monument, to wit:

<blockquote>
GEN'L JOHN MILLER
BORN JUNE 30, 1798.
MORTALLY WOUNDED AUG. 30, 1862.
WHILE GALLANTLY RALLYING A DISORDERED COLUMN OF SOLDIERS
BEARING THE BANNER OF THE UNION.
DIED SEPT. 6, 1862.
" 'BRAVE, GENEROUS, AND AFFECTIONATE, HE COMMANDED THE ADMIRATION OF THE VIRTUOUS WHEN LIVING; AND IN DEATH THEIR UNFEIGNED REGRET.'
</blockquote>

"A letter from the Treasury Department, Washington City, bearing date September 2, 1862, signed by the Commissioner of Internal Revenue was forwarded to General John Miller, Richmond, Ky., notifying him of his appointment by the President of the United States as Collector of Internal Revenue . . . but four days after the date of this letter and commission, General Miller died. . . .

"In 1840, the great celebration of the Settlement of Kentucky was held at Boonesborough with a Military Encampment consisting of all the Volunteer and Amateur Military Companies of the State in attendance for a week or more. It was a State occasion and celebration and attended by large crowds, besides the military array and display. General Miller was made commandant of the encampment, considered quite a distinction, as there was much discussion as to who would be the proper man to conduct it. General Leslie Combs, of Lexington, Kentucky, was one of his subaltern officers. . . .

"General Miller was a prominent merchant of Richmond, Ky., from his early manhood until a very short time before his end. In his mercantile life he made many horseback trips from his native town to Baltimore, Philadelphia, and other Eastern cities for merchandise. On one of these Eastern trips, in 1835, he arrived from Baltimore in Philadelphia on the evening of March 13, 1835, and stopped at the United States Hotel. A letter in his own hand, written by him at 10 o'clock P. M. the next day, at said hotel, to his wife Elizabeth, begins in this way: 'Having an opportunity to send you a letter by the Hon. Davy Crockett, I drop you a line.' Col. Crockett, the Representative from Tennessee, was then figuring upon a large scale in the East, receiving great ovations of immense crowds and the night this letter was written General Miller attended the theater on Arch Street to witness a reception given Colonel Crockett, who when he (Crockett) took his seat in the box was cheered for several minutes heavily. 'Go ahead,' etc., etc., rang from side to side by an immense crowd, which General Miller writes was much the largest he had ever seen in the city, and he had the pleasure of an introduction of Colonel Crockett by Representative Mr. Low. . . .

"He owned and occupied as his home, till just before his death, the handsome and desirable property on Lancaster Avenue, now owned and occupied by William W. Watts, Esquire; on the site of the old mansion Mr. Watts has erected a large palatial residence."—W. H. Miller, *History and Genealogies*, pp. 75-78.

82. THE ELEVENTH KENTUCKY CAVALRY, C. S. A.

As might be expected under the circumstances many young men of Madison County, who, for one reason or another, had not yet entered the Confederate service before the Battle of Richmond, responded to General Kirby Smith's call for a regiment of cavalry to be recruited from Madison and adjoining counties.

It appears that on Sunday, August 31, the day following the battle, the movement to recruit this regiment got under way. On that day certain influential men of Madison County recommended David Waller Chenault, a farmer who lived near Foxtown, as the most suitable person to organize this cavalry unit.

Ten days later (September 10) the regiment consisting of nine companies of some 800 men was organized at a sort of barbecue and picnic in a grove on the Big Hill pike near and beyond Woodlawn, the old home of Colonel William Rodes (built in 1822. See the county map). Because of the fine spring and other favorable conditions this location was suitable to army encampments, and both Federals and Confederates took advantage of it.

In the final organization of the regiment (November 9, near Knoxville) David W. Chenault was elected Colonel; Joseph T. Tucker, of Winchester, Lieutenant Colonel; and James B. McCreary, of Madison County, Major. The regiment was soon (accepted on November 18) joined to General John H. Morgan's cavalry brigade. Chenault was killed while bravely fighting at Green River Bridge on July 4, 1863, and Tucker and McCreary were advanced to colonel and lieutenant colonel respectively. Still later (July 19) at Buffington Ford in Ohio above the rapids at the mouth of the Kanawha about one-half of Morgan's command was captured and in a few days Morgan and others of his force surrendered.

Morgan and about sixty of his officers were placed in the penitentiary at Columbus, Ohio. The most of the soldiers were confined at Camp Chase, near Columbus, Ohio, and Camp Douglas, then in the environs of Chicago. For more than a year, therefore, many of the Boys in Gray from Madison County were confined as prisoners of war.

General Basil Wilson Duke's *Morgan's Cavalry* gives the best account of Morgan's exploits, the experiences of his officers in the Ohio penitentiary, Morgan's escape, and other matters pertaining to his officers and men. See also his *Reminiscences* (New York, 1911). Duke was an officer on Morgan's staff. The information about the organization of the regiment was taken from an account by Anderson Chenault Quisenberry in a scrapbook belonging to Mrs. James W. Caperton.

Chapter XXV

83. Miller's *History and Genealogies,* p. 451, says of Cabell Chenault, who was an uncle of the author of the original account of *Old Cane Springs:* "Cabell Chenault joined the Confederate army in 1862; died in the service at Monticello, Ky.; was a handsome man and a brave soldier."

84. OTHNIEL RICE OLDHAM.

"Othniel Rice Oldham enlisted in the Confederate army, Captain Thomas B. Collins' Company F. 7th, afterwards 11th Kentucky Cavalry, Colonel D. Waller Chenault, General John H. Morgan's command, two of his sons being in the same army. He was a kind-hearted good man, and had many friends.

"An incident of his army life was, that he and his cousin and comrade, Thomas M. Oldham, on a certain occasion whilst stationed at Monticello, were granted a leave of absence, and bethought themselves to make their way to their homes in Madison County to see their wives and children. On the way, they were intercepted, arrested, and carried to Cincinnati and there imprisoned, tried, and sentenced as spies to suffer the penalty of death; but through the interposition and persistent efforts of a lady [Miss Juan Phillips, Monticello, Kentucky] who afterwards became the wife of Rev. Milton Elliott, aided by General Speed S. Fry, their lives were spared, and they were finally released after taking the oath of allegiance and fidelity to the United States Government . . ."—W. H. Miller, *History and Genealogies,* p. 525.

Mr. Othniel Oldham appreciated Miss Phillips' efforts to save him and his cousin "so much that he begged her to call on him if ever he could be of any assistance." Thirty years later she told Mr. Oldham that a nephew of a kinswoman, but no blood relative of hers, and the kinsman of a former Federal and Confederate Congressman, was wrongfully convicted of a crime and had been sentenced to serve a long term in the Arkansas penitentiary. Governor James P. Eagle, of Arkansas, had married Mr. Oldham's niece, and consequently Mr. Oldham believed he would have no difficulty in getting the boy pardoned. Governor Eagle, in answer to his letter, however, said that from what he remembered of the case he would not be justified in issuing a pardon. Soon thereafter Governor Eagle visited Mr. Oldham in Kentucky, and the old soldier pleaded as earnestly for the boy's freedom as Miss Phillips had pleaded for his own thirty years before, with the result that the governor promised to go over the evidence again. Soon Mr. Oldham received a telegram advising him that the boy had been pardoned. He at once rode many miles to place the telegram in the hands of the boy's benefactor, who had become Mrs. Milton Elliott and was then residing at Kirksville, Madison County, where her husband was conducting a high-class academy.—Clipping from the *Arkansas Eagle*, April 6, 1918. Substantiated by Mr. Milton Elliott, the son of Rev. Milton Elliott and Mrs. Juan Phillips Elliott, who lives in Lexington, Kentucky.

Mr. Oldham was living in Richmond with his son-in-law, John Cabell Chenault, when he received Governor Eagle's telegram informing him that he had pardoned the young man whose release from prison he had sought at the request of his former benefactor, Miss Juan Phillips, then Mrs. Milton Elliott, of Kirksville, Madison County. It was along in the afternoon, the weather was pleasant and the old gentleman was out in the yard. As soon as he had read the message, without a word to anyone, he went to the barn, saddled and mounted an "outlaw" horse, which Mr. Chenault had accepted a little earlier as a fee from a client, and rode away.

As Mrs. Chenault (the beautiful, black-eyed Nettie of the story) saw her father, who was then nearly eighty years old (he died in 1900 in his eighty-fourth year), suddenly leaving on this dangerous horse, she cried to him to return. Mr. Oldham, however, did not heed her but went on. The next morning at the breakfast table his little grandson, Joe Prewett, heard him say, "Well, John, I am ready to die, I have paid the last debt I owe." Then he told the family why he had ridden away so suddenly the previous afternoon and where he had gone.—Statement by Joe Prewett Chenault, August 15, 1936.

Mr. Milton Elliott, who was formerly principal of the Lexington High School and Assistant Professor of English of Transylvania College, often heard his mother tell of her part in saving the lives of the Oldham cousins. The account as told by the son is as follows:

"Micajah Phillips, a prominent and well-to-do citizen, lived at Monticello, Kentucky. His home was hospitable and the officers of both Confederate and Union armies frequently visited him. When the Oldhams, who had been guests of Mr. Phillips, determined to return to Madison County, they notified Miss Juan Phillips, the daughter of their host, of their intention and indicated that, if caught, they would say that they were cattle buyers. If this story did not effect their release, they wanted Miss Phillips to know exactly why they were returning home, which they had told her was because of illness in their families. She was to testify, therefore, that the men were not spies, if there were occasion for such testimony.

"The Oldham cousins were captured in a short while after leaving Monticello. Soon thereafter, and providentially it may seem, two Union officers, a colonel and a lieutenant, came to the Phillips home, where Miss Juan overheard the lieutenant say: 'Colonel, what will be done with those two men?' The colonel replied: 'Much sympathy is felt for them and they seem like fine men, but they were caught within our lines without a pass and will probably be executed as spies.'

"Miss Phillips, though naturally timid, knocked at the door of the colonel's room and said, 'Pardon me, Colonel, but were the men the lieutenant referred to Messrs. Othniel and Thomas Oldham?' The colonel replied, 'Young lady, what do you know about it?' Miss Phillips then said, 'I know they are not spies; they are gentlemen and if you permit them to be executed, you will have innocent blood on your hands.' She further referred them to her father, who corroborated her statement.

"The colonel forthwith sent a courier to have the execution delayed until further investigation."—Written statement by Milton Elliott, August 3, 1936.

85. MAJOR JAMES B. MCCREARY AND MISS JUAN PHILLIPS.

Major McCreary kept a diary covering his experiences from August 30, 1862, to the time of his exchange near Savannah, Georgia, late in 1864. The entire composition has much literary merit and is indeed a rare bit of narration. In the light of what has already been said about Miss Phillips an account of his association with her is very interesting.

On March 8, 1863, the young officer wrote: "Met today Miss Juan Phillips at Mrs. Hall's. She is a lovely blue-eyed, fine-formed maiden with flowing curls. Also late this evening, when taking a walk with Lieut. Ransom stopped at a house where we heard music and again met Miss Juan. Had a good time. That name makes a thrilling, witching tale of Byron's come running through my head. I have a presentment that Juan and I will come to know each other well ere my soldier lot be cast in another land."

More than a month later McCreary's regiment was camped one mile from "Monticello . . . at 'Camp Juan.' I shall always remember my stay in Monticello," he wrote, "as an oasis springing up amid the desolation of war, cheering and charming my soldier life."

There had already been some fighting in and around Monticello, but there was to be more, and the gallant major from Madison County had the coveted privilege of defending the home of the beautiful Juan after whom he had christened his camp not far away. On May 2 he penned this entry: "Fighting still continues on this day. Tucker was pursued with his detachment through Monticello. On the hill . . . as the Yankees were pressing Tucker, I charged them and by a strange coincidence drove them back and from the house of Miss Juan Phillips where they had sheltered themselves to fire on our men. This is a strange life. The house, where, in pleasing dalliance I had spent many happy hours and where I had reason to believe those who liked me lived, became the rampart, behind which those seeking my life fight . . ."

But a soldier's fortune is very uncertain and in the case of Major McCreary the god of war did not permit him to linger long among the alluring enchantments of Monticello. Morgan's men had work in other places. Nevertheless, the bold officer found his way back to the capital of Wayne County on May 28, where by invitation he "took tea" with another charming lady to whom he alludes as Miss Emma C. This was the lady's birthday, "and the dainties of her supper, the hospitality of her parents, and the cheerful music made me feel," his diary says, "as if I had returned, after many weary wanderings, to a place nearly allied to my own sweet home."

Evidently, however, Major McCreary had returned to Monticello to see his charming Juan, for on the morrow his diary received the following significant impression: "This rainy day was spent with fair Juan. Ah! How unlike the day is her sunny face and sparkling eyes. The hours flew by on angel's wings, and on the morning of the 30th, sad yet happy I tore myself from these endearing scenes, it may be forever, and again sought the rugged scenes of the forest bivouac."

This was the last time the young major referred to Miss Phillips in his diary. The gallant and fearless Morgan moved northward and at Green River Bridge the brave and handsome Colonel Chenault fell mortally wounded, and thereafter until the end of the Ohio raid Tucker and McCreary were colonel and lieutenant colonel, respectively.

It is interesting to note in passing that among the many young women whose hospitality McCreary enjoyed during the period covered in his diary Miss Juan Phillips received his most ardent consideration. What a contrast was his happiness in her company and in the environs of Monticello with the gloom and horrors which awaited him and his fellow officers in the Columbus penitentiary after the Ohio raid!

This unique diary of the major and lieutenant-colonel, who later became the Governor of Kentucky twice and a United States Senator, was published in the *Register* of the Kentucky Historical Society in the April and July, 1935, numbers. Unfortunately the transcriber for the *Register* caused "Juan" to be spelled "Inan" in every reference to Miss Phillips.

86. CURTIS FIELD BURNAM.

Curtis Field Burnam (1820-1909) graduated from Yale in 1840, was admitted to the Richmond, Kentucky, bar in 1842, and served in the Kentucky legislature in 1851-53 and 1859-63 (Senate). He was a delegate to the convention which nominated John Bell for the presidency in 1860 and helped carry the State for the American Party. As a strong Union man he did much to cause the legislature to refuse repeatedly to call a convention to consider the proposition of secession.

In 1863 General John H. Morgan captured Mr. Burnam in the historic Phoenix Hotel, of Lexington, Kentucky, but offered

COL. JAMES B. McCREARY
Governor of Kentucky, 1875-1879, 1911-1915; United States Senator, 1903-1909.

MRS. MILTON ELLIOTT
(nee Juan Phillips)

She was instrumental in saving the lives of two citizens of Old Cane Springs, who had been condemned as spies. She is also mentioned frequently in Colonel McCreary's Diary.

Mrs. Margaret Jane (R. C.) Boggs, age 91; Mrs. Margaret Adams, age 84. They remember much of events in Madison County during the early 1860's.

The Fort at Boonesborough. Reproduced from an illustration in Lewis Collins' "Historical Sketches of Kentucky," published in 1847.

him his freedom if he would take the oath of allegiance to the Confederacy. He refused and expected to be sent to a Southern prison, when General Morgan told him that he could have his liberty if he would effect the release of General Morgan's younger brother, who was a prisoner of war at Camp Chase, Columbus, Ohio. Mr. Burnam accepted the offer and immediately went to Washington and effected the exchange.

President Lincoln appreciated Mr. Burnam's services for the Union in Kentucky and received him in his office several times on his numerous trips to Washington. On one of these visits to the White House, according to Miss Lucia Burnam, one of his daughters (born 1854), Mr. Burnam had his son Thompson S. (born 1852) with him. During the interview Mr. Lincoln took an apple from a supply near at hand and ate it without even offering one to the boy, who never forgot the incident and often related it thereafter.

Mr. Burnam secured pardons for persons in Kentucky during and especially after the war. His daughter, Miss Lucia, of Richmond, states that he had a part in securing the pardon of Othniel and Thomas Oldham of Old Cane Springs, who were about to be executed as spies in 1863. Miss Burnam relates having heard a Confederate sympathizer's wife, Mrs. Jonathan Estill, of Madison County, say: "It is a good thing we have Mr. Burnam, who can get pardons for us."

Mr. Burnam was held in high esteem by Kentucky Confederates after the war. He was the author of the law establishing the Confederate Home at Pewee Valley. Another service as legislator was his support in 1906 of the bill creating two state schools for the training of teachers in Kentucky, one of which was located in Richmond. Perhaps the most important recognition of his ability was his appointment as First Assistant Secretary of the Treasury in 1875, in which position he served until Secretary Bristow resigned in June, 1876. Mr. Burnam enjoyed other honors including the presidency of the Kentucky Bar Association.—Robert Burnam, *In Memoriam Curtis Field Burnam.*

87. JAMES W. CAPERTON.

Colonel James W. Caperton (1824-1909) was the son of William H. Caperton, who was an eminent Kentucky lawyer and orator, a United States District Attorney (1853-1857), and an intimate friend of Henry Clay. He attended Centre College and then graduated in law at Transylvania, having studied under the able legalists Chief Justice Robertson and Thomas A. Marshall. Soon after graduation he formed a law partnership with his father, whose boon companion he was until the father's death on July 4, 1862.

The Capertons supported Lincoln for the presidency in 1860 and spoke in behalf of the Republican candidate. Since Kentucky cast only 1,364 votes for Lincoln in this election out of a total of 146,216, such support in Madison County by two eminent lawyers and slave owners was appreciated, and consequently James W. and Curtis F. Burnam, his law partner after his father's death, found Lincoln very considerate of their requests during the war.

Colonel Caperton worked heroically with his father to assuage the cholera epidemic in 1849. It has been said that he always took the side of the defense in a lawsuit. Notwithstanding the fact that his business (he was president of the Richmond National Bank for twenty years) and law interests kept him out of politics, he was a delegate to the Republican conventions which nominated Grant (1872), Hayes (1876), Garfield (1880), and McKinley (1896) for the presidency.

At a meeting of the Madison County Bar on April 20, 1909, to honor Colonel Caperton, who had just passed away, United States Senator James B. McCreary said of him: "His life was full of good illustrations and he came fully up to Blackstone's aphorism, 'act honestly, live honorably, and render to every man his due.' He was universally conceded to be an able lawyer."

On Monday morning, October 29, 1919, handsome oil portraits of W. H. Caperton and his son, James W., were placed in the Madison County Circuit Court room by Mrs. James W. Caperton and her daughter, Mrs. Paul Burnam. "The presentation speech was made by Attorney A. R. Burnam, Hon. W. B. Smith responding on behalf of the bar, and Judge W. R. Shackelford accepted the handsome portraits on behalf of the court."—A memory and scrapbook belonging to Mrs. James W. Caperton containing clippings from the Louisville *Courier-Journal* and the Lexington *Herald;* also the Richmond *Daily Register,* October 27, 1919.

88. GENERAL BURBRIDGE.

General Stephen Gano Burbridge was born in Scott County, Kentucky, in 1831, and attended Georgetown College. He practiced law, engaged in the mercantile business and operated a large farm in turn until the war began, when he raised the 26th Kentucky Infantry and became its colonel. After Shiloh he became brigadier-general and later he helped check Bragg in Kentucky and participated in the Vicksburg campaign.

After the victories in Mississippi, Burbridge was transferred to Arkansas "and led the charge at Arkansas Post that resulted in its capture, planting the American flag upon the fort." This emblem had been placed in his hands for that purpose as a tribute to his gallantry by General A. G. Smith. Soon after the fall of Port Gibson, where he was also conspicuous, he was placed in command of the military district of Kentucky. On July 4, 1864, he was thanked and made a major-general for his service against General John H. Morgan.

As military commander in his native State, General Burbridge was very unpopular, and apparently justly so. Naturally his task was difficult, but the long list of cruel executions and other apparent excessive measures charged against him, even by a Harvard professor, Nat T. Shaler, cause one to wonder whether President Lincoln really knew what was going on in Kentucky. Suffice it to say that Burbridge never returned to his native State to live after the war.—Appleton's *Encyclopedia of American Biography*, Vol. I, p. 449. For a severe arraignment of General Burbridge's administration in Kentucky see E. Polk Johnson, *A History of Kentucky and Kentuckians*, pp. 369-374.

89. Thomas Oldham was a farrier in Thomas B. Collins' company. There were seven other Oldhams enlisted in this company from Madison County, namely, J. F. Oldham (first lieutenant), J. R., Preston, Richard, James, Othniel R., and J. T. The records show that Nathan Deatherage enlisted in Captain Joseph Chenault's company.—Copy of record apparently furnished Nathan B. Deatherage by General Basil W. Duke, now in possession of the writer.

Chapter XXVI

90. Miller's *History and Genealogies,* p. 314, says of Robert Christopher Harris Covington: ". . . After his marriage in the year 1862 he enlisted in Chenault's company [regiment], Duke's Brigade, Morgan's command of the Confederate army, and died in the service of brain fever, at Monticello, Kentucky, March 22, 1863, where his remains were burried. . . ." The records referred to above in note 89 show that R. C. H. Covington was second lieutenant in Captain Thos. B. Collins' Company F, of Chenault's regiment. (Also see page 236.)

91. The writer has published an article on "President Lincoln's Clemency" in the *Journal of the Illinois State Historical Society,* Vol. XX (January, 1928), pp. 547-568. He has rewritten and extended this article and expects to publish it again in 1937 as a chapter of a book entitled *Pardon and Amnesty During the Civil War and Reconstruction.* See "Pardoning the Leaders of the Confederacy" by J. T. Dorris, in the *Mississippi Valley Historical Review,* Vol. XV, pp. 3-21 (June, 1928), and note 95 under Chapter XXVIII.

92. The likeness of Mary Ann Oldham facing page 36 was made from an enlarged picture which had been developed from a tin-type that she had made for Nathan Deatherage while he was a prisoner in Camp Douglas. Nathan was in this military prison for more than eighteen months. Early in 1865 he was sent to Richmond, Virginia, where he was paroled, after which he walked to his home in Madison County. (See note 40.)

Chapter XXVII

93. A Madisonian's Response to the Draft.

"A True Kentuckian. The Provost Marshal of the Eighth District of Kentucky, having called upon those whom he had enrolled to show cause for exemption—if cause there were—was waited on by a large crowd, nearly all of whom were rebels, many of them having served several months in the rebel army, but considered themselves unfit for the hardships of the tented field.

Hereupon, the Provost Marshal was favored with the following letter:

"Richmond, Ky., December 17, 1863.

"Captain Robert Hays, Provost Marshal Eighth District, London, Kentucky:

"Dear Sir: I have seen your advertisement giving the people desiring exemption from the coming draft an opportunity to lay in their complaints, &c. Now, sir, I have never had the honor of your acquaintance, but I can refer you, for the truth of what I am about to say, to my worthy friend, James D. Foster, surgeon, and a member of your honorable Board. My complaints are as follows, viz.:

"I have no broken limbs. I have no chronic diseases, such as inflammatory rheumatism, chronic inflammation of the stomach, phthisic, white swelling, &c. I am not blind in either eye. I am not knock-kneed. I am not bandy-shanked. I am not bow-legged. I have no bad teeth, and can bite off a cartridge. I stand straight on my pastern joints. I have never been drilled in the Southern army, and never been so fortunate as to belong to the sympathizing party in Madison. I have no impediment in my speech. I am neither near-sighted nor far-sighted. I can hear well; I can hear the ring of a musket as well as the ring of a silver dollar. In short, I am sound in wind and limb. I am about twenty-eight years old. I am a housekeeper, and have a wife (a good Union woman), and no children living. I am a citizen of Madison County, Kentucky, from which you want two hundred and thirty-nine soldiers. I am as brave as any man who is no braver than I am. One of my legs is as long as the other, and both are long enough to run well. I am for the 'last man and the last dollar,' 'nigger or no nigger'; especially the last man. If you have a good musket marked 'U. S.', send it down here, and I am ready to bear it in defence of the Union. I am no foreigner, and claim all the papers that entitle me to 'go in.'

"WILLARD DAVIS."

—Moore, Frank: *Anecdotes, Poetry, and Incidents of the War,* p. 335.

94. In the matter of Negro substitutes in the Union army, E. M. Coulter, *op. cit.* p. 205, says that "the order allowing Negroes to substitute for whites made it easy for the Provost Marshals to do business on their own account among Kentuckians who had no scruples against letting a Negro do their fighting. To curb the outside substitute brokers the legislature made it a misdemeanor, punishable by a fine of $1,000 and one year imprisonment to take a substitute out of the State."—Also see Fred Albert Shannon, *The Organization and Administration of the Union Army*, pp. 164-165.

Chapter XXVIII

95. Securing the Release of Confederate Prisoners.

It was natural for persons in the South who had relatives and friends in northern military prisons to try to secure their release, when an early exchange seemed unlikely, as was often the case in 1864-65. There is positive evidence that such releases were actually effected by the law firm of Burnam and Caperton.

In "Family Records" (three typed volumes), by Mrs. James W. Caperton, Vol. I, p. 42, Mrs. Caperton has recorded the following account by her husband: Some time in 1864 Colonel Caperton was engaged to go to Washington to get the President to release a number of prisoners from Camp Douglas. Mr. Lincoln received Mr. Caperton cordially and, after learning his visitor's mission, said, "Caperton, when Seward sees this list he will think I am recruiting for the Southern army." He allowed the request and Mr. Caperton went to Chicago and secured the release of the prisoners on his list.

Two incidents connected with this mission of Colonel Caperton's are worth relating. While he was waiting outside the President's office, he noticed a man in distress farther down the line. On inquiry he learned that the man's "son was to be shot the next morning as a spy, unless he could secure a pardon from Mr. Lincoln." Colonel Caperton at once gave the anxious father his place and in a little while the man came out of the President's office beaming with joy, for his petition had been granted and his son was saved.

The other instant is of similar import. Colonel Caperton took his group of released prisoners from Camp Douglas to an eating place nearby, where he discovered that there were fifteen men instead of the fourteen on his list. It happened that there was a man by the name of Kavanaugh who was to be released. When his name was called by the officer at the gate another man from Arkansas by the same name also responded. When Colonel Caperton discovered the error, he said, "Young man, I had nothing to do with getting you out of that prison, and if you will take the oath of allegiance, as these other men have done. . . . I will certainly not put you back." The man took the oath and Colonel Caperton gave him money to pay his way home. In due time this money was refunded.

Unfortunately Mr. Caperton's fee book contains no record of this case. Mrs. Caperton, however, has his checks of withdrawals from his bank for that year and she believes a check payable to himself for $800 and dated February 1, 1864, was for money to meet the expense of this trip to Washington and Chicago. Often the lawyers had to furnish the released prisoners money to pay their expenses home.

Fortunately the fee book of Burnam and Caperton for 1865 is available. It shows that in January and February, 1865, this law firm was engaged by a number of persons in and near Madison County to secure the release of their Confederate kinsmen from Camp Douglas. Messrs. Burnam's and Caperton's friendship with President Lincoln apparently encouraged this action. At any rate the firm agreed to procure the release of some thirty-four prisoners. It was a strictly business proposition in every instance and the fee was $100.00 in nearly every case. The exceptions were $50.00 for each of two others, and $150.00 for the release of two more.

Mr. Burnam went to Washington and obtained the President's order for the releases and Mr. Caperton took the approved list to Camp Douglas. In all, the liberty on parole of twenty prisoners was secured, seventeen from Camp Douglas and three from other prison camps—Fort Delaware, two, and Rock Island, one. Several prisoners whose freedom the lawyers had undertaken to secure were released before Caperton arrived in Chicago and consequently his firm received nothing for those cases.

It should be noted that Burnam and Caperton also received (February 21, 1865) $300.00 for obtaining permission from the Federal authorities to allow Cabell Chenault's sons, David and Anderson, and Ira N. Scudder, escaped rebel prisoners, to take the oath of allegiance to the United States. These men on returning to Madison County were in danger of being arrested and returned to the prison camps from which they had escaped.

The fees which this law firm charged for services in these instances were not exorbitant, when compared with charges in similar cases at that time. "It appears that one hundred and fifty dollars was the usual fee charged by" pardon attorneys who obtained pardons for persons excepted from President Johnson's general amnesty of May 29, 1865, as stated in "Pardon Seekers and Brokers: A Sequel of Appomattox," by the writer, in *The Journal of Southern History,* Vol. I, p. 286.—The above information was obtained from one of the fee books of the law firm of Curtis F. Burnam and James W. Caperton, now in the possession of Mrs. J. W. Caperton, Richmond, Kentucky.

96. It is interesting to note that a large number of people in Madison have relatives in McClain County, Illinois. Evidently this fertile part of the Prairie State very early attracted many settlers from Madison County. Miller Park, in Bloomington, the county seat of McClain, was given to the city by James Miller, an early settler of Bloomington, who was a native of Virginia and a relative of Millers in Madison County.

97. The minutes of Cane Spring Church show no preaching in the months of January, May, September, October, and November, 1864. In March of that year "a few met but did no business." There were only four services in 1865. The War between the States apparently made a difference for a time in religious devotion in Old Cane Springs, if the minutes of its old church are to be relied on in that respect. Yet back in the late forties and early fifties there were months in every year when no services were recorded in the minutes.

Aunt Ann Bradley (see note 49) states that she remembers when the colored folks were allowed to use Old Cane Spring Church on Sundays occasionally for their services. This was apparently before they built a church in the community.

98. See page 81.

99. See note 95.

100. W. H. Miller's *History and Genealogies,* p. 451, says: "David Chenault was a Confederate soldier in Colonel D. Waller Chenault's Regiment; [was] taken prisoner on the Ohio raid and confined in Camp Douglas, but made his escape [and] was recaptured. He married Mary Bullock of Illinois in 1865 and lives on the outskirts of Richmond."

101. Miller also says on the same page: "Anderson Chenault joined the Confederate army at 19 years of age, was captured on General Morgan's Ohio raid, escaped from Camp Douglas, [was] recaptured and tried at Louisville, Ky., as a rebel spy, but was released. In 1866 he married Bettie Fogg, of Woodford County, Ky., and settled down to farming in Madison County, Ky...."

102. The Madison County Marriage Book B, pp. 215-236, gives seven marriages for August, twenty for September, eleven for October, fourteen for November, and thirteen for December, 1865, or sixty-five for these five months. For the corresponding months of 1864 there was a total of thirty-nine.

103. THE DEATHERAGE-OLDHAM WEDDING.

The marriage book referred to above states that Nathan Bird Deatherage and Mary Ann Oldham were married on November 9, 1865, "in the presence of Jonathan P. Estill and John Chambers" by Reverend "W. M. Riddell, M. B. C." The wedding evidently was a great social event in Old Cane Springs. Nath and Mary Ann were popular young people and their parents were among the most substantial citizens of the community. Mrs. Margaret Jane Boggs (see note 78) and Mrs. C. L. Searcy, who lives at Elliston (see map), were present. They were about twenty and thirteen years old respectively.

Mrs. Boggs states that the attendance was estimated at five hundred. She ought to remember the occasion well for she refused a proposal of marriage that night by her escort, a young Mr. Black, and an older sister lost an underskirt which she had removed in order that she might look more slender and attractive. She failed to find the garment when she was ready to return home.

Miss Polly Gilbert planned and carried out the wedding program, serving and all. Her success was generally acclaimed, and was long afterwards favorably commented on. Mrs. Boggs and Mrs. Searcy did not attend the infare. Mrs. Searcy was too ill the next day, apparently from excesses of the previous occasion. Robert Turpin (see note 49) was present, however, and believes that two or three hundred people attended.

Nathan and Mary Ann went to housekeeping on a farm near their parents but on the west side of Muddy Creek. There they lived happily until Mary Ann's death, June 5, 1869.—See map of Old Cane Springs.

104. Finally it might be said that Nathan Deatherage died childless; and, moreover, it might also be noted that there is not a Deatherage, Oldham, Chenault, Noland, or Chambers living in Old Cane Springs today. In fact, most of the ante-bellum family names in that community are gone. The farms there are smaller and more numerous, of course, and many are cultivated by white tenants. Only a few residences of that early day remain and they are rather dilapidated. Furthermore, where there were formerly so many Negroes not a person of color can now be found.

Indeed the community has undergone a great change since the War between the States and the abolition of slavery. Perhaps such a transformation would have come anyway, for surely the slaves would have been emancipated before 1900, even if there had been no war with its concomitant and subsequent economic and social results. This question, then, arises: Would Old Cane Springs have been any different today if freedom had come later, unaccompanied by warfare?

ADDENDA

A

COLONEL JAMES B. McCREARY'S INTEGRITY

A FEW YEARS AGO the writer found the following accounts in a quantity of James B. McCreary's "papers." The quarters in Richmond which the former Governor of Kentucky and United States Senator had occupied as an office were being prepared for another occupant and many items from his files were thrown into a trash can on the street below. The two articles published here were typed but unsigned and not dated. They had been written, evidently, to record for all time certain of the Colonel's experiences as a Confederate prisoner of war in the Ohio penitentiary and in Fort Delaware. Efforts to ascertain their authorship have been futile. Fortunately the papers were saved.

There is no question about McCreary's being cast into a dungeon for possessing a case knife. Furthermore, it is certain that he and other officers were later transferred to points near the Atlantic coast to be exchanged. Nevertheless, the graphic and laudatory accounts of his refusal to reveal the identity of the man who gave him the knife and of his refusal to accept the President's parole on condition that he leave the United States and remain away until the end of the war, are so remarkable that one desires to ascertain their authorship and the source of the information contained therein. The eulogies of McCreary might be accepted as plausible evidence that he himself did not write the articles, if it were not for penciled interlineations in the original manuscripts in his own hand, as attested by Mr. Henry Cosby, who was the Colonel's secretary while he was United States Senator. Evidently McCreary emitted the information contained in the articles and sanctioned the sentiment expressed therein. Perhaps he wrote both papers. At any rate, they merit publication.

It is interesting to note that General Basil W. Duke referred to Colonel McCreary only once (and that very indirectly) in his *Morgan's Cavalry*, which he published first in 1867. And strange to say he omitted any reference to him in his *Reminiscences* in 1911, after McCreary had been Governor of Kentucky and United States Senator. Some significance must be given these omissions of his fellow officer and prisoner, since he mentioned many others of lesser rank. McCreary mentions Duke in his "Journal," which the *Register* of the Kentucky State Historical Society published in April and July, 1935.

I

On the morning of July 2nd, 1863, General John H. Morgan's division of cavalry, twenty-eight hundred strong, rose at the break of day. A few miles apart the two brigades composing the division had spent the night on the bank of the Cumberland River, in Wayne County, Ky. The stream was full from shore to shore, and great nests and piles of driftwood, interspersed with thousands of logs, floated by on their way to the ocean. A thrill of joy stirred every heart and quickened every fiber when the order came to these expatriated Kentuckians to turn their faces homeward.

The Federals on the north side of the river, quieted by the tremendous currents that flowed in the stream, were less vigilant in their watch. When these hardy Kentuckians, these men of brave hearts, rode down to the edge of the stream, some unsaddled their horses, drove them into the swift currents and forced them to head their way for the other side. There was small opposition to prevent these newcomers from landing. The Federals were not sure where General Morgan's men would cross, and so, peacefully, unsuspectingly, they slept in their tents, trusting to luck and high water to hold back these daring invaders.

The Eleventh Kentucky Cavalry was in the Second Brigade, then commanded by Adam R. Johnson, of the Tenth Kentucky Cavalry. James B. McCreary, then Major, was acting as Lieutenant Colonel of this regiment. The stream was half a mile wide. A small ferryboat and a few canoes constituted the means of transportation across the turgid stream. The ferryboat could at best carry a small portion of the soldiers, and a large majority of them, flinging their clothes into the ferryboat, hung onto the sides; others holding their horses by the manes and tails to prevent being swept down by the swift tides essayed to cross and overtake the horses that had passed on before in this perilous swim.

As the first detachment of the second brigade reached the opposite bank, the Federal picket stationed on the north side undertook to resist the landing. Some of the Confederates who were in the ferryboat and in the canoes rushed into line, while those who were naked and had swum, despising the role of laggards and not stopping to dress, seized their muskets and their cartridge boxes and rushed at the foe. The strange sight of clothesless men engaged in combat, paralyzed the enemy. They had never before seen soldiers go into conflict clothed only in nature's garb, and it seemed to them that warriors, fully grown and armed, were just born into the world and must have come down from some spirit land weird and strange to rush to combat.

Among scenes like these began the thousand-mile march which constituted Morgan's Ohio raid. It did not take long for General Morgan and his followers to discover that their presence was not only unwelcome and expected, but was to be resisted to the bitter end. In a little while dead horses, dead troopers, broken wagons, abandoned clothing and haversacks along the roadway from Burksville to Columbia gave mute proof not only of war's terrors but of its baneful consequences.

The enthusiasm of home-going gave renewed courage and aroused increasing vehemence in these Kentuckians, who were facing their homes; and they were ready and determined to ride over anything that obstructed the way toward their friends farther up in the settlement.

Picket firing and occasional volleys from the hilltops marked the pathway to Columbia, twenty-six miles from Burksville. The remainder of the second of July after the crossing of the Cumberland River, and the third of July were consumed in reaching the Federal stockade at Green River, several miles from Lebanon. Here was stationed the Twenty-fifth Michigan Infantry, commanded by Colonel O. B. Moore. The stockade was well constructed, with great skill, and protected by an impassable line consisting of trees and rifle pits and some sharpened pieces of wood, with wires and fencing protected by heavy brush. Against this a couple of regiments were hurled, but in vain. When surrender had been demanded of Colonel Moore, the Federal commander, he returned the laconic answer, that "the Fourth of July was no day for a Union soldier to entertain such a proposition." He was a brave, gallant, and fearless foe, and his patriotic and valorous response won the respect of his enemies. The tone and words of his reply foreboded trouble. The Confederates were not long in finding out that he was prepared in action to back up his words of eloquent defiance.

General Morgan was compelled in a little while to do what his judgment now told him he should have done in the outset, that was to leave the stockade and infantry alone. They were really not in his way, could do him no damage if left unmolested, and could join in no pursuit when once he had passed them by. They could only follow on foot, and the swift riding raiders would in a few hours leave them far behind. In thirty minutes' fighting more than forty men were killed and forty-five wounded. Of the enemy nine were killed and twenty-six wounded. Colonel Chenault of the 11th Kentucky, Major Brent of the 5th, Captain Tribble of the 11th, Lieutenant Cowan of the 3rd, Lieutenants Holloway and Ferguson of the 5th, were among the valiant and gallant officers who laid down their lives on that day for their country. A full description of this battle has already been given.

In any protracted war all commands which extensively participate have their dark days, and in some respects, outside the disaster at Buffington Island, sixteen days later, the darkest day that ever came to General Morgan's division was this sad Fourth of July. For a little while it checked the enthusiasm and stilled the quickened heartbeats of the returning exiles. On the morrow at Lebanon there would be other sorrowful experiences and the hope of home-going would temporarily vanish, when at Lebanon the head of the column turned west instead of continuing east.

On this grim day at Green River Stockade the 11th under Chenault and the 5th under Colonel Smith were asked to do the impossible. They stood until standing was no longer wise or even brave. The Federal commander reported that the fighting lasted three hours, but the real fighting lasted less than an hour; and with something less than seven hundred men engaged, about forty-five were killed and the same number wounded. This was a distressing percentage of mortality under the circumstances of the battle.

Chenault, impetuous, gallant, died close up to the enemy with his face to the foe. Major Brent, of the 5th Kentucky, so full of promise, was killed as he rode up to salute Colonel James B. McCreary, who succeeded Chenault in command of the 11th. Captain Tribble, of Christmas raid fame, was among the men who gave their lives on this field for the Southland. As he rose to salute the Colonel, who had become such by the death of Chenault, and waved his hand to let him know that he would be ready when the order came, he fell, crushed by a bullet that crashed his brain.

None of those who saw these dead brought out under the flag of truce, and the wounded carried in blankets from out of the woods and from the ravines and laid along the turnpike road from Columbia to Lebanon, will ever forget the harrowing scene. When they looked upon the dead, with their pallid faces turned heavenward, and their pale, motionless hands folded across their stilled breasts, poignant grief filled every heart. It did not take long to bury, or arrange for burial for, the dead. Humanity would care for the wounded, and war's demands bade the remaining soldiers press forward, and by midnight the division camped a few miles out from Lebanon to rest for the conflict on the morrow.

The 11th Kentucky was a magnificent regiment. It had been recruited in Madison, Clark, Estill, and Wayne counties, and was filled with men of courage, ambition, patriotism, and loyalty to the Southern Cause. Most of them had volunteered when Kirby Smith and Bragg invaded Kentucky in June and July, 1862. They had been at Hartsville. They had been on the Christmas raid. They had been in many conflicts in Tennessee during General Morgan's operations from December, 1862, to June, 1863. They had become hardened to the privations and sacrifices of real war, and they had learned to obey, and they rejoiced to fight for their beloved Southland.

Colonel James B. McCreary had volunteered in the 11th Kentucky, as a private, and he carried a musket for some months, then became Adjutant, and a little later Major of this splendid regiment, and then became Colonel when Colonel Chenault was killed. On the thousand miles which marked this raid of General Morgan, through Kentucky to Indiana and

Ohio, his conduct as Colonel had elicited the admiration of General Morgan, who assigned him important duties. On the 19th of July, 1863, came the disastrous defeat at Buffington's Island. Many wondered why this battle should have gone so sorely against the Confederates. True, the men composing it had ridden with ceaseless speed for nineteen days and nights, and hindsight, which is so much better than foresight, reasoned why General Morgan did not cross the Ohio River when he reached its banks on the evening of July 19th. It was just one of war's happenings, and backward vision pointed out how readily it might have been avoided. But the crossing of the river at night, swollen by late rains and guarded by gunboats, might have caused serious losses. It is possible a few hundred men would have been drowned in the passage, but that would have been nothing compared to the loss of this splendid division at this time in the history of the war.

Amongst the prisoners captured at Buffington's Island, was Colonel James B. McCreary, with a large number of officers, including General Duke, Commander of the first brigade. The prisoners were transferred down the Ohio River in steamboats, carried to Cincinnati, and then later transferred to the Columbus penitentiary. The people of Ohio and Indiana had never felt the touch of war, and when Morgan's "terrible men" rode through their towns and villages, tore up the railroads and burned their mills, destroyed public property and fired back at the people who fired at them, and killed a man here and there, it was regarded as dreadful evidences of savagery and brutality. Along the line of the march there was hardly an hour that some reckless gunner had not fired into General Morgan's line of march, and the dropping of a soldier here and there gave proof of the sure aim of these amateur defenders. Intense feeling had been excited against Morgan's men and at one place later on the populace of a large town threatened and actually started to mob the defenseless prisoners, but the courage and sagacity of the commander of the Federal guard prevented this outrage.

This feeling in Ohio was so intense that under the influence of C. S. Todd, then Governor of Ohio, all of Morgan's officers were carried to the Ohio penitentiary and confined in a new store building just finished, many of them remaining as long as nine months. None of these men seemed to remember what the people of the South suffered from raids in the Southland, and the cry of "Vengeance!" went up, and Morgan's men were compelled to submit to these shameful and unjustifiable wrongs. The story of the escape of General Morgan from the Ohio penitentiary with his six companions is one of the most thrilling and dramatic of all the events of the war.

It is natural that among men so high-spirited, so brave, so intelligent and enterprising, that efforts to escape should be made. Nine-tenths of all the officers of Morgan's men were from Kentucky. Their families were well to do and they supplied them an abundance of money which they spent freely. Some of the captives had managed to bribe their guards to get knives, which were case knives, and when well ground down they became formidable weapons; and among those who had gotten the knives was Colonel James B. McCreary. After General Morgan's escape the cells of all these prisoners were searched and Colonel McCreary was found in the possession of a knife. The demand was made that he should give the name of the person from whom he had received it, either by gift or by purchase. This the gallant young officer flatly refused to do, preferring any punishment to the betrayal of the man who had helped him in his extremity. It was in the midst of winter and the Ohio penitentiary in those days not altogether comfortable, was cold and dreary. The officer urged Colonel McCreary to surrender this name and he promised him if he should do so that he would escape punishment. Firmly and flatly the Confederate refused to divulge the name of the giver of the knife. He was told that if he persisted in this course that he must suffer solitary confinement in an underground dungeon, fitted up for the most hardened criminals. To all this he responded: "You may kill me if you will, but I shall not betray the man who gave me the knife." Under guard, in the roughest manner, he was hurried away to the dungeon, without fire, without any convenience or comfort—no bed, no cot, no blanket. There in darkness and stillness in these awful surroundings he awaited the orderings of what seemed to him to be a slow living death.

On the second day an officer appeared and opened the small gate which did not even let in any light, and the young Colonel was asked if he would reveal the name required. The thermometer down in the cell was hovering around zero. Still, almost speechless, he whispered through the grating, "I will die before I will give the name." Then a cup of water and a piece of stale bread were passed to the small shelf on the inside of the door. When the bearer of the message went away leaving him to the horrors of what appeared then to be his death-chamber, he at first walked from side to side of the cell where he could hear only the sound of his own footsteps on the stone floor. With no voice, no response, he felt the stupor which precedes death by freezing. He stamped and walked and flapped his hands against his body and bent his limbs to drive off the stupor. Minutes lengthened into hours, hours—seemingly—into weeks. The prisoner felt he was to be neglected and left alone to die amid these horrible and gruesome surroundings, but his courage never failed. On the third day the messenger came again and asked him if he was ready to reveal the name of the man who gave him the knife. Numb with cold, practically unable to speak, he could only mutter back that he had no answer to make to any such infamous proposition. Another cup of water and another piece of stale bread were passed in, but these were to be untouched. The limbs of the prisoner were now stiff with cold. His jaws had lost their power to move, and thus the hours passed until finally nature could not withstand the awful strain and he sank down helpless on the floor. Unconscious, moaning and groaning, he lay there apparently in the throes of death.

At this time the surgeon passed through the corridor upon which the dungeon was situated and heard the moanings of the now insensible man. He demanded of the guard to know who was in the cell. He ordered the door opened and then went in and with kind and merciful hands lifted the helpless form, now stiff, rigid, and speechless. He ordered the man carried from this place of brutality and horror to the hospital, and nourished and brought him back to life. He entered vigorously in the protest against this merciless conduct of the guards of the penitentiary. He ordered Colonel McCreary restored to his cell.

Only a man of iron constitution, only a man of unconquerable will, only a man with the noblest sense of honor and the highest spirit of integrity could have passed through such an ordeal. Only a hero that God had made could have faced the horrors of the situation and gone down practically unto death with the name of the giver of the knife unspoken. The man who had given him the knife was nothing but an ordinary private Federal soldier. He had neither position nor money. The Confederate might have betrayed him and his punishment would not have been quite so severe as that of the Confederate, but a spirit of Southern honor in this man prompted this prisoner to his noble and heroic deed.

II

Early in 1864 Morgan's officers were moved to Johnson's Island, Sandusky, Ohio.

There had been arrangements made for an exchange, [and] Morgan's officers were transferred to more convenient places where they might readily be sent to the boats which the Federals used to convey the prisoners to the mouth of the James River and there exchanged in return for their own soldiers.

Doctor E. R. McCreary, the father of James B. McCreary, was a man of wealth and much social influence among the statesmen of that day in Kentucky. Connected with many of the most distinguished families of that Commonwealth, he was enabled to bring influence to bear upon Mr. Lincoln and to secure from him an agreement that if Colonel McCreary would accept a parole and go abroad and not return to the United States during the continuance of the war he would be released.

At this time the mother of Colonel McCreary was an invalid. She was suffering from an incurable disease. Colonel McCreary was an only son. The mother was unable to travel to Washington to meet her boy, but the father went, with his soul all filled with the desire to do something to stay the hand of disease which was striking down his life's companion and hour by hour eating out her life. He knew that there could be no medicine more potent in her possible restoration than the removal of her love from prison hardships and war's dangers.

When the father of Colonel McCreary was ready to start upon his journey the grief of his wife was well nigh indescribable. The longing for her boy and the suffering which came from disease filled her soul with acutest anguish, and, pressing her face against that of her devoted husband, she pleaded and prayed that he should not return without letting her see her child, or at least getting an assurance that he should be removed from the sufferings, dangers, and privations of war, and if she could not see his face that she might know that his life would be spared and after the war he could return to his father and mother and his home. Armed with the necessary authority to make the proposition to the young officer, the sorrowing and hopeful father hastened to Fort Delaware and secured an interview with his son. Laying before him the distressing and sad condition of his mother, he brought with him not only her written but her spoken words of pleading, that he would comfort her in her dying hours and listen to the persuasions of his father and remove himself from further participation in the war. The father, with the tenderness and love only a parent can feel, put his arm around his son, and with his head resting upon his boy's shoulder, he told, as only a physician could describe, the ailments and malady of the loving mother, five hundred miles away in her Kentucky home.

He reminded his boy that he was the last of his race, that if he should die the name would become extinct and the family tree be lopped off. He said to him, "My son, I do not ask you to desert your Cause. I only ask you to accept this parole which I have obtained from President Lincoln and to leave this country until the cessation of hostilities."

It required an almost superhuman courage to resist this appeal. With the resplendent courage that had marked the history of this young officer when he fell down unconscious on the stone floor of a dungeon in the Ohio penitentiary to save an humble man from whom he bought a knife, he replied:

"Father, I took an oath to fight for the Confederate States of America until the war should be ended. It was not one month or six months, but until the end of hostilities. Should I now accept this parole and go away it would be practical desertion of the Cause to which I have pledged my services, my honor, my life. The immeasurable love I have for my mother, my reverence and affection for you, would prompt me to yield to your request, but should the war end and I return to the State of Kentucky, I could never look again in the face of the thousand men that I led at Hartsville, Green River, Lebanon, Buffington Island, and through the States of Indiana and Ohio, nor could I ever face again these associates rendered near and dear to me as brothers by a common sacrifice and the common dangers through which we passed. Father, oh, father, do not tempt me to do this thing. I would be unworthy of the name you bear and which you have transmitted to me. I would be unworthy of the ancestors whose graves would be about us in our birthplace in Madison County, the home of our people for so many years, and when I would go and visit the spot where my dead are sepulchred, as I stood above their ashes I would despise myself for having deserted the Cause for which I had in my young manhood pledged my loyalty and my faith and my life. I would be an exile in my own State and among my own people, and among the soldiers that I led in battle. My heart is torn by these conflicting emotions. With deepest love for my mother and tenderest regard for your wishes I would do anything that honor does not forbid. My record as a soldier, my pride as a patriot, cry out against this proposal. Father, father, for you and my mother, I dare not do this cowardly act."

The Federal officer in charge of the young soldier, touched by the distress of the father, urged upon the young soldier acquiescence to his wishes, but the boyish Confederate Colonel turned to him and said: "If the thing were reversed and you were in my place, would you prove disloyal to your country and to the cause to which you had pledged your life, and go away in voluntary exile and leave your people to fight out the struggle while you enjoyed a life of ease and plenty in a foreign land?"

The Federal soldier replied, "I would not."

"Then," said Colonel McCreary, "I will not," and turning to his father, with tears streaming down his cheeks, he said, "Father, father, this temptation is almost greater than I can bear. Do not press it on me. You would not love and respect me, and my mother would not love and respect me, and the world would say I was unworthy of the name of McCreary if I were to do this. I will go back and bear the burdens and the privations that will come in this war, and if I die on the battlefield or in the hospital, I shall perish with the consciousness that I brought no shame upon my ancestry, my name, or my country."

The father returned to the sad and stricken home, depressed that he had failed in his mission, yet proud of the son who had borne so fiery an ordeal without surrendering his convictions. The mother lived to see her son return home and then met death serenely with the knowledge that her only son had proved himself a patriot and man of honor.

B

LETTERS WRITTEN BY PRISONERS OF WAR IN CAMP DOUGLAS

THESE LETTERS speak for themselves. Those by Nathan Deatherage to his parents were selected from fifteen extant, the last of which is dated October 30, 1864. His letter of December 3, 1863, suggests that he had just written to his "sweetheart,"

Mary Ann Oldham. Unfortunately their letters to each other appear not to exist.

The letter by James Davis to his brother, John, in Madison County, appears to be the only one extant from his hand. It is in the possession of Mrs. Lyman Parrish, the daughter of John Davis, to whom it was written.

The letters have been edited slightly.

Camp Douglas, Illinois
November the 23rd, '63

Dear Father,

I have been looking for a letter from home for two weeks. It has been two weeks today since I got the last letter from home. I thought I would write you a few lines to let you know how I am getting along. I am well at present. I had the yellow ganders last week. It made me sick a little, but I am well now. All the boys are well, of your acquaintance. Bob Shearer is well. I got a letter from Bob Covington last Saturday. I told him to tell Mother to send me a box of provisions but you need not send them. They won't let them come in. I want you to send me five dollars. You will have to send it in a letter. I reckon the people have quit coming up here; it is very safe in a letter. Father, if you have a chance I want you to send me two pair of twill cotton drawers. Bob said in his letters that Mother had got my miniature. I am very glad of that. I am doing very well now. I have moved in James Davis' mess. They have got a small room and a cooking stove. It is very much better in a small room than a large one. I want to fix up, for I believe we are here for all the winter. I have never got a letter from any of my uncles yet; I wrote to Uncle Billy twice. Father, I have not got much to write this time. You must write soon. Give me all the news. Give my best respects to Jose Woods and Billy Covington. Tell them both to write; Will Jackson also. Give my best respects to all the neighbors. Give my love to all the family. Tell Uncle George Simmons to write. Tell him the reason he cannot write. He is too busy sitting by Miss Nancy McCoy. Please write soon, no more at present. This is from your son.

N. B. DEATHERAGE.

P.S. James Oldham is well and fat. We both got the clothes you sent us.
N. B. DEATHERAGE.

Camp Douglas, Ill.
December the 3rd, 1863

Dear Mother,

I have been looking for a letter from you for four weeks. I thought I would write you a few lines to let you know how I am getting along. I am well at present, all the boys are well of your acquaintance. Bob

Shearer is getting well. I got a letter from Bob Covington several days ago and he said that you all were well. I got a letter from Mag Newland a day or two ago. Bob Covington said you got my miniature. I was glad of that. It has been very cold here for the last week, but is getting warmer. It was the coldest spell that we ever had since we have been here. Cull Maupin and Crate are up here. They came to see their brothers. I heard that Doctor Webb and Rayner came home. I understand that they took the oath. I am sorry for our regiment. I do not know what we will do if all the commissioned officers take the oath. I believe it will play out entirely. You need not send me anything to eat. They are not admitted to come in. I wrote in my other letter for Father to send me five dollars; if he has not sent it tell him to send it. I have three dollars and a quarter owing to me in here, but I can't get it for some time. If I can't get home against Christmas I must have some money to buy firecrackers and (sweethearts) sweet cakes. I made a mistake. I have sweetheart in my head so much I put it down in place of sweet cakes. You must excuse my foolishness. I got all the clothes you sent me the last time. I need two pair of drawers but if you have not sent them I can buy them here for 40 cents a pair. The cotton will cost you more than that a yard. I have no more to write. Give my best respects to Jose and Nannie. Tell them to write. Give my best respects to all the neighbors. Tell Will Jackson to write and Billy Covington. Tell Uncle George to write. Jo Simmons, James Davis, Jim Oldham are well. Give my love to the family. Kiss all the children for me. Sam and Kile in particular. Please write soon.

N. B. D.

Camp Douglas, Illinois
January the 14th, 1864

Dear Mother and Father,

I received your kind and welcomed letter dated Dec. the 28th. I would have written sooner but we are only allowed to write but one letter in every 13 days. Christmas is over. We had a fine time. You wanted to know what we had for dinner. We had coffee, sugar corn, bread and gravey. I would not have anything better. It is very cold here, New Years Day was the coldest day that I ever saw. I am well and doing well. All the boys are well but one or two. The talk is here now that we are going to Point Lookout. I dread the trip. I would rather stay here until spring than to be exchanged this winter. You have no idea how cold it is here. I received a letter from Mag Newland the other day. I am sorry I cannot write to her. I will have to quit writing to my friends. What time I have I have to write to you. Tell the boys to eat their pies, cakes, can-peaches; but I would not swap places with them. They have the best eatables, but we enjoy ours better than they do. We have no stock to feed and do not have to run out in the cold. We have nothing to do but draw rations and cook them and then go to eating. I understand that there is not any well men in Madison Co., and that the conscript is scaring them very bad. Tell the boys that it is all over with them, so they will be cut off from their can-peaches if they don't watch out. Tell cousin Will Jackson I would like to capture him the best in the world. Tell Sally, Nancy and Molly that it is too cold to make rings. Kiss them for me, and Sam, and Kile in present order. Ask Josh Woods when he is going to have his sale, if he don't get his tobacco. He is broke—his heart anyhow. Mother, you must write often even if I can't. Be sure to direct your letter to the 7th Ky. (prisoners of war). Do not forget that is the reason I do not get any more letters. Send the drawers on in haste. Tell all my friends to write; but I cannot write to them. Tell me something about the boys that go out to take the oath. We hear a heap of talk about them. James Davis, James Oldham, and Jo Simmons are well. Please write soon and often. No more at present. I remain your loving son until death.

N. D.

Camp Douglas, Illinois
Feb. the 20, '64

Dear Father,

It has been some time since I have written to you and I thought I would write you a few lines to let you know how I am getting along. I am well at present. I had a very bad cold a few days ago. The smallpox has broke out in camp. There was one in my mess that had it and since died. He was taken out on the 11th and died on the 18th. It was old Pap John Hill. I was sorry to hear of his death. He was a good soldier. There were three other cases taken out on the same day from our regiment. James Freeman was another. He is getting along very well. We have all been vaxinated since. Mine did not take. I will be vaxinated again. It has been very cold here for several days. It is warm now. I am willing to be exchanged now at any time. Not that we are treated bad, but I want to get around and see John. We are treated fine here now and plenty to eat. They will let us have money now. They have put up another shop. I want you to send me some money the first chance you get. I never received the drawers you sent me. I fear I never will. I received a letter from Mother on 12th dated the 6th. I have never answered it. This is our writing day. I want you to answer this for I have not received one from you for several months. Tell Will J. I received his letter but cannot answer. Feb. the 24th. The box of clothes has come in but we never got them. They were confiscated. It is against orders for citizens in Chicago to send anything in. James Bonney got his coat and pants. Bob Tevis got his coat. The clothes were issued to the infantry. You need not send me any more drawers. When I get some money I can buy them at 50 cents a pair. James Davis has got the mumps. Answer as soon as you get this. I remain your true son.

NATHAN DEATHERAGE
Co. B. 7, Ky. Cav.

Camp Douglas, Ill.
April the 21st, 1864

My Dear Father,

I received a letter from Mother dated the 12th a few days ago, which I was glad to receive. I am sorry to hear of the misfortune of Jack Willougby's family. I and James Davis received a box of provisions yesterday. I guess Grandma Nell sent it. Tell her I am a thousand times obliged to her. We are all well and getting along fine. There is fine weather sure now, warm and comfortable. Father, I want you to go to town and get Roland to make me a pair of number one boots. I want them doubled in the foot, coarse, fine foot, citizen boot with tolerable high top. No. 8. My boots are nearly worn out. I do not want to go to Dixie bare-footed. Also send me a pair of socks, silk handkerchief. Send them as quick as you can. I remain your true but absent son.

N. B. DEATHERAGE

P.S. Father, do your best for me in the boots. Send with haste.

Camp Douglas, Ill.
June the 12th, '64

Dear Father and Mother,

It has been some time since I've heard from you. I received a letter from Tiff Chenault yesterday. He said you had not received a letter from me for some time. I have written. I cannot tell the reason why you do not get them. I am well and doing well as any other man in a Northern prison. All the boys are well, of your acquaintance. The health of them is very good. There was 54 dead here in the month of May of different diseases. Mother, you can send me two pair of checked cotton shirts, two pair of drawers, twill cotton. I am afraid this letter will be detained on the road. We hear the Rebels are in Ky. Tell Tiff Chenault to send me a photograph of Col. Chenault. If I had one I would not take anything for it. I thought so much of him. I loved him like a father. He treated me as if I was one of his children. Please write soon and often. Tell Jose and Sam to write. Give my love to the family. No more.

NATHAN DEATHERAGE
Co. B 64 North Carolina

P.S. Tell Tiff I will write to him as soon as I can. I would be a thousand times obliged if he would send the photograph of Col. D. W.

N. B.

[Note: At the time of writing this letter Mr. Deatherage appears to have been attached to "Co. B 64 North Carolina."]

Camp Douglas, Illinois
Oct. the 30th, 1864

Dear Mother

I received your letter of the 11th of this month. I was glad to hear from you to learn that you were well. I have not received any answer from my last letter. Answer them as soon as you get them and I will get it before next writing day. I am well and doing well. All the boys are well, of your acquaintance. You need not send me clothing until I write for them. I never received any letter from Ret. Tell her she must write again. Mother, you wanted a photograph, but I cannot send it. Eatables are of more importance to me than a photograph is to you or any of your friends. I wish I could write little Nannie a letter. Tell her I will write her one yet. I have no more to write. Tell Jose, please, to write one more letter. I will answer. I guess we are here for the winter. I hope not. Give my love to all the family. Write soon and often. I remain your true son until death.

N. B. DEATHERAGE
Co. B, 7th Ky. Cav.
Barracks, No. 29.

Camp Douglas, Ill.
Nov. 16th, 1863

Dear Brother:

Yours of the seventh inst came in due time. You are entirely excusable for not writing sooner. I heard of the sickness in your family and entertained great fears that Lester would not get well. I am truly glad to hear that she is getting well. My health is very good. There is considerable sickness in camp caused mostly by being destitute of clothing, blankets. There has been many deaths since we have been here. Five in our Regiment and that is very small compared with some other Regiments.

The hospital arrangements are very good but one has to be very sick before they are allowed to go there. We have been getting plenty to eat, but I understand our rations are to be cut off in retaliation. I don't know that there is any truth in the report. I notice some very doleful stories in the Chicago papers in regard to their men who are prisoners in the Confederacy. I have no doubt those papers greatly exaggerate the true state of things I don't doubt that the Confederacy is doing the best for them that they can. If they retaliate on us of course we will have to stand it, hard though it be. I would be very much pleased if you would send me a box of provisions. I would like a ham or two, some nice light bread, some cakes, etc. and etc. If you should send it put in some good documents to read, that is not of much use to you. Send "Pollock's

Course of Time." I think I have one there. I prefer religious books to any others. Write soon and give me all the news.

Yours,

Please send a jar of butter. J. D.   JAMES DAVIS

C

THE ELEVENTH KENTUCKY CAVALRY, C. S. A. (PART OF MORGAN'S MEN. RECRUITED AND TEMPORARILY ORGANIZED AT RICHMOND, KENTUCKY, SEPTEMBER 10, 1862.)

The records below appear to have been copied for Nathan B. Deatherage, of Madison County, from records prepared by General Basil W. Duke, from the original rolls on file at Washington, D. C. The copies published here are in the writer's possession. It will be seen that Companies A, B, F, G, and H are largely made up of citizens of Madison County. No information for Companies C and J exists in the manuscript records used. Perhaps the confusion is due to a reorganization of the regiment after its union with General Morgan's army. See the note signed by Colonel Joseph Tucker after the list of officers below.

FIELD AND STAFF OFFICERS OF THE 11th CAVALRY, KENTUCKY VOLUNTEERS, C. S. ARMY

Name	Rank	Date of Appointment or Commission	Remarks
D. W. Chenault	Colonel	Sept. 10, '62	Killed July 4, '63, at Bacon Creek Bridge, Ky.
Jos. T. Tucker	Colonel	July 4, '63	
Jos. T. Tucker	Lt. Colonel	Sept. 10, '62	
Jas. B. McCreary	Lt. Colonel	July 4, '63	Paroled.
Jas. B. McCreary	Major	Sept. 10, '62	
G. M. Webb	Surgeon	Sept. 10, '62	Deserted Oct., '63. Took oath to U. S. in prison on plea of ill health.
A. Raines	A Surgeon	Sept. 10, '62	Deserted Oct., '63. Took oath to U. S. in prison.
B. W. Taylor	A Surgeon	Sept. 1, '64	
Wm. M. Riddle	Chaplain	Sept. 10, '62	Resigned Feb., '63.
R. Williams	A. C. S.	Sept. 10, '62	Out of Office July 1, '63, by Act of Congress.
B. A. Tracy	A. Q. M.	Sept. 10, '62	
Wm. L. Hickman	Adjutant	Sept. 10, '62	

Note: "The 11th Ky. Cav. was organized on the 10th day of September, 1862, and was mustered into service, Sept. 10, '62, at Richmond, Ky. It was raised by Col. D. W. Chenault, who acted under authority granted him by Major Gen. E. Kirby Smith, and was subsequently ordered by him to report to Brig. Gen. Jno. H. Morgan under whom it served, in all operations of his division, to the conclusion of the Ohio raid, when the larger portion of it was captured, in the fight at Buffington Island, and immediately afterwards. It was composed exclusively of Kentuckians."

Signed by Basil W. Duke, Brig. Gen.

Note: "After regiment was ordered to report to Brig. Gen. Morgan, Cos. D and G were consolidated, and an addition of other companies caused a change to be made in the letters of some of the companies. At the death of Col. Chenault the regiment numbered 500 effective men."

Signed by Joseph Tucker, Colonel.

MUSTER ROLL OF COMPANY A, 11th CAVALRY, KENTUCKY VOLUNTEERS, C. S. ARMY

Name	Rank	Mustered in When	Mustered in Where	Remarks
Gordon C. Mullens	Captain	Sept. 10, '62	Richmond, Ky.	
Allen A. Rankins	1st Lieut.	Sept. 10, '62	Richmond, Ky.	
Sidney P. Cunningham	2nd Lieut.	Sept. 10, '62	Richmond, Ky.	
Rodney Haggard	2nd Lieut.	Sept. 10, '62	Richmond, Ky.	
Wm. W. Baldwin	1st Sergt.	Sept. 10, '62	Richmond, Ky.	
Joel Quisenbury	2nd Sergt.	Sept. 10, '62	Richmond, Ky.	
John D. Reed	3rd Sergt.	Sept. 10, '62	Richmond, Ky.	Deserted in E. Tenn., Nov. 17, 1862.
John Doyle	4th Corp.	Sept. 10, '62	Richmond, Ky.	Died in Ky., Nov. 25, '62, Camp Fever.
Wm. A. Oliver	1st Corp.	Sept. 10, '62	Richmond, Ky.	
Josephus Oliver	2nd Corp.	Sept. 10, '62	Richmond, Ky.	
Rob't Quisenbury	3rd Corp.	Sept. 10, '62	Richmond, Ky.	
Ellis G. Baxter	4th Corp.	Sept. 10, '62	Richmond, Ky.	
Adkinson, Jos. R.	Teamster	Sept. 10, '62	Richmond, Ky.	
Baker, Thomas	Private	Sept. 10, '62	Richmond, Ky.	Died in Ky., Oct. 10, '62, Camp Fever.
Baker, Pleasant	Private	Sept. 10, '62	Richmond, Ky.	
Baker, Stanley	Private	Sept. 10, '62	Richmond, Ky.	
Brock, Allen	Private	Sept. 10, '62	Richmond, Ky.	
Brock, Francis	Private	Sept. 10, '62	Richmond, Ky.	
Brock, Wm.	Private	Sept. 10, '62	Richmond, Ky.	
Bush, Clifton	Private	Sept. 10, '62	Richmond, Ky.	
Baldwin, W. L.	Private	Sept. 10, '62	Richmond, Ky.	
Brown, Harden	Private	Sept. 10, '62	Richmond, Ky.	
Brown, Henry	Private	Sept. 10, '62	Richmond, Ky.	
Baxter, Luke	Private	Sept. 10, '62	Richmond, Ky.	Deserted in Ky., Nov. 17, '62. Went to Federal lines.
Combs, Walter	Private	Sept. 10, '62	Richmond, Ky.	
Cooper, John	Private	Sept. 10, '62	Richmond, Ky.	
Chisem, Wm.	Private	Sept. 10, '62	Richmond, Ky.	
Collins, Edward	Private	Sept. 10, '62	Richmond, Ky.	
Cooper, McGown	Private	Sept. 10, '62	Richmond, Ky.	
Dixon, Wm.	Private	Sept. 10, '62	Richmond, Ky.	
Freeman, Jas.	Private	Sept. 10, '62	Richmond, Ky.	

Old Cane Springs 233

		Mustered in		
Name	Rank	When	Where	Remarks
Glover, John	Private	Sept. 10, '62	Richmond, Ky.	
Gorden, David	Private	Sept. 10, '62	Richmond, Ky.	
Hampton, E.	Private	Sept. 10, '62	Richmond, Ky.	
Hampton, Jesse	Private	Sept. 10, '62	Richmond, Ky.	
Hampton, Jos.	Private	Sept. 10, '62	Richmond, Ky.	Wounded in Ky., Nov. 17, 1862 — died Nov. 30, '62.
Haggard, W. L. (s)	Private	Sept. 10, '62	Richmond, Ky.	
Haggard, J. P.	Private	Sept. 10, '62	Richmond, Ky.	
Johnson, Jas.	Private	Sept. 10, '62	Richmond, Ky.	
Hall, Achilles	Private	Sept. 10, '62	Richmond, Ky.	
Jackson, Jno. H.	Private	Sept. 10, '62	Richmond, Ky.	Pro. Sergt. Major, Sept. 10, '62.
King, Robert	Private	Sept. 10, '62	Richmond, Ky.	
King, Jeff. C.	Private	Sept. 10, '62	Richmond, Ky.	
Kelley, Jas.	Private	Sept. 10, '62	Richmond, Ky.	Wounded and prisoner at Hartsville, Tenn., Dec. 7, '62 (Lost leg).
Kenny, Wm. C.	Private	Sept. 10, '62	Richmond, Ky.	
Lisle, Braxton	Private	Sept. 10, '62	Richmond, Ky.	
Lisle, Jas. H.	Private	Sept. 10, '62	Richmond, Ky.	
Meredith, Henry	Private	Sept. 10, '62	Richmond, Ky.	From Duke's Reg't, Dec. 22, '62.
Mullins, Jas. H.	Private	Sept. 10, '62	Richmond, Ky.	
Oliver, James	Private	Sept. 10, '62	Richmond, Ky.	
Perkins, Minot	Private	Sept. 10, '62	Richmond, Ky.	
Paradove, Colby	Private	Sept. 10, '62	Richmond, Ky.	
Paradove, J. W.	Private	Sept. 10, '62	Richmond, Ky.	
Quisenbury, U. J. (T)	Private	Sept. 10, '62	Richmond, Ky.	
Ragland, Nath.	Private	Sept. 10, '62	Richmond, Ky.	
Ragland, Thomas	Private	Sept. 10, '62	Richmond, Ky.	
Ragland, Milton	Private	Sept. 10, '62	Richmond, Ky.	
Ragland, Harry	Private	Sept. 10, '62	Richmond, Ky.	
Rash, A. Clay	Private	Sept. 10, '62	Richmond, Ky.	
Railsback, Edw.	Private	Sept. 10, '62	Richmond, Ky.	
Railsback, David	Private	Sept. 10, '62	Richmond, Ky.	Sergeant.
Rutlidge, James	Private	Sept. 10, '62	Richmond, Ky.	
Simpson, Richard	Private	Sept. 10, '62	Richmond, Ky.	
Stevens, Solomon	Private	Sept. 10, '62	Richmond, Ky.	
Stevens, Benjamin	Private	Sept. 10, '62	Richmond, Ky.	To Cook. Duke's Reg't, Dec. 2, '62.
Stevens, Michael	Private	Sept. 10, '62	Richmond, Ky.	
Stokley, Edward	Private	Sept. 10, '62	Richmond, Ky.	"Deserted in Middle Tenn."
Schooler, John	Private	Sept. 10, '62	Richmond, Ky.	
Trusle, Armstead	Private	Sept. 10, '62	Richmond, Ky.	
Thomas, Charles	Private	Sept. 10, '62	Richmond, Ky.	Died Jan. 11, '63, Tenn.
Thomas, Lewis	Private	Sept. 10, '62	Richmond, Ky.	
Trusle, Simeon	Private	Sept. 10, '62	Richmond, Ky.	
Waller, Wm.	Private	Sept. 10, '62	Richmond, Ky.	Deserted in Ky., Nov. 17, '62. Went to Federal lines.
Woosley, Lewis	Private	Sept. 10, '62	Richmond, Ky.	

Note: Only one roll of this company on file, covering time from Sept. 10, '62, to Dec. 31, '62.

MUSTER ROLL OF COMPANY B, 11th CAVALRY, KENTUCKY VOUNTEERS, C. S. ARMY

Name	Rank	Mustered in When	Mustered in Where	Remarks
Joseph Chenault	Captain	Sept. 10, '62	Richmond, Ky.	Killed May 8, '63.
A. H. Tribble	Captain	Sept. 10, '62	Richmond, Ky.	Killed July 4, '63.
Isham A. Fox	1st Lieut.	Sept. 10, '62	Richmond, Ky.	
Charles Stone	2nd Lieut.	Sept. 10, '62	Richmond, Ky.	
Dudley Tribble	2nd Lieut.	Sept. 10, '62	Richmond, Ky.	
James P. White	1st Sergt.	Sept. 10, '62	Richmond, Ky.	
Robt. Samuels	2nd Sergt.	Sept. 10, '62	Richmond, Ky.	
Andres McCord	3rd Sergt.	Sept. 10, '62	Richmond, Ky.	
Squire Tevis	4th Sergt.	Sept. 10, '62	Richmond, Ky.	
John Hill	5th Sergt.	Sept. 10, '62	Richmond, Ky.	
Michael Hennesee	1st Corp.	Sept. 10, '62	Richmond, Ky.	
T. B. Shearer	2nd Corp.	Sept. 10, '62	Richmond, Ky.	
James Davis	3rd Corp.	Sept. 10, '62	Richmond, Ky.	
John Jones	4th Corp.	Sept. 10, '62	Richmond, Ky.	
Robt. Rice	Forage Mas.	Sept. 10, '62	Richmond, Ky.	
Wm. Berry	Forage Mas.	Sept. 10, '62	Richmond, Ky.	
Baxter, Edward	Private	Sept. 10, '62	Richmond, Ky.	Co. Farrier.
Berry, Sam'l	Private	Sept. 10, '62	Richmond, Ky.	
Biggerstaff, Wm.	Private	Sept. 10, '62	Richmond, Ky.	
Berry, Wm.	Private	Sept. 10, '62	Richmond, Ky.	
Coby, Chas.	Private	Sept. 10, '62	Richmond, Ky.	
Cosby, Jas.	Private	Sept. 10, '62	Richmond, Ky.	
Cosby, Jno.	Private	Sept. 10, '62	Richmond, Ky.	
Cosby, Oliver W.	Private	Sept. 10, '62	Richmond, Ky.	
Cosby, A. S.	Private	Sept. 10, '62	Richmond, Ky.	
Carter, G. W.	Private	Feb. 2, '63	Albany, Ky.	
Deboe, Western	Private	Sept. 10, '62	Richmond, Ky.	
Deatherage, Nathan	Private	Sept. 10, '62	Richmond, Ky.	
Davis, Joe	Private	Sept. 10, '62	Richmond, Ky.	
Dickerson, Wm.	Private	Sept. 10, '62	Richmond, Ky.	Deserted at Smithville, Tenn., Jan. 3, '63.
Duerson, Thompson	Private	Sept. 10, '62	Richmond, Ky.	
Dozier, Peter	Private	Sept. 10, '62	Richmond, Ky.	
Fowler, Thos.	Private	Sept. 10, '62	Richmond, Ky.	
Ferrell, Zack	Private	Sept. 10, '62	Richmond, Ky.	Deserted Nov. 20, '62, in Middle Tenn. Post Oak.
Ferrell, John	Private	Sept. 10, '62	Richmond, Ky.	Supposed captured at Springfield, Ky., Dec. 20, '62.
Ferrell, Anderson	Private	Sept. 10, '62	Richmond, Ky.	
Fox, Wm.	Private	Sept. 10, '62	Richmond, Ky.	
Fox, Jno.	Private	Sept. 10, '62	Richmond, Ky.	
Farris, Wm.	Private	Sept. 10, '62	Richmond, Ky.	Deserted in Ky., Sept. 10, '62, took oath to U. S.
Garrett, Chas.	Private	Sept. 10, '62	Richmond, Ky.	
Griffey (Griffith) Dan	Private	Sept. 10, '62	Richmond, Ky.	Deserted Nov. 16, '62, in Ky.
Goodman, Wishfred	Private	Feb. 27, '63	Albany, Ky.	Re-enlisted.
Hardin, Leroy J.	Private	Sept. 10, '62	Richmond, Ky.	
Huguely, Jas.	Private	Sept. 10, '62	Richmond, Ky.	
Huguely, Squire	Private	Sept. 10, '62	Richmond, Ky.	
Hicks, David	Private	Sept. 10, '62	Richmond, Ky.	
Hockaday, Jas.	Private	Sept. 10, '62	Richmond, Ky.	
Hill, John	Private	Sept. 10, '62	Richmond, Ky.	
Jones, Wm.	Private	Sept. 10, '62	Richmond, Ky.	Deserted at Big Hill, Ky., Oct. 17, 1862.
Jones, James	Private	Sept. 10, '62	Richmond, Ky.	

Old Cane Springs 235

Name	Rank	Mustered in When	Mustered in Where	Remarks
Jones, Andrew	Private	Sept. 10, '62	Richmond, Ky.	
Jones, Anderson	Private	Sept. 10, '62	Richmond, Ky.	
Kester, G. R.	Private	Sept. 10, '62	Richmond, Ky.	
Lear, Benjamin	Private	Sept. 10, '62	Richmond, Ky.	Substitute for Jas. Trimble.
Lanter, Newton	Private	Sept. 10, '62	Richmond, Ky.	
Musleman, J. E.	Private	Feb. 27, '63	Albany, Ky.	Re-enlisted.
Mattingly, W. E.	Private	Sept. 10, '62	Richmond, Ky.	
Newby, Jno.	Private	Sept. 10, '62	Richmond, Ky.	
Newkirk, Cyrus	Private	Sept. 10, '62	Richmond, Ky.	
Perkins, Meredith	Private	Sept. 10, '62	Richmond, Ky.	
Pence, Alex	Private	Sept. 10, '62	Richmond, Ky.	Co. Blacksmith.
Permertier, J. W.	Private	Feb. 19, '63	Knoxville, Tenn.	Conscripted.
Russell, Alex	Private	Sept. 10, '62	Richmond, Ky.	
Rice, John	Private	Sept. 10, '62	Richmond, Ky.	
Rice, Thomas	Private	Sept. 10, '62	Richmond, Ky.	
Rames, Olyett	Private	Sept. 10, '62	Richmond, Ky.	Asst. surgeon, Dec. 31, '62.
Shanks, Tilmon	Private	Sept. 10, '62	Richmond, Ky.	Deserted Nov. 10, '62, Richmond, Ky.
Smithheart, Wesley	Private	Sept. 10, '62	Richmond, Ky.	Deserted Dec. 30, '62, Columbia, Ky.
Shearer, Jno.	Private	Sept. 10, '62	Richmond, Ky.	Deserted Nov. 1, '62, took oath to U. S.
Simmons, Jos. P.	Private	Sept. 10, '62	Richmond, Ky.	Orderly Sergt. to Col.
Scudder, Ira W.	Private	Sept. 10, '62	Richmond, Ky.	Comp. Sergt.
Shaw, Sidney	Private	Feb. 10, '63	Knoxville, Tenn.	From Buckner's Body Guard.
Shaw, Harrison	Private	Feb. 10, '63	Knoxville, Tenn.	From Buckner's Body Guard.
Shearer, James	Private	Sept. 10, '62	Richmond, Ky.	
Turner, Reuben	Private	Sept. 10, '62	Richmond, Ky.	
Turner, Robert	Private	Sept. 10, '62	Richmond, Ky.	Assigned to Battery, Dec. 1, '62 (Byrn's).
Turner, James	Private	Sept. 10, '62	Richmond, Ky.	Deserted Jan. 10, '63, Smithville, Tenn.
Turner, Will	Private	Sept. 10, '62	Richmond, Ky.	Assigned to Battery, Dec. 1, '62 (Byrn's).
Turner, John	Private	Sept. 10, '62	Richmond, Ky.	Deserted Dec. 30, '62, Columbia, Tenn.
Trimble, James	Private	Sept. 10, '62	Richmond, Ky.	Furnished Substitute (Benj. Lear).
Tevis, Robert	Private	Sept. 10, '62	Richmond, Ky.	
Tillett, Tine	Private	Sept. 10, '62	Richmond, Ky.	Deserted Richmond, Ky., Sept. 10, '62.
White, Jacob	Private	Sept. 10, '62	Richmond, Ky.	
Wade, James	Private	Sept. 10, '62	Richmond, Ky.	Assigned to Battery, Dec. 1, '62 (Byrn's).
Williams, Richard	Private	Sept. 10, '62	Richmond, Ky.	Commissary.
Wood, Hiram	Private	Feb. 20, '63	Knoxville, Tenn.	Substitute for J. W. Permertier.
Woolcot, Ezekial	Private	Feb. 20, '63	Monticello, Ky.	

Note: "Only two rolls of this company (B) on file, covering time from Sept. 10, '62, to Apr. 30, '63."

Stationed Mch. 7, '62, and June 2nd, '63, at Camp Williams, Near Albany, Clinton Co., Ky.

MUSTER ROLL OF COMPANY D, 11th CAVALRY, KENTUCKY VOLUNTEERS, C. S. ARMY

Name	Rank	Mustered in When	Where	Remarks
J. L. N. Dickens	Capt.	Sept. 10, '62		Prisoner.
W. Wiseman	1st Lieut.	Sept. 10, '62		Prisoner.
J. M. Riddle	2nd Lieut.	Sept. 10, '62		Deserted—took oath to U. S.
W. Winburn	2nd Lieut.	Sept. 10, '62		Reduced to ranks and deserted.

Note: "No rolls of this Co. (D) on file. The above names taken from roster."

MUSTER ROLL OF COMPANY E, 11th CAVALRY, KENTUCKY VOLUNTEERS, C. S. ARMY

Name	Rank	Mustered in When	Where	Remarks
R. C. Terril	Capt.	Sept. 10, '62		Wounded and captured.
G. W. Ransom	1st Lieut.	Sept. 10, '62		Supposed killed Mi'ss'y Ridge.
G. W. Maupin	2nd Lieut.	Sept. 10, '62		Discharged, Nov., '62.
Seth Maupin	2nd Lieut.	Sept. 10, '62		Wounded and captured.

Note: "No rolls of Co. E on file, the above names taken from roster."

MUSTER ROLL OF COMPANY F, 11th CAVALRY, KENTUCKY VOLUNTEERS, C. S. ARMY

Name	Rank	Mustered in When	Where	Remarks
Thos. B. Collins	Captain	Sept. 10, '62	Richmond, Ky.	Supposed to be in Canada.
J. F. Oldham	1st Lieut.	Sept. 10, '62	Richmond, Ky.	Prisoner.
R. J. Park	2nd Lieut.	Sept. 10, '62	Richmond, Ky.	Prisoner.
C. H. Covington	2nd Lieut.	Sept. 10, '62	Richmond, Ky.	Died Mch. 22, '63, Brain Fever.
James H. Tevis	2nd Lieut.	Sept. 10, '62	Richmond, Ky.	April 1, '63.
Joseph Collins	Order Sergt.	Sept. 10, '62	Richmond, Ky.	
Jas. Tevis	1st Sergt.	Sept. 10, '62	Richmond, Ky.	
Jas. Caldwell	2nd Sergt.	Sept. 10, '62	Richmond, Ky.	
Thos. Dejarnett	3rd Sergt.	Sept. 10, '62	Richmond, Ky.	
W. B. Benton	4th Sergt.	Sept. 10, '62	Richmond, Ky.	
J. K. Sams	4th Sergt.	Dec. 31, '62	Bardstown, Ky.	Appt. Feb. 1, '63.
S. C. Broaddus	1st Corp.	Sept. 10, '62	Richmond, Ky.	
J. T. Jones	1st Corp.	Sept. 10, '62	Richmond, Ky.	Appt. Feb. 1, '63.
R. Caldwell	2nd Corp.	Sept. 10, '62	Richmond, Ky.	
A. G. Fife	3rd Corp.	Sept. 10, '62	Richmond, Ky.	
Rob't Miller	4th Corp.	Sept. 10, '62	Richmond, Ky.	
James Miller	Blacksmith	Sept. 10, '62	Richmond, Ky.	
Thos. Oldham	Farrier	Sept. 10, '62	Richmond, Ky.	
Asbell, John	Private	Mch. '62	Richmond, Ky.	
Benton, John	Private	Sept. 10, '62	Richmond, Ky.	Died Mch. 25, '63, Monticello, Ky., Brain Fever.
Benton, Van	Private	Sept. 10, '62	Richmond, Ky.	
Broaddus, T. C.	Private	Sept. 10, '62	Richmond, Ky.	Deserted, Jan. 30, '63, Albany, Ky.

Old Cane Springs

Name	Rank	Mustered in When	Mustered in Where	Remarks
Butler, Geo.	Private	Sept. 10, '62	Richmond, Ky.	
Beck, Peter	Private	Feb. 1, '63	Albany, Ky.	
Bronston, J. C.	Private	Sept. 10, '62	Richmond, Ky.	Deserted, Feb. 10, '63, Albany, Ky.
Benton, W. B.	Private	Sept. 10, '62	Richmond, Ky.	Deserted, Jan. 30, '62, Albany, Ky.
Cosby, Jas.	Private	Sept. 10, '62	Richmond, Ky.	
Coulter, Jas. W.	Private	Sept. 10, '62	Richmond, Ky.	
Covington, Chas.	Private	Sept. 10, '62	Richmond, Ky.	
Cohran, Jas. G.	Private	Feb. 13, '63	Monticello, Ky.	
Coldiron, H. W.	Private	Sept. 10, '62	Richmond, Ky.	From Co. H, Feb. 20, '63.
Collins, Jos.	Private	Sept. 10, '62	Richmond, Ky.	
Embrey, Joel	Private	Sept. 10, '62	Richmond, Ky.	From Co. H, Feb. 1, '63.
Grugg, Wm.	Private	Sept. 10, '62	Richmond, Ky.	
Giltner, David	Private	Mch. 1, '63	Albany, Ky.	
Hutchinson, Jno.	Private	Sept. 10, '62	Richmond, Ky.	
Hall, Elihu	Private	Sept. 10, '62	Richmond, Ky.	
Horn, Wiley	Private	Sept. 10, '62	Richmond, Ky.	
Harris, Anderson	Private	Sept. 10, '62	Richmond, Ky.	
Jones, Joseph	Private	Sept. 10, '62	Richmond, Ky.	
Jones, Meredith	Private	Sept. 10, '62	Richmond, Ky.	
Judy, M. B.	Private	Sept. 10, '62	Richmond, Ky.	
Kurtz, Jacob	Private	Sept. 10, '62	Richmond, Ky.	
Kavanaugh, Arch	Private	Feb. 9, '63	Albany, Ky.	
Mize, J. B.	Private	Sept. 10, '62	Richmond, Ky.	
McKee, Owen	Private	Sept. 10, '62	Richmond, Ky.	
Million, Travis	Private	Sept. 10, '62	Richmond, Ky.	Deserted, Jan. 18, '63, at McMinnville, Tenn.
Meeks, Samuel	Private	Mch. 13, '63	Monticello, Ky.	
Norman, Jas.	Private	Sept. 10, '62	Richmond, Ky.	
Oldham, J. R.	Private	Sept. 10, '62	Richmond, Ky.	
Oldham, Preston	Private	Sept. 10, '62	Richmond, Ky.	
Oldham, Richard	Private	Sept. 10, '62	Richmond, Ky.	
Oldham, Jas.	Private	Sept. 10, '62	Richmond, Ky.	Detailed Asst. Wagon Master, Dec. 20, '62. Brigade Wagon Master.
Oldham, O. R.	Private	Sept. 10, '62	Richmond, Ky.	
Oldham, J. T.	Private	Sept. 10, '62	Richmond, Ky.	
Portwood, Thomas	Private	Sept. 10, '62	Richmond, Ky.	
Price, Benj.	Private	Sept. 10, '62	Richmond, Ky.	
Pearce, Silas	Private	Mch. 13, '63	Monticello, Ky.	
Rownan, Robt.	Private	Sept. 10, '62	Richmond, Ky.	
Sams, J. K.	Private	Jan. 1, '63	Bardstown, Ky.	
Semones, Jno.	Private	Mch. 1, '63	Albany, Ky.	
Turpin, Andrew	Private	Sept. 10, '62	Richmond, Ky.	
Turpin, Sam	Private	Sept. 10, '62	Richmond, Ky.	
Thorp, Harris	Private	Sept. 10, '62	Richmond, Ky.	
Troxell, Granville	Private	Apr. 5, '63	Monticello, Ky.	
White, Durrett	Private	Sept. 10, '62	Richmond, Ky.	
White, Daniel	Private	Sept. 10, '62	Richmond, Ky.	
Watts, Jas.	Private	Sept. 10, '62	Richmond, Ky.	
Wilder, Wm.	Private	Sept. 10, '62	Richmond, Ky.	Deserted, Jan. 20, '63, at McMinnville, Tenn.

		Mustered in		
Name	Rank	When	Where	Remarks
Woods, Alex	Private	Sept. 10, '62	Richmond, Ky.	Died, Nov. 13, '63, near Knoxville, Tenn.
Wright, O. F.	Private	Mch. 1, '63	Monticello, Ky.	

Note: Only 2 rolls of this Co. on file covering time from Sept. 10, '62, to Feb. 28, '63.

Note: Mch. 7, '63, Co. was stationed at Albany, Ky. Apr. 15, '63, Co. was stationed at Monticello, Ky.

MUSTER ROLL OF COMPANY G, 11th CAVALRY, KENTUCKY VOLUNTEERS, C. S. ARMY

		Mustered in		
Name	Rank	When	Where	Remarks
James Mitchell	Captain	Sept. 10, '62	Richmond, Ky.	
Thos. Wells	Captain	Sept. 10, '62	Richmond, Ky.	Prisoner.
G. W. Bowen	1st Lieut.	Sept. 10, '62	Richmond, Ky.	
Alfred Williams	1st Lieut.	Sept. 10, '62	Richmond, Ky.	
Thos. J. Current	2nd Lieut.	Sept. 10, '62	Richmond, Ky.	
W. A. Bedford	2nd Lieut.	Sept. 10, '62	Richmond, Ky.	
D. H. Clowers	2nd Lieut.	Sept. 10, '62	Richmond, Ky.	Reduced to ranks and deserted.
Milo Wells	2nd Lieut.	Sept. 10, '62	Richmond, Ky.	Killed, Nov. 13, '64, Bulls Gap, Tenn.
Chas. C. Rule	1st Sergt.	Sept. 10, '62	Richmond, Ky.	
Chas. R. Shawhan	2nd Sergt.	Sept. 10, '62	Richmond, Ky.	
Wm. Kendall	3rd Sergt.	Sept. 10, '62	Richmond, Ky.	
Thos. J. Howard	1st Corp.	Sept. 10, '62	Richmond, Ky.	
Gano Leer	2nd Corp.	Sept. 10, '62	Richmond, Ky.	
Wm. H. Current	3rd Corp.	Sept. 10, '62	Richmond, Ky.	
L. Lair	4th Corp.	Sept. 10, '62	Richmond, Ky.	
Bedford, Thos.	Private	Sept. 10, '62	Richmond, Ky.	
Bedford, A. W.	Private	Sept. 10, '62	Richmond, Ky.	
Bowman, Jno.	Private	Sept. 10, '62	Richmond, Ky.	
Batterton, Jas.	Private	Sept. 10, '62	Richmond, Ky.	
Breedon, F. M.	Private	Sept. 10, '62	Richmond, Ky.	
Clay, J. C.	Private	Sept. 10, '62	Richmond, Ky.	
Current, N.	Private	Sept. 10, '62	Richmond, Ky.	
Current, Jesse	Private	Sept. 10, '62	Richmond, Ky.	
Demmitt, J. H.	Private	Sept. 10, '62	Richmond, Ky.	
Demmitt, J. W.	Private	Sept. 10, '62	Richmond, Ky.	
Davis, Jno.	Private	Sept. 10, '62	Richmond, Ky.	
Fretwell, L. J.	Private	Sept. 10, '62	Richmond, Ky.	
Godman, R. F.	Private	Sept. 10, '62	Richmond, Ky.	
Gregory, Geo.	Private	Sept. 10, '62	Richmond, Ky.	
Hanby, B.	Private	Sept. 10, '62	Richmond, Ky.	
Hoover, R. J.	Private	Sept. 10, '62	Richmond, Ky.	
Honey, Jesse	Private	Sept. 10, '62	Richmond, Ky.	
Hinton, Jos.	Private	Sept. 10, '62	Richmond, Ky.	
Hamilton, Sam	Private	Sept. 10, '62	Richmond, Ky.	
Kelley, Jas.	Private	Sept. 10, '62	Richmond, Ky.	
Neal, Emberson	Private	Sept. 10, '62	Richmond, Ky.	
Penn, Jno.	Private	Sept. 10, '62	Richmond, Ky.	
Phillips, Wm.	Private	Sept. 10, '62	Richmond, Ky.	
Ross, Wm.	Private	Sept. 10, '62	Richmond, Ky.	

	Name	Rank	Mustered in When	Where	Remarks

Name	Rank	When	Where	Remarks
Sullivan, P. C.	Private	Sept. 10, '62	Richmond, Ky.	
Smizer, Sam	Private	Sept. 10, '62	Richmond, Ky.	
Shawhan, Geo.	Private	Sept. 10, '62	Richmond, Ky.	
Smith, W. D.	Private	Sept. 10, '62	Richmond, Ky.	
Tate, Jas.	Private	Sept. 10, '62	Richmond, Ky.	
Turner, Cyrus	Private	Sept. 10, '62	Richmond, Ky.	
Talbott, Chas.	Private	Sept. 10, '62	Richmond, Ky.	
Wilson, R.	Private	Sept. 10, '62	Richmond, Ky.	
Wilson, Jas.	Private	Sept. 10, '62	Richmond, Ky.	
Wilson, David	Private	Sept. 10, '62	Richmond, Ky.	

Note: Only one roll of this company on file covering time from Sept. 10, '62, to Dec. 31, '62.

Note: March 17, 1863, Co. was stationed at Monticello, Ky.

MUSTER ROLL OF COMPANY H, 11th CAVALRY, KENTUCKY VOLUNTEERS, C. S. ARMY

Name	Rank	When	Where	Remarks
Augustus Magee	Captain	Sept. 10, '62		Killed, Nov. 13, '64. (Captured at Springfield, Ky.)
Frank A. West	1st Lieut.	Sept. 10, '62		Killed, July 4, '63.
F. M. Louderback	2nd Lieut.	Sept. 10, '62		Sept. 4, '63, took oath while prisoner.
Cash M. Taylor	2nd Lieut.	Sept. 10, '62		Oct., '63, captured at Springfield, Ky. (Sept. 4, '64.) Died in prison, '63.
E. C. Elliott	1st Sergt.	Sept. 10, '62	Mt. Sterling, Ky.	
W. M. Newby	2nd Sergt.	Sept. 10, '62	Richmond, Ky.	
Sidney Knatzer	3rd Sergt.	Sept. 10, '62	Richmond, Ky.	
Milford Jackson	4th Sergt.	Sept. 10, '62	Richmond, Ky.	
John McCoy	1st Corp.	Sept. 10, '62	Mt. Sterling, Ky.	
B. F. McCoy	2nd Corp.	Sept. 10, '62	Mt. Sterling, Ky.	
Thos. Smar	3rd Corp.	Sept. 10, '62	Mt. Sterling, Ky.	
Reuben Munday	4th Corp.	Sept. 10, '62	Richmond, Ky.	Captured Springfield, Ky.
Ashcraft, Lewis	Private	Sept. 10, '62	Mt. Sterling, Ky.	
Alexander, Jacob	Private	Sept. 10, '62	Richmond, Ky.	
Breakhill, Phillip	Private	Sept. 10, '62	Mt. Sterling, Ky.	
Browning, Jas.	Private	Sept. 10, '62	Mt. Sterling, Ky.	
Browning, Jno.	Private	Sept. 10, '62	Mt. Sterling, Ky.	
Browning, Ben	Private	Sept. 10, '62	Mt. Sterling, Ky.	
Benson, Jno.	Private	Sept. 10, '62	Mt. Sterling, Ky.	
Claypole, E. C.	Private	Sept. 10, '62	Mt. Sterling, Ky.	
Chism, Thos.	Private	Sept. 10, '62	Mt. Sterling, Ky.	
Coats, Amos	Private	Sept. 10, '62	Richmond, Ky.	
Coats, Isiah	Private	Sept. 10, '62	Richmond, Ky.	
Cusick, Rob't.	Private	Sept. 10, '62	Richmond, Ky.	
Cocks, Robin	Private	Sept. 10, '62	Richmond, Ky.	
Coleiron, W. H.	Private	Sept. 10, '62	Richmond, Ky.	
Fitch, John	Private	Sept. 10, '62	Richmond, Ky.	

		Mustered in		
Name	Rank	When	Where	Remarks
Fraley, John	Private	Sept. 10, '62	Mt. Sterling, Ky.	
Hamilton, Pat	Private	Sept. 10, '62	Mt. Sterling, Ky.	
Hamilton, Dolphus	Private	Sept. 10, '62	Mt. Sterling, Ky.	
Hayes, Geo.	Private	Sept. 10, '62	Mt. Sterling, Ky.	
Hunt, Wm.	Private	Sept. 10, '62	Mt. Sterling, Ky.	
Judd, John	Private	Sept. 10, '62	Mt. Sterling, Ky.	
Jenkins, Chas.	Private	Sept. 10, '62	Richmond, Ky.	
Kelly, Thos.	Private	Sept. 10, '62	Richmond, Ky.	
Lewis, William	Private	Sept. 10, '62	Richmond, Ky.	
Louderback, Wm.	Private	Sept. 10, '62	Mt. Sterling, Ky.	
McCoy, V. B.	Private	Sept. 10, '62	Mt. Sterling, Ky.	
Meadows, Wesley	Private	Sept. 10, '62	Mt. Sterling, Ky.	Captured at Springfield.
McMahan, Henry	Private	Sept. 10, '62	Mt. Sterling, Ky.	Deserted.
Madox, Geo.	Private	Sept. 10, '62	Richmond, Ky.	
Madox, Josiah	Private	Sept. 10, '62	Richmond, Ky.	
Newby, Jesse	Private	Sept. 10, '62	Richmond, Ky.	
Newby, Jas.	Private	Sept. 10, '62	Mt. Sterling, Ky.	
Maden, Wm.	Private	Sept. 10, '62	Mt. Sterling, Ky.	
Rice, Daniel	Private	Sept. 10, '62	Mt. Sterling, Ky.	
Rice, Marion	Private	Sept. 10, '62	Mt. Sterling, Ky.	
Ryan, John	Private	Sept. 10, '62	Mt. Sterling, Ky.	
Roberts, Merill	Private	Sept. 10, '62	Richmond, Ky.	
Roberts, Mack	Private	Sept. 10, '62	Richmond, Ky.	
Roberts, Squire	Private	Sept. 10, '62	Richmond, Ky.	
Sims, Geo.	Private	Sept. 10, '62	Richmond, Ky.	
Simons, Jno.	Private	Sept. 10, '62	Mt. Sterling, Ky.	
Taylor, Shelby	Private	Sept. 10, '62	Richmond, Ky.	
Wade, Pope	Private	Sept. 10, '62	Richmond, Ky.	
Webb, Jas.	Private	Sept. 10, '62	Mt. Sterling, Ky.	
Wood, Sam	Private	Sept. 10, '62	Mt. Sterling, Ky.	
Wood, J. W.	Private	Sept. 10, '62	Mt. Sterling, Ky.	
Wood, Vince	Private	Sept. 10, '62	Mt. Sterling, Ky.	
Wood, J. M.	Private	Sept. 10, '62	Mt. Sterling, Ky.	
Woods, James W.	Private	Sept. 10, '62	Mt. Sterling, Ky.	
Wood, Augustus	Private	Sept. 10, '62	Mt. Sterling, Ky.	

Note: Roll dated Monticello, Ky., Mch. 17, 1863. The name of James A. Louderback appears upon the Roster as 2nd Lieut. of Co. H, Chenault's 11th Ky. Cav., while the name appears as F. M. Louderback upon Co. rolls. "This Co. (H) was in the service for 12 mo. under Brig. Gen. Marshal. At the expiration of their enlistment they enlisted in this regiment (Col. D. W. Chenault's 11th Ky. Cav.). During recent raid in Ky., Capt. Augustus Magee and 2nd Lieut. Louderback were captured at Springfield, Ky., and are now in Camp Chase."

Note: Only one roll of this Co. on file, covering time from Sept. 11, '62, to Dec. 31, '62. The name appears as Augustus Magee, as captain on Co. roll and as G. H. Magee on Roster.

MUSTER ROLL OF COMPANY I, 11th CAVALRY, KENTUCKY VOLUNTEERS, C. S. ARMY

		Mustered in	
Name	Rank	When	Remarks
Jack May	Captain	Sept. 10, '62	Shot while in prison.
T. C. Corbin	1st Lieut.	Sept. 10, '62	Supposed to be dead.
M. Rein	2nd Lieut.	Sept. 10, '62	Left in Ky.

Note: No rolls of Co. I on file. Above names taken from Roster.

MUSTER ROLL OF COMPANY K, 11th CAVALRY, KENTUCKY
VOLUNTEERS, C. S. ARMY

Name	Rank	Mustered in When	Remarks
B. S. Barton	Captain	Sept. 10, '62	Prisoner.
Harrison Moles	1st Lieut.	Sept. 10, '62	Killed in Tenn.
F. Frost	2nd Lieut.	Sept. 10, '62	Killed Sept., '63.
T. B. Corbett	2nd Lieut.	Sept. 10, '62	

D

DEATHS IN THE ELEVENTH KENTUCKY CAVALRY AT CAMP DOUGLAS

These names are given just as Nathan B. Deatherage copied them under the several company headings. A check, however, will show that his company assignments are not correct in every instance. Furthermore, it will be seen that names appear in his list which are not in the preceding muster rolls. Perhaps those not appearing enlisted in the several companies after the September, 1862, recruiting. It seems that the Eleventh Kentucky Cavalry became the Seventh about the time of the Ohio raid.

Co. A.

Richard Simpson	Dysentery	Jan. 14, 1864
James Freeman	Smallpox	Feb. 25, 1864
John Cooper	Smallpox	May 6, 1864
John Paridove	Dysentery	Aug. 26, 1864
James H. Mullins	Heart disease	Sept. 18, 1864
Thos. Calicut	Smallpox	Nov. 13, 1864
James Oliver	Chronic diarrhea	Nov. 17, 1864
Jesse Hampton	Smallpox	Dec. 19, 1864

Co. B.

James Wilson	Old sores	Feb. 18, 1864
John Hill (Pap)	Small Pox	Feb. 19, 1864
Anderson Ferrel	Smallpox	March 10, 1864
H. K. Anderson	Smallpox	March 20, 1864
John Rice	Smallpox	April 12, 1864
Sam Berry	Dropsy	Aug. 18, 1864
John Asbell	Consumption	Nov. 25, 1864

Co. C.

John W. Flims (?)	Congestive chill	Jan. 8, 1864
Gen. O. B. Tracy	Chronic diarrhea	Feb. 17, 1864
John Daugherty	Pneumonia	Oct. 2, 1864
Robt. Knox	Chronic diarrhea	Oct. 21, 1864
J. N. Aldrige	Typhoid fever	Oct. 31, 1864

Co. E.

George McDaniels	Dysentery	Oct. 7, 1863
William Huse	Measles	Oct. 29, 1863
Steve Adair	Measles	Nov. 24, 1863
George Vaughn	Smallpox	Nov. 30, 1863
George W. Moore	Typhoid	Dec. 28, 1863
G. J. Elmore	"Debillity fever" Smallpox	Jan. 2, 1865

Co. F.

Thos. Hamilton	Pneumonia	Sept. 27, 1863
Joel W. Watts	Pneumonia	Feb. 25, 1864
A. B. Benton	Smallpox	March 14, 1864
James P. Norman	Pneumonia	Oct. 26, 1864
Samuel Turpin	Smallpox	Nov. 26, 1864

Co. G.

Geo. Maddox	Heart disease	Feb. 18, 1864
Jacob Hurst	Smallpox	March 9, 1864
James K. Newby	Smallpox	March 29, 1864
James Wards	Inflamation of bowels	Oct. 31, 1864
John Woods	Chronic diarrhea	Dec. 15, 1864
William Lewis	Scrofula	Jan. 31, 1865

Co. H.

N. P. Bell	Measles	Nov. 10, 1863
John Wade	Measles	Nov. 12, 1863
S. W. Frost	Debility	March 26, 1864
E. Turpin	Smallpox	March 27, 1864
George Gayford (?)	Smallpox	March 27, 1864
W. R. Barton	Typhoid	Nov. 10, 1864
Neury Rigner	Chronic diarrhea	Dec. 28, 1864
John Franklin	Smallpox	Dec. 29, 1864
John Fitch	Chronic diarrhea	Dec. 30, 1864

Co. D.

Joseph Clowers (?)	Diarrhea	Oct. 7, 1863
Robert Shearer	Brain fever	Dec. 25, 1863
John Allen	Smallpox	Feb. 20, 1864

BIBLIOGRAPHY USED IN PREPARING NOTES AND ADDENDA

GENERAL WORKS

Appleton's *Encyclopedia of American Biography*. 6 Vols. New York, 1900.

Burnam, Robert: *In Memoriam Curtis Field Burnam*. Louisville, 1909.

Clay, Cassius Marcellus: *The Life of Cassius Marcellus Clay, Memoirs, Writings, and Speeches*. Cincinnati, 1886.

Collins, Richard H.: *History of Kentucky*. 2 Vols. Cincinnati, 1874.

Confessions of Edward W. Hawkins, A Detail of Crimes Unparalleled in History for one of His Age—Hanged before he was 21 years of Age; His Address on the Gallows, printed by the Irvine, Kentucky, *Tribune*, 1906.

Coulter, E. Merton: *The Civil War and Reconstruction in Kentucky*, Chapel Hill, 1926.

Dorris, Jonathan Truman: *A Glimpse at Historic Madison County and Richmond, Kentucky*. Richmond, Ky., 1934.

Dorris, J. T.: "Central University, Richmond, Kentucky," A Reprint from the *Register* of the Kentucky State Historical Society, Vol. 32, No. 99 (April, 1934).

Dorris, Jonathan T. (Editor): *Three Decades of Progress, Eastern Kentucky State Teachers College*. Frankfort, 1936.

Duke, Basil W.: *History of Morgan's Cavalry*. Cincinnati, 1867.

Duke, Basil W.: *Reminiscences*. New York, 1911.

Encyclopedia Britannica, 14th Edition, Vol. 23.

Fairchild, E. H.: *Berea College, An Interesting History*. Cincinnati, 1883. First published in 1875.

Fee, John G.: *Autobiography of John G. Fee*. Chicago, 1891.

Jenkins, William Sumner: *Pro-Slavery Thought in the Old South*. Chapel Hill, 1935.

Johnson, E. Polk: *A History of Kentucky and Kentuckians*. Chicago, 1912.

Littell, William: *The Statute Law of Kentucky.* 5 Vols. Frankfort, 1809-1819.

Martin, Asa Earl: *The Anti-Slavery Movement in Kentucky, Prior to 1850.* Louisville, 1918.

McDougle, Ivan E.: *Slavery in Kentucky, 1792-1865.* Reprinted from the *Journal of Negro History,* Vol. III. 1918.

Miller, W. H.: *History and Genealogies of the Families of Miller, Woods, Harris, Wallace, Maupin, Oldham, Kavanaugh, and Brown,* with *Interspersions of notes of the Families of Dabney, Reid, Martin, Broaddus, Gentry, Jarman, Jameson, Ballard, Mullins, Michie, Moberley, Covington, Browning, Duncan, Yancey, and Others.* Lexington, 1907.

Moore, Frank: *Anecdotes, Poetry and Incidents of the War North and South.* New York, 1867.

Moore, Frank: *The Rebellion Record, A Diary of American Events.* 8 Vols. New York, 1862.

Peters, Dewitt: *Kit Carson's Wild West.* New York, 1880.

Rank, George W.: *Boonesborough; Its Founding, Pioneer Struggles, Indian Experiences, Transylvania Days and Revolutionary Annals.* Louisville, 1901.

Rogers, John A. R.: *Birth of Berea, A Story of Providence.* Philadelphia, 1903.

Shannon, Fred Albert: *The Organization of the Union Army.* Cleveland, 1928.

Townsend, W. H.: *Lincoln and His Wife's Home Town.* Indianapolis, 1929.

Weatherford, W. D.: *The Negro from Africa to America.* New York, 1924.

Williams, John Augustus: *Life of Elder John Smith with Some Account of the Rise and Progress of the Current Reformation.* Cincinnati, 1870.

Wilson, Henry: *History of the Rise and Fall of the Slave Power in America.* 3 Vols. Boston, 1875.

NEWSPAPERS, MAGAZINES, SCRAPBOOKS, ETC.

Confederate Veteran, Vol. XXXVI, No. 8 (August, 1928).

Journal of Southern History, Vol. I, No. 3 (August, 1935), "Pardon Seekers and Brokers: A Sequel of Appomattox," by J. T. Dorris.

"Memory and Scrapbook": A collection of clippings, etc., pertaining mostly to the Caperton, Phelps, and Burnam families, prepared by Mrs. James W. Caperton (nee Katherine Phelps), in the possession of Mrs. Caperton.

Register, Kentucky State Historical Society, Vol. 32, No. 99 (April, 1934), "Central University, Richmond, Kentucky," by J. T. Dorris; Vol. 33, Nos. 103 and 104 (April, July, 1935), "Governor James B. McCreary's War Time Journal."

Richmond *Daily Register*, October 27, 1919.

MANUSCRIPTS

"An Accumulation of Evidence." Being a manuscript book bound in three volumes (vellum) prepared by Mrs. James W. Caperton (nee Katherine Phelps) and pertaining to the families from which Mrs. Caperton is descended and to which she is allied by marriage, covering five generations. The work has many fine full-page photographs. Three copies of each volume were prepared.

Autograph Album, originally owned by Miss Clara B. Wherritt. Covers period 1857-1886. Now in possession of the writer.

Bogie Family: A Genealogy of the descendants of Thomas Bogie of the Shire of Fife, Scotland, through Andrew Bogie, born 1733. Prepared by Elbert Perry Brink and belongs to Jesse Bogie, Richmond, Kentucky.

County Court Records, Madison County, Kentucky, Vol. 1. In the County Clerk's office.

Deatherage, Nathan Bird. Sundry letters, records, etc., relating to Mr. Deatherage, in possession of J. W. Deatherage, Richmond, Kentucky.

Eleventh Kentucky Regiment (cavalry), C. S. A. Copy of record of enlistments, desertions, deaths, etc. In possession of the writer.

Fee Book of the law firm of Curtis Field Burnam and James W. Caperton, Richmond, Kentucky, covering the period from the spring of 1863 to the autumn of 1869. In possession of Mrs. James W. Caperton.

French Tipton Papers. Seven volumes and an index volume written in preparation of a history of Madison County, Kentucky, but never finished. Ten years' work by French Tipton. Also scrapbooks, scores of photographs, hundreds of letters, etc. In possession of the writer.

Madison Female Institute Minutes of Board of Trustees, 1857-1917. One volume. In possession of the writer.

Marriage Book B, Madison County, Kentucky, County Clerk's office.

Methodist Church (South) Quarterly Conference Record Book, Madison County, Kentucky. 1811-1845. Original in possession of Rev. W. E. Arnold, Winchester, Kentucky. Two typed copies in possession of the writer.

Miller, W. H. Seven large volumes of notes including an index volume, written in preparation of his *History and Genealogies,* including other matter. In the library of the Eastern Kentucky State Teachers College.

Old Cane Spring Baptist Church of Christ Records, Madison County, Kentucky. 4 volumes. In possession of the writer.

Republican (Tates Creek) Baptist Church Records, Madison County, Kentucky. 5 volumes. Original are all kept in the church. Two typed copies of first four volumes are in the possession of the writer.

Will Books J and R, Madison County, Kentucky, County Clerk's office.

MAP

Map of Madison County, Kentucky, compiled and published by D. G. Beers and Co., Philadelphia, 1876. This 38 inch by 54 inch wall map contains the nine precincts in color; the towns, villages, streams, toll houses, country stores, country churches and schools; the ferries, Indian mounds, mills, distilleries, and ponds; the cemeteries, caves, the farms with owners' names and often the number of acres; the historic places, the census for 1870 for both whites and colored in each precinct and the town of Richmond; and the roads of every sort. The subscribers and their business notices; the plats of every village and town with the locations of homes, schools, churches, and business places, and offices along the roads and streets, with the names of the owners are also given. It is a most remarkable map for its contents and manner of presentation. Several copies exist.

INDEX

INDEX

Abney, Jonathan, 29
Adams, Captain, 71, 78, 94, 109
Adams, George, 131
Adams, Mrs. Margaret Ann, 192
Adams, P. K., 189
African religion, spirits in, 163
Album, an autograph, 195
Alfred, Cabell Chenault's, 11
Allegheny Mountains, 159
Allen, Noland's, 44
Amazing Grace, singing of, 55
America, colored race in, 59
American flag, 207
American Missionary Association, 142
American Party, the, 204
American Tract Society, 142
Amos, Uncle, 11, 18
Andy, Cabell Chenault's, 15
Appomattox, surrender at, 127
Arkansas Eagle, 201
Arkansas penitentiary, 200
Arkansas Post, 207
Army, Bragg's in Kentucky, 89
Army, Southern, moving northward, 87
Arnett, J. B., 193
Arnold, Rev. W. E., 188
Atlanta, 75
Augusta, college at, 141
Austin, L. A., 195
Autumn, a Kentucky, 37
Ayres, Dr. Jeremiah, 77, 93ff., 134, 185
Ayres Seminary, 134

Ballard, Captain P. P., 68, 127, 183
Baptist Association, 48
Bard of Federal Hill, 136
Barnes, Eugene, 137
Barnes, Henry, 110
Barren County, Kentucky, 86
Barton, William E., 147
Basket dinners, 179
Bath County, Kentucky, 172
Battle of Richmond, 194, 196, 197, 198
Bear, Uncle Caesar's, 65
Bearwallow, 85, 184
Beecher, Henry Ward, 147, 150
Beechers, sister of the famous, 136
Bell, John, 204
Bennett, J., 188
Berea, a school at, 14

Berea College, 135, 156, 168
Bereans, the, 151, 154, 194
Berea, town of, 147
Big Bend of Kentucky River, 142
Big Bend schoolhouse, 170
Big Hill, 82, 85, 106
Big Hill pike, 190, 199
Black, a young Mr., 213
Blackstone's aphorism, 206
Blanton, Rev. Lindsay Hughes, 148
Bloomington, Illinois, 124
Blue Grass region, 150
Boggs, E. C., 193, 194
Boggs, Mrs. Margaret Jane, 192, 2
Boggs, William, 193
Bogie, Andrew, 135, 137, 158
Bogie, James, 135, 158
Bogie, the widow, 137
Bogie's Mill, 6, 23, 135
Bonney, James, 228
Bonnie Blue Flag, 69, 73
Boone, Daniel, 134, 159, 170
Boone, Fort, 133
Boonesborough, 22, 132, 134, 159, 197
Boughton, John F., 153
Bourbon County, Kentucky, 72
Boxankle, 189
Boyle, General, 186
"Boys in Blue," 194, 196
"Boys in Gray," 194, 196
Bracken County, Kentucky, 141
Bradley, Aunt Ann, 171, 212
Bragg, General, 87, 98, 109, 191,
Bragg's Army, 94
Brandenburg, W. C., 134, 169
Brandenburg, Wilson, 194
Breck, Charley, 89
Brent, Major, 220
Bristow, Secretary, 205
Broaddus, Andrew, 178
Broaddus, Elbridge, J., 57, 178
Brock Negroes, the, 8, 27
Brown, John, 150
Buckner, Simon Bolivar, 182
Buffington Island, 166, 221
Bullock, Miss Mary, 127, 213
Burbridge, General, 11, 112, 113, 120, 207

250   Index

Burgess, John Daniel, 67
Burksville, Kentucky, 219
Burnam, Attorney A. R., 206
Burnam and Caperton, law firm of, 127, 210
Burnam, Curtis F., 51, 63, 111, 204
Burnam, Miss Lucia, 205
Burnam, Mrs. Curtis F., 112
Burnam, Mrs. Paul, 206
Burnam, Rollins, 181
Burnam, Thompson S., 205
Bybeetown, 83
Byrd, Colonel William, 132
Byron's *Juan,* referred to, 203

Caesar, Old, 26, 137, 161, 171
Calk, William, 160
Calloway, Richard, 159
Camp Boggs, 193
Campbell, Alexander, 176
"Camp Boone Hollow," 170
Camp Chase, 128, 165, 199, 205
Camp Douglas, 123, 165, 166, 199, 205, 208, 210, 213
Camp Juan, 203
Camp meeting, 46
Camp Nelson, 81, 185
Candee, Rev. George, 154
Cane Spring Church, Old, 4, 56, 62, 66, 137, 173, 212
Caperton, James W., 111, 181, 205
Caperton, Mrs. James W., 194, 199, 206, 210
Caperton, W. H., 205, 206
Carnegie, Andrew, 147
Carolina, South, 116
Cassius M. Clay Battalion, 62, 180
"Castlewood," 194
Cavalry, General John H. Morgan's, 218
Cavins, grandfather, 6
Cavins, Josephine Prewett, 20, 23, 132
Cedar hills, 48
Cedar rail fences, 169, 182
Cemetery, at Camp Nelson, 192
Cemetery, Indian Fort, 158
Cemetery, the Richmond, 192
Census for 1870, 136
Central University, 148
Centre College, 148, 206
Chambers, Ann, 178
Chambers, Captain John, 5, 18, 19, 22, 134, 178
Chambers, John, 178, 213
Chenault, Anderson, son of Cabell, 11 16, 123, 127, 212, 213
Chenault, Cabell, 10, 11, 16, 17, 20, 21, 58, 72, 127, 212

Chenault, young Cabell, 11, 16, 121, 200
Chenault, Captain Joseph, 207
Chenault, David, son of Cabell, 8, 11, 16, 123, 127, 212, 213
Chenault, David, of Gallatin, Tenn., 85
Chenault, Colonel David Waller, 109, 114, 165, 166, 199, 200, 229
Chenault, Elder David, 138, 173, 174, 176
Chenault, Harvey, 36, 77, 171
Chenault, Jephtha, 77
Chenault, Joe Prewett, 201
Chenault, John Cabell, 169, 201
Chenault, Josephine, 3, 26
Chenault, Mrs. John Cabell, 201
Chenault, plantation of, 44
Chenault, Robert, 3, 21, 63, 64, 86, 132, 170
Chenault, Tiff, 229
Cherokees, 133
Cheshire, Ohio, 166
Chicago, Illinois, 123, 199, 210
Chicago papers, 230
Chitlins, 77
Christmas of 1860, 56ff.; of 1863, 226; of 1864, 124, 126
Christmas raid, the, 220
Church, manner of seating, 51
Church, Republican Baptist, 186
Cincinnati, 75
Civil War, a vision of, 152
Clark, George Rogers, 160
Clay, Cassius M., home of, 3; emancipationist, 14, 156; defends White House, 62, 180; encouraged Fee, 142, 147; declined to aid Fee, 146; delivered Washington Centennial address, 149; candidate for Vice-Presidency, 149
Clay, General Green, 149, 159, 160
Clay, Henry, 141, 206
Cobb, Harvey, 172
Coffey, Major W. A., 184
College Hill, 133
College Hill Seminary, 134
Collins, Captain Thomas B., 114, 200, 207
Collins, Josiah, 176
Columbia, Kentucky, 166, 219
Columbus penitentiary, 204, 221
Combs, General Leslie, 198
Confederate Army, expected in Kentucky, 87
Confederate hide-out, 170
Confederate Home, 168, 205
Confederate Military History, 190
Confederate prisoners released, 211
Confederates, 64

Index

Confederate States of America, 125, 224
Conscripts in Madison County, 228
Constitutional Convention, state, 157
Cornelison, Jephtha, 89
Cornelison, Robert, 192, 194
Corn shucking, 43
Cosby, Henry, 217
Coulter, Dr. E. Merton, 210
County Court of Madison, 191
Courthouse, Madison County, 132, 150
Covington, Bob, 226, 227
Covington, Captain Robert C. H., 116, 208
Covington, Coleman, 169
Covington, Mr., 144
Covington, Robert, 162
Covington, Robert, a Revolutionary soldier, 170
Covington, William Q., 41, 92, 107, 162, 169, 170
Covington's factory, 146
Crockett, Hon. Davy, 198
Cuba, 160
Cuff, Cabell Chenault's, 171
Cumberland Gap, 184, 185, 190
Cumberland River, 219
"Cumberland View," 194
Cunningham, John, 72, 75
Cynthiana, Kentucky, 43

Danville, Ky., 111
Darwin, Charles, 173
Daughters College, 137
Davis, Jas. S., 153, 155, 226, 228, 229
Davis, John, 226
Davis, President Jefferson, 74
Davis, Willard, 209
Deatherage, Amos, 5, 33, 80, 165
Deatherage, J. W., 168, 178
Deatherage, Killis, 34, 35
Deatherage, Mrs. Amos, 127
Deatherage, Nathan Bird, 34, 35, 42, 51, 69, 82, 105, 107, 108, 109, 124, 128, 165ff., 207, 208, 213
Decorum, a church, 173
Devil's backbone, the, 34, 103
Dillingham, Henry, 51
Dillon, Captain Boston, 94, 184
Distillery, 161, 193
Dixie, 69
Dixie Highway, 194
Donovan, Dr. H. L., 194
Doylesville, 184
Dripping Springs, 142
Dudley, Captain Ambrose, 87, 89
Duke, General Basil Wilson, 199, 207, 217, 221
Dunn, Robert, 194

Eagle, Governor James P., 200
Eastern Kentucky State Teachers College, 132
Edwards, G. L., 185
Egyptians, monuments of, 139
Eleventh Kentucky Cavalry, C. S. A., 109, 193, 200, 218, 231ff.
Eliot, President of Harvard, 147
Elliott, Milton, 201, 202
Elliott, Mrs. Milton, 201
Elliott, Rev. Milton, 200, 201
Ellison, J. B., 127, 194
Elliston precinct, 136
Elliston, village of, 170, 213
Elm, the, 134
Emancipation Proclamation, 120
Embree, Allen, 176
Enquirer, Cincinnati, 60, 78
Estill County, knobs of, 67, 72, 109, 161
Estill, James, 159, 194
Estill, Jonathan P., 213
Estill, Mrs. Jonathan, 205
Estill, Samuel, 161

Fairchild, E. H., 147
Fayette County, 6, 132
Federals, 84, 197
Federal Stockade at Green River, 219
Fee book, lawyer's, 211
Fee, John G., effect of teachings, 14; expulsion of, 14, 150; mobbed, 14; preaching on Christian Union, 142; regarded as a "Radical" 146; in the East, 150; again driven away, 155; an abolitionist, 156; concerning mob episode, 168, 169
Fees for the release of prisoners, 211, 212
Ferry, the Red River, 134
Fields, Mr., 142, 143
Flat Woods Church, 173, 176
Floyd, Jonathan, 175
Fluty, Robert, 72, 75
Fogg, Miss Bettie, 127, 213
Fort Delaware, 211, 217, 224
Fort Sumter, 180
Foster, James D., 209
Four Mile pike, 178
Fox hunt, 168
Fox hunters, 35
Fox, John, 166
Foxtown, 3
Freeman, James, 228
French Tipton Papers, 183
Frost, William Goodell, 147
Fry, General Speed S., 200
Fugitive Slave Law, 156

Garden of Eden, 4
Garfield, nomination of, 206
Garrard County, Kentucky, 142
Garrison, an abolitionist, 156
Gentry, Nancy, 165, 189
Georgetown College, 207
Ghosts, 33, 34
Gibbs, Mrs. A. R., 193
Gilbert, Miss Polly, 214
Giles, Amos Deatherage's, 50
Golden, James, 121
Governor, petitioned, 152, 154
Grant's Army, 166
Granville, Ohio, 195
Grape-vine route, 69, 71, 82
Greeley, Horace, 149
Green River Bridge, 166, 204
Green River Stockade, 220
Griffin, Charles E., 153
Griggs, Sam, 161
Griggs, W. C., 177
Grinstead, Mathew D., 133

Hagerd, James, 173
Hall, Mrs., 203
Hamilton Norris Homestead, 179
Hammonds, Colonel, 165
Hanson, J. G., 153, 154
Harper's Ferry, 150
Harris, Dick, 172
Harris, Dr. John, 172
Harris, John, teacher, 38
Harris, Mrs. Nancy, 182
Harrison, Colonel John Noland's, 19, 46, 50
Harrison County, 42
Harrod, James, 134, 159
Harrodsburg, 159
Harry, David Chenault's, 8, 27
Harry of the West, 136
Hart, Augustine, 20, 35, 57, 82, 118, 165, 169
Hart, Joel T., 137
Hart, Thomas M., 21, 137, 159
Hartsville, 220
Hawkins, hanging of, 27
Hawkins, Edward W., 161
Hayes, E. T., 153
Hayes, nomination of, 206
Hays, Captain Robert, 209
Hayti, 140
Henderson, John, 175
Henderson, Judge Richard, 134, 160
Herd, G. W., 193
Hickey, William, 174
Hickory Lick, 196
Hill, Pap John, 228
Hisle, Willis, 48, 49, 56, 109

Holloway, William, 154, 194
Home Guards, 66, 70, 78, 81, 101, 109, 182, 184
Honeymooning, 168
Horses, Thoroughbred saddle, 108
Howard's Creek, 3, 5, 36
Hoy, William, 131
Huffman, Phil A., 133
Hughes, Polly, 158
Huguely, Jake, 171
Huguely, John, 122
Humphrey, Robert Chenault's, 122, 127
Hutchins, Dr. William J., 147

Illinois Country, 160
Inaku of the Niger valley, 164
Indian mounds, 135
Indians, Hueco, 133
Infare, the Deatherage-Oldham, 214
Irvine, David C., 51
Irvine, Kentucky, 72, 161
Irvine, William, 157, 160
Ivani, the, 164

Jackson, General Israel, 33, 73, 103
Jackson, Joe, 110
Jackson, Mrs. General Israel, 33
Jackson, Will, 226
Jake, Cabell Chenault's, 30, 94ff., 170
James River, 223
Jefferson, the equalitarian, 138
Jenkins, Dr. William Sumner, 138, 140
Jerry, a black boy, 21
Jerry, a waggoner, 11
Jessamine County, 132
Jesse, Captain, 189
Jett, Mrs. Shelby, 174
John Brown, 147
Johnson, Adam R., 218
Johnson, E. Polk, 207
Johnson, J. J., 133
Jones, Robert, 142, 145, 146

Kansas, warfare similar to that in, 155
Kansas Territory, 161
Kavanaugh, a man named, 211
Kavanaugh Armstrong home, 193
Kavanaugh's woods, 106
Kentucky, information relating to, 132; wealth and culture in, 57; invasion of, 220
Kentucky Appellate Court, 148
Kentucky Historical Society, 204
Kentucky hospitality, 36, 42, 126
Kentucky Infantry, 26th, 207
Kentucky River, 3, 22, 134
Kingsley, Mary, 163
Kirkersville, Ohio, 195

Index

Kirksville, 201
Kit Carson, 178
Knife, in possession of McCreary, 222

Lancaster, Kentucky, 195
Lane Seminary, 141
Lane, Senator James H., 180
Lariemore, John, 36, 39
Lebanon, Kentucky, 166
Lee, Gen. Robert E., 166, 167, 190
Letcher, Cabell Chenault's, 18, 19
Letters, by Confederate prisoners, 225ff.
Lewis, A. K., 43
Lewis Chapel, 142, 170
Lewis County, 142
Lexington *Herald,* 206
Lexington, Kentucky, 204
Library, Berea College, 149
Life, Swinglehurst, 153
Lincoln, President, 6, 8, 12, 44, 60, 114, 117, 119, 120, 121, 156, 180, 181, 205ff.
Lion of White Hall, 136
Lion Run branch, 26
Lipscomb, Major Nathan, 189
Lipscomb, Nancy, 189
Lipscomb, Nathan, 165
Lipscomb, Susannah J., 165
Lipscomb, William, 133
Liquor, the use of, 170
"Little Brown Jug," 170
Louisville, 148
Louisville *Courier-Journal,* 206
Low, Representative, 198
Lyell, Sir Charles, 173

Madison County, 3, 22, 131, 136, 149, 150, 206
Madison County Bar, 206
Madison County Court room, 206
Madison Female Institute, 108, 167, 191ff.
Madison, James, 131
Manson, General M. D., 190
Manuals, anti-slavery, 142
Marriages, number of, 213
Marsh, Mr., 142, 143
Marshall, Thomas A., 206
Martin, Asa Earl, 141, 163
Martin, David G., 169
Martin, Jack, 5, 36, 37, 134
Massa's in the Cold, Cold Ground, 48
Matthew, John Huguely's, 122
Maupin, Cull, 227
Maupin, Socrates, 194
McClain County, Illinois, 212
McCord, Mrs. Nanny May, 167
McCoy, Nancy, 226

McCreary, Dr. E. R., 223
McCreary, James B., 199, 202, 218, 220
McCreary, Mrs. E. R., referred to, 223
McDougle, Dr. Ivan E., 137, 162
McKinley, nomination of, 206
McKinney, Colby, 5, 43
Methodists, Quarterly Conference of Madison County, 186
Methodist Church, split of, 188
Mexican War, 149
Michigan Infantry, 25th, 219
Milford, 131
Military Board, 183
Military roads, 185
Miller, Colonel John, 131
Miller, General John, 109, 193, 196
Miller Park, Bloomington, Ill., 212
Millie, Aunt, 6, 170
Million precinct, 136
Mills, on Silver Creek, 136
Minerva, Aunt Creech Sally's, 73
Mississippi, victories in, 207
Missouri, 161
Moberly, Dr. Thomas S., 51, 100, 101, 189
Mobs, irresponsible men, 144
Money, 228
Monticello, Kentucky, 110, 200, 202
Moore, Colonel O. B., 219
Morgan, General John Hunt, 109, 121, 165, 189, 190, 199, 200, 204, 207
Morgan's Cavalry, 199
Morgan's men, 117
Morgan's officers, 223
Morgan's Ohio raid, 219
Morgan's "terrible men," 221
Mount Sterling, 166
Mount Vernon, Kentucky, 142
Mount Zion Church, 109, 191, 194, 197
Muddy Creek, 4, 22, 23, 39, 80
Muddy Creek hill, 45
Mullins, a slave buyer, 30, 31
My Old Kentucky Home, 48

Navy yard, 62
Negroes, held as criminals, 7; free are no good, 9; marrying of, 12; sold only on request, 13; satisfied, 15; happy children of, 16; seen not as poor slaves, 16; tied together, 31; happy, 36, 37; eating, 50; contented servants, 55; part of church reserved for, 55; bright-faced and happy, 57; considered as restless and unhappy, 58; as Christians, 59; high types of, 61; report actions of Home Guards, 67; doing chores, 80; interest in plantation, 81; work on roads, 85ff.;

return from road work, 87; rejoice over return of master, 108; appreciative of Lincoln, 120; as draft substitutes, 121, 122; indignant at being substituted for whites, 122; influenced to join Federal army, 122, 123; will never sing as before, 125; good ones will never be equaled again, 126; condition of free, 141; admitted to school at Berea, 147; brought into Kentucky, 163; a guard of, 167; singing of, 170, 171; allowed to make money, 171; teaching them to read, 172; sold down South, 29, 172

Negro substitutes, 210
Nellie Gray, 58
Nellie Was a Lady, 48
Nelson, General William, 84, 108, 185, 190, 191
Newland, Mag, 227
New Orleans, 160
New Providence Church, 186, 188
New York *Tribune*, 149
Nigeria, customs in, 164
Noland, Captain Nathan, 5, 25, 43, 48, 60, 61, 92, 98, 111, 134, 167, 181
Noland-Chambers graveyard, 167
Noland, Colonel John, 5, 18, 19, 111, 134, 138, 167
Noland, Elbridge, 26
Noland, Green, 26, 32, 134, 161, 170
Noland, James, of Clark County, 51, 52
Noland, James, son of Captain Nathan, 26
Noland, John, 175
Noland, John, attorney of Richmond, 135
Noland, John Black, 5, 134, 135, 161
Noland, Mary, 167
Noland, Temperance, 178
Noland, William, 175
Noland's Creek, 189
Norris, Hamilton, 180
Norris-Hisle family reunion, 179
Norris, Walter, 5, 39, 60, 170, 180
Norris, Will, 179, 180
North, expense of transportation from, 158; interference with slavery, 85; invasion of, 190; mutterings in the, 56
North District Association, 173, 176

Oath of Allegiance to United States, 114, 184, 200
Oberlin College, 147
Ogg, W. C., 161
Ohio, 161

Ohio Annual Conference Rule, 186ff.
Ohio penitentiary, 199, 217
Ohio raid, 204, 213
Ohio River, 74, 124, 166
Ohio Volunteer Infantry, 95th, 195
Old Black Joe, 48
Old Cane Springs, named, 3; fertility of, 37; name justified, 37; inhabitants of, 38; good people of, 59; fighting men in, 61; God-fearing people in, 62; hospitality of, 67; melodies heard in, 80; custom to visit sick in, 92; freedom, peace, and happiness in, 96; excitement over the Oldham convictions in, 116; the heroine of, 117; desolation in, 124; changed, 125; prosperity and happiness to return to, 128; life in, 170
Oldham, Abner, 133, 160
Oldham, Charles, 41
Oldham, Eleanor Bird ("little Nettie"), 40, 83, 117, 169
Oldham, Hezekiah, 161, 189
Oldham, James, 41, 65, 88, 189, 228
Oldham, Kie, 34, 41, 65, 88
Oldham, Mary Ann, 36, 74, 77ff., 91, 93, 108, 111, 116, 124, 128, 167, 169, 208, 213
Oldham, Mrs. Othniel, 88, 111
Oldham, Othniel, 5, 23, 34, 39, 66, 99ff., 106, 111, 169, 200, 202, 205
Oldham, Susan, 40, 111, 169
Oldham, Temperance, 169
Oldham, Thomas, 111, 200ff.
Oldham, Thomas Moberly, 41
Oldhams in Captain Collins' Company, 207
"Old hams," 185
Olds, T. W., 195
Olmsted, opinion of, 158
Onesimus, 140
Origin of Species, Darwin's, 173
Ottaway, Moberly's, 45
"Outlaw" horse, an, 201
Oxford, Ohio, college at, 141

Pace, J., 188
Palmer, Thomas, 109, 191
Panorama of Kentucky River, 167
"Papers" of James B. McCreary, 217
Pardons, sought for the Oldhams, 116
Paris, Kentucky, 43
Parker, A. G. W., 153
Parole, obtained from Lincoln, 217, 224
Parrish, Mrs. Lyman, 226
Parrish, S. D., 192
Perryville, battle of, 109, 191
Pewee Valley, 205

Index

Philadelphia Centennial, 133
Philemon, 140
Phillips, Micajah, 202
Phillips, Miss Juan, 111, 200ff.
Phoenix Hotel, 204
Pike, Oldham's, 45, 66, 88, 99ff., 107, 112, 171, 191
Pine Mountain, battle of, 88, 89, 189
Plantation, kinds of work on, 11; neglected, 124
Pleas, Lariemore's, 44, 67
Point Lookout, 227
Pollock's *Course of Time*, 230
Poosey precinct, 3, 136
Port Gibson, 207
Postoffice, at the Rock House, 75
Potomac River, 166
Pottery, at Waco, 133
Prairie State, the, 212
Prather, Philip, 188
Predestinarian Baptist Church of Christ, 177
Presbyterian Church, a separation in, 148
"President Lincoln's Clemency," an article, 208
Prewett, Sally, 132
Prison camps, locations of, 184
Provost judge, 86
Provost Marshals, 210
Pud, Chambers', 45

Quisenberry, Anderson Chenault, 199
Quisenbery, James, 173

Ranck, George W., 134
Ransom, Lieutenant, 203
Rebel prisoners, escaped, 212
Rebels, 63, 67, 127
Rebels in Kentucky, 229
Red House, village of, 171
Red River, 3, 36
Red River road, 22, 39
Reed, J. D., 153
Register, Kentucky Historical Society, 218
Religious service, first recorded in Kentucky, 134
Reminiscences, of General Basil W. Duke, 178
Rennels, Henry H., 174
Richardson, a Mr., 171
Richmond, battle of, 190
Richmond cemetery, 167
Richmond Ice Company, 192
Richmond, Kentucky, 57, 63, 109, 131, 132, 146
Richmond National Bank, 206
Richmond, Virginia, 166

Riddell, W. M., 213
Robertson, Chief Justice, 206
Rock House, 65, 69, 70, 77, 94, 102, 124, 170, 182, 184, 185
Rock Island, Illinois, 211
Rodes, Colonel William, 194, 199
Rodes, Robert, 159
Rogers, Ben, 194
Rogers, John A. R., 14, 147, 150, 194
Rogersville, skirmish at, 190
Roosevelt, Theodore, 147
Rupard, Rev. William, 52, 62, 174, 181

Sally, Aunt Creech, 27ff., 64, 71ff., 77, 93, 95, 122, 162, 170
Sally, old man Harry's wife, 27
Salt, 77, 172
Sam, Aunt Creech Sally's, 29, 32, 77
Santa Fe, 178
Santo Domingo, 140
Sarah, a Negro girl, 188
Savannah, Georgia, 202
Saw mill, in Richmond, 169
Schaoff, General, 197
School, 38
Schurz, Carl, 147
Scott, Cabell Chenault's, 50
Scott County, Kentucky, 207
Scudder, Ira N., 212
Searcy, Mrs. Chas. L., 162, 213
Secessionists, 180
Seward, 210
Shackelford, Judge W. R., 206
Shaler, Nat T., 207
Shannon, Fred Albert, 210
Sharpe's rifles, to Berea, 150
Shearer, Ann, 58
Shearer, Bob, 226
Shearer, Nannie, 58
Shiloh, 207
Shortening bread, 77
Silver Creek, 3, 6, 7, 21, 23, 43, 135, 161
Simmons, George, 226
Simmons, Joe, 227, 228
Slate Lick Springs, 155
Slaughter, Gabriel, 174
Slave code of 1798, 162
Slave, refuses punishment, 172
Slavery, 13, 140
Slaves, term not common, 12, 85; used on roads, 84ff.; marriage among, 137; number in Kentucky, 157; importation forbidden, 162; increase of population, 162; trade in, 162, 163; number of, in Madison, 179
Smith, Elder John ("Raccoon John"), 176

Smith, General A. G., 207
Smith, General Kirby, 105, 108, 190, 198
Smith, Gerret, 147
Smith, Hon. W. B., 206
Smith, John, 153
Soldiers, wanted from Madison County, 209
Somerset, Kentucky, 113
South, demands of, 56; people of the, 63; cause doomed, 125
Southern Confederacy, 189
Southern ethnologists, 139
Speedwell, Madison County, 51
Springs, 37
Stanford, Kentucky, 113
State Guards, 182
Stormes, Mrs. John E., 196
Substitutes, white, 121
Swing Low, Sweet Chariot, 48, 59
Sycamore, the, 4, 37, 132, 133, 160
Sycamore Hollow, 132

Tates Creek Association, 176
Taylor's Fork, of Silver Creek, 131
Tennessee, Confederate army in, 69
Tennessee Conference, 188
Tennyson's Brook, 178
Terrill, Daniel Maupin, 194
Tevis, Bob, 228
Texas, annexation of, 149
Texas Seminary, 133
Texas, village of, 3, 5, 14, 60, 72, 81, 171
Thomas Palmer home, 193
Thompson, G. M., 174
Those Golden Slippers, 59
Thrall, Miss Clara, 196
Thrall, Robert, 195
Tiley, Dudley, 65, 84
Tipton, French, 133, 160
Tobacco, 131, 157, 159
Todd, C. S., 221
Torry, W. H., 153
Townsend, W. H., 163
Transylvania College, 201
Transylvania Colony, 134
Transylvania Company, 159
Tribble, Alexander, 194
Tribble, Captain Alexander, 166, 194, 220
True American, the, 136
Tucker, Joseph T., 199, 203
Turley, Green, 194
Turley, Robert, 192
Turner, Squire, 157
Turnpike, Richmond and Irvine, 4

Turpin, Hayden, 5, 170
Turpin, Robert, 170, 214

U. C. V., reunions of, 167
Uncle Tom's Cabin, 136
Union Church, an anti-slavery, 147
Unionists, 182
Union precinct, 136
Union Soldiers, return of, 127
Union Stockyards in Cincinnati, 179
Union troops in Kentucky, 84
Union, village of, 82
United Baptist Church of Christ, 176
United States mail, 74
United States Navy Yard, 180
University Hall, 148

Vaccination, 228
Veterans of the Confederacy, 168
Vicksburg campaign, 207
Violet, General Jackson's, 33, 73, 75

Waco, Madison County, 3, 82, 83, 133
Waco-Red River road, 3
Waco, Texas, 133
Wagon train, General Morgan's, 114
Walden, Mrs., 25
Walden, the miller, 24, 161
Wallace, Alfred Russell, 173
Wallace, C. C., attorney, 135
Wallace, William Reid, 67
War between the States, 3, 56, 133, 136
Ward, Dick, 27
Wash, Captain Noland's, 48
Washington Centennial Address, in New Haven, 149
Washington County, Kentucky, 133
Washington, D. C., 115, 180
Washington, George, 131
Water power in Kentucky, 158
Watts, William W., 198
Wayne County, Kentucky, 203
Webb, Doctor, 227
Wedding, Deatherage-Oldham, 128, 213
Weddle, George, 25, 160
Weddle's Mill, 23, 184
Wetherford, President W. D., 158, 163
Wherritt, Miss Clara B., 195
Wherritt, Samuel H., 196
Whig, a Henry Clay, 184
Whiskey, 24; cost of, 43; Walden's, 46
White House, the, 62, 180, 205
White Oak, the church at, 173
White, William, 174
Whizaker, the spotted mule, 6, 10, 25, 74, 75, 171
Wild Cat Mountain, battle of, 64, 182

Williams, Alf, 160, 161
Williams, A. W., 133
Williams, John Augustus, 137
Willoughby, Jack, 229
Wills, pertaining to slaves, 138
Wilson, Vice-President Henry, 180
Winchester, Kentucky, 30, 31, 72
Wolford, Colonel, 91
Woodford County, Kentucky, 213
"Woodlawn," 194, 199
Woods, Archibald, 194
Woods, Josh, 226, 228
"Woodstock," 194
Writing day in prison, 228

Yale University, 149
Yankee Doodle, 72, 77, 81
Yankees, 64, 67, 75, 85, 107, 122, 167
Yellow Rose in Texas, the, 58
Yorktown, 131

Zollicoffer, General, 64

THE MADISON COUNTY SESQUICEN-TENNIAL ANNIVERSARY. 1786-1936.
(Celebrated October 13-17, 1937.)

I. THE BOONESBOROUGH CHAPTER OF DAUGHTERS OF THE AMERICAN REVOLUTION

IN ANY STATEMENT concerning the commemoration of Madison County history the Boonesborough Chapter of the Daughters of the American Revolution deserves mention. At least some of the accomplishments of this worthy organization should be given. In 1907, the chapter inscribed the names of the earliest settlers of Boonesborough on a large Bedford stone within a fifty foot square, surrounded by a stone wall, on the site of Fort Boone. Twenty-four years later these ladies placed a handsome bronze tablet commemorating the founding of Boonesborough, on a large stone setting near the Madison County end of the Boonesborough Memorial Bridge. In April, 1937, they unveiled a beautiful bronze tablet honoring Daniel Boone, in the Thomas Jackson Coates Administration Building of the State Teachers College in Richmond. A few weeks later the Chapter also dedicated a granite marker on the site of Fort Twetty, near Richmond, where Indians killed two of Boone's party on March 25, 1775.

The officers of the Chapter are:
HONORARY REGENT, Mrs. James W. Caperton, who for thirty-one years has been chairman of the organization's Boonesborough Monument Committee.
REGENT, Mrs. John Gibson Phelps.
FIRST VICE-REGENT, Mrs. W. S. Broaddus.
SECOND VICE-REGENT, Mrs. Allen Zaring.
TREASURER, Miss Mattie Tribble.
RECORDING SECRETARY, Mrs. Robert Dunn.
CORRESPONDING SECRETARY, Miss Florence Burnam.
HISTORIAN, Mrs. Jerry B. Noland.
REGISTRAR, Mrs. J. G. Bosley.

II. THE MADISON COUNTY HISTORICAL SOCIETY

The Madison County Historical Society was organized and incorporated in 1933 by the writer, who became and remained its president until July, 1937. The organization's objectives, as stated at the outset, include the preservation of things of historic value; the acquisition of a museum; the dissemination of information about the history of the county; the marking of historic places in the county; and the establishment of a national monument and park at Boonesborough. The society took a conspicuous part in the Daniel Boone Bicentennial Celebration in 1934, its president having initiated and directed the movement which caused the General Assembly to create the Daniel Boone Bicentennial Commission. Four members of the society became and three remain members of the commission.

Madison County Sesquicentennial 259

Early in 1936, the society determined to sponsor a fitting recognition of the hundred and fiftieth anniversary of the organization of Madison County. The county's fiscal court was influenced to authorize the celebration; but, owing to lack of general interest, the affair was deferred until the autumn of 1937, when the sesquicentennial of the making of the Federal Constitution might also be commemorated. Sometime after the movement for the celebration had been revived, the Board of Directors of the society was reorganized with the following officers and members: President, Dr. W. J. Moore; Vice-President, Mrs. Grant E. Lilly; Secretary, Mr. Edward Wayman; Treasurer, Mr. David J. Copeland. Other members, Superintendent W. F. O'Donnell, Dr. C. A. Keith, Mr. H. Bennett Farris, Judge John Noland, Mrs. Joe Head, and Dr. J. T. Dorris.

This board created a special organization to plan and direct the celebration, and engaged the John B. Rogers Producing Company, of Fostoria, Ohio, to produce a historical pageant for the occasion. Hon. Cassius M. Clay, of Bourbon County, Counsel for the Reconstruction Finance Corporation, Washington, D. C., delivered the county sesquicentennial address, and Dr. Shelton Phelps, President Winthrop College, Rock Hill, South Carolina, the address on the Constitution.

III. SESQUICENTENNIAL COMMITTEES
(Chairmen only)

GENERAL CHAIRMAN	Mr. B. E. Willis
PRESIDENT HISTORICAL SOCIETY	Dr. W. J. Moore
HISTORIAN	Dr. J. T. Dorris
FINANCE	{ Mr. David J. Copeland { Mr. H. Bennett Farris
TICKET SALES	Judge Kirk Moberly
PUBLICITY	Mr. James A. Miller, Jr.
HOMECOMING	Mr. Elmer Deatherage
INVITATIONS	Miss Issie D. Million
DECORATIONS	Mr. Edward Wayman
CONSTITUTION	Judge John Noland
SELECTION OF MISS MADISON	Mr. Leslie Thomson Bennett
HISTORICAL EXHIBITS	Mrs. R. G. Woods
MINISTERIAL	Rev. Clyde L. Breland
POLICE AND TRAFFIC	Chief W. B. Lackey
PROPERTIES	Dr. Dean W. Rumbold
TALENT	Miss Field Shackleford
COSTUMES	Miss Louise Rutledge
MUSIC	Prof. James E. Van Peursem
MILITARY EPISODES	{ Maj. Chas. W. Gallaher, U.S.A. { Dr. J. H. Rutledge
FOX HUNT	Mr. A. R. Denny
PRINTING	Mr. A. F. Scruggs
RECEPTION	Mrs. Grant E. Lilly
SESQUICENTENNIAL BALL	Dr. Harvey Blanton